Collins
English for Exams

D1612363

SKILLS FOR THE TOEIC® TEST

Speaking and Writing

Collins

HarperCollins Publishers
77-85 Fulham Palace Road
Hammersmith
London W6 8JB

First edition 2012

Reprint 10 9 8 7 6 5 4 3 2 1 0

© HarperCollins Publishers 2012

ISBN 978-0-00-746058-8

Collins® is a registered trademark of HarperCollins Publishers Limited.

www.collinselt.com

A catalogue record for this book is available from the British Library.

Editorial Services: Content*Ed Publishing Solutions, LLC

Writing Services: Content*Ed Publishing Solutions, LLC and Creative Content, LLC

Typeset in India by Aptara

Printed in China by South China Printing Co.

Contents

Guide to the Writing Test

About the Writing Test
Challenges and Solutions

How to Use This Book

Collins Skills for the TOEIC® Test: Speaking and Writing and its companion edition, *Listening and Reading*, offer a comprehensive guide to the TOEIC (Test of English for International Communication). If you use this series to prepare for the test, you will be able to improve your score on the TOEIC test and demonstrate your skills in using English in a business setting.

No matter the level of your English, *Collins Skills for the TOEIC® Test* provides you with all the tools you need to succeed on the test. Here's a glimpse of the learning tools included in this book.

» Skill-specific *Challenges and Solutions* sections. These sections offer strategies and suggestions to help you learn how to overcome the most common challenges in each section of the test.

» *Quick Guide* question overviews. Each lesson provides a brief summary of the question type in an easy-to-read chart so that you can quickly understand what is important to know in order to answer the questions correctly.

» *Walk Through* samples. Clear, visual and / or audio examples show you the types of questions, passages, and responses you can expect to find on the test. Knowing what to expect is an important part of preparing for the test.

» *Get It Right* presentations. These presentations give an overview of the most important steps, skills, and language needed for doing well on each question. They include useful vocabulary and expressions that you can use when answering the questions and provide tips and tasks for noticing and understanding the important elements of each question type.

» *Progressive Practice*. For each question type, carefully designed activities gradually prepare you for the TOEIC test. This step-by-step practice builds the knowledge and skills you need for a good score and encourages independent learning while working up to TOEIC testing levels.

  • *Get Ready* activities walk you through the steps you will need to follow to respond to each question effectively and offer extensive support and models to follow along the way.

  • *Get Set* activities allow you to respond to TOEIC-style test questions more independently, but still offer additional support and modeling to help you as you go.

  • *Go for the TOEIC Test* activities put you in an authentic test situation and allow you to practice what you have learned in a simulated test environment.

» Skill-specific *Practice Test* sections. At the end of each section, you'll be able to put your skills for the test to use by taking a timed practice test. These practice tests will help you identify your weaknesses so you can know what areas to focus on before the actual test.

» *Quick Tips.* Throughout the book, you'll see *Quick Tips*, which offer best-practice strategies and useful advice on how to approach certain activity types and perform better on the test.

» Dictionary definitions. *Collins COBUILD Advanced Dictionary* definitions are provided throughout the book to help you understand words and build your knowledge of vocabulary that may be found on the TOEIC test and in business settings where English is the language of communication.

» Answer Key and Audio Scripts. Found at the back of this book, these tools will help you check your answers as you prepare for the TOEIC test and offer opportunities for reading along with the scripts to improve pronunciation, intonation, and other speaking skills.

Tips for Success

Start getting ready to take the TOEIC test by following these tips.

» **Find out where you can take the test.** Begin by asking the organization requiring the test information if the TOEIC test can be administered on its premises. There are also test sites around the world with specific test dates available. Finally, if neither of these options is available in your country, you or your organization can contact ETS to find out how it can make the test available.

» **Find out the score requirements for your organization.** Your organization will decide how to use the score you receive on the TOEIC test.

» **Start to study early.** The more you practice, the more you will improve your skills. Give yourself at least one or two months to review the materials and complete <u>all</u> of the practice activities in this book. Try to spend at least one hour a day studying. Remember, by using this book, you are on your way to good scores on the TOEIC test!

» **Time yourself.** When you do exercises and *Practice Test* sections in this book, track the time used to match TOEIC test requirements. By practicing in a timed setting, you will feel more comfortable with the time limits of the actual test.

» **Listen to the audio.** For practice activities, you can listen to the audio as many times as you need to in order to understand the concepts taught in this book. As you listen, or after you listen, read along in the script. This can help improve your listening comprehension. However, stay with the audio and listen only once when you do the Speaking *Practice Test* section. You cannot go back in the actual test, so this will help you get used to the process.

» **Complete all the exercises in this book.** The practice activities have been designed to develop specific skills that will help you perform better on the test. Also, don't be afraid to make your own notes on the page. For example, writing down the definitions of words you don't know will help you remember them later on.

Overview of the TOEIC® Test

The TOEIC test measures your proficiency in the type of English used in business settings around the world. The test does not evaluate your knowledge of the English language. Rather, it measures your ability to <u>use</u> English in a variety of business settings.

The TOEIC test is divided into two smaller, timed tests: Listening and Reading, and Speaking and Writing. The Listening and Reading Test is a paper and pencil test. The Speaking and Writing Test is administered on a computer. Each test evaluates key skills that you will need in order to use English in a business setting, regardless of where in the world this might be. You can choose to take either test first and the other second. You may also opt to take only the test that is needed to gauge your skills in a specific area, listening and reading or speaking and writing.

Speaking and Writing

The speaking and writing portion of the TOEIC test takes approximately 2 hours to complete.

- Speaking Section = 20 minutes

- Writing Section = 60 minutes

- Filling out forms = approximately 30 minutes

For the Speaking and Writing Test, you will be tested on a computer. You will complete each task by responding into a microphone or typing your response on-screen. You cannot go back and rerecord or retype most task responses.

Speaking Section

The Speaking Test is first on the computer-based TOEIC Speaking and Writing test. The Speaking Test consists of 11 tasks total and lasts about 20 minutes.

Questions 1–2:	Read a Text Aloud
Question 3:	Describe a Picture
Questions 4–6:	Respond to Questions
Questions 7–9:	Respond to Questions Using Information Provided
Question 10:	Propose a Solution
Question 11:	Express an Opinion

You will wear a headset with both earphones and a microphone during the test. You should speak clearly and carefully to be sure your speech is heard correctly by the scorers. You will be given the opportunity before you start to check that your microphone is in the best position and at the best levels to record your responses. Should you have any technical issues before or during the test, you will be able to call an administrator for help.

You will be expected to speak for a specific amount of time on some of the tasks and will be given a specific amount of time to prepare for some of the tasks. The audio program will indicate when preparation and speaking times begin and end. An on-screen timer may also be used to help you gauge how much time you've used and how much time you have left to speak.

Writing Section

The Writing Test is last on the computer-based Speaking and Writing Test. The Writing Test consists of eight tasks total and lasts about one hour.

Questions 1–5:	Write a Sentence Based on a Picture
Questions 6–7:	Respond to a Written Request
Question 8:	Write an Opinion Essay

The test is given on a standard English-language keyboard. You should therefore practice typing and working with this type of keyboard (called a QWERTY keyboard) if possible to ensure that you will be able to perform well on the test day. A QWERTY keyboard is the most common English keyboard layout, and you can check to see if you have this version by looking at the first six letters that are located at the top left edge of the keyboard. The letters should read Q-W-E-R-T-Y. If you do not have a QWERTY keyboard, you may wish to find one on which you can practice before you take the test.

In the Writing Test, you will be expected to complete specific tasks in a certain amount of time. When your time is over, a pop-up window will notify you that your time is finished and that you will need to move to the next question. As with the Speaking Section, an on-screen timer may also be used to help you gauge how much time you've used and how much time you have left to write.

If at any given point during the test you are unsure how to do a task, you can click on the "Help" button to get information about how to do the test. You can also call an administrator for help with technical issues.

Scoring for Speaking and Writing

You will receive a score for each section of the Speaking and Writing Test. Each score is based on a scale of 1–200, given in increments of 10. The individual task scores, which are most often referenced in this book, are rated based on performance and range from 0–5 for the task types listed below.

Speaking

Questions 1–2:	Score range 0–3
Question 3:	Score range 0–3
Questions 4–6:	Score range 0–3
Questions 7–9:	Score range 0–3
Question 10:	Score range 0–5
Question 11:	Score range 0–5

Writing

Questions 1–5:	Score range 0–3
Questions 6–7:	Score range 0–4
Question 8:	Score range 0–5

In addition to this scaled score, you will receive an indication of your general skills and abilities in the skills. The Speaking Test has 8 levels of proficiency, and the Writing Test has 9 levels of proficiency. These proficiency levels are based on common general English skills for speaking and are assigned according to the total scaled scores a test taker receives.

Listening and Reading

The TOEIC Listening and Reading Test takes approximately 2.5 hours to complete.

- Listening Section = 45 minutes

- Reading Section = 75 minutes

- Filling out general forms for taking the test = approximately 30 minutes

For the Listening and Reading Test, you will receive an answer sheet and a test booklet. The Listening and Reading Test is a multiple-choice test. You will mark each answer by filling in the oval on your answer sheet, <u>not by marking the test booklet.</u> You must fill in the oval completely. Look at the example. This test taker has marked (B) as the answer.

You <u>must</u> use a #2 pencil to mark your answers on the answer sheet. For security reasons, you may <u>not</u> use a mechanical pencil. You may <u>not</u> use a pen, either.

You can erase an answer if you decide a different answer is the correct one. If you change your mind, be sure to erase the answer completely. <u>Never</u> cross out an answer. The machine that scores the test will count that as two answers, and two answers are always wrong.

Listening Section

The Listening Test is first on the TOEIC paper and pencil test. The Listening Test consists of four parts and 100 questions total. The Listening Test lasts 45 minutes. You <u>cannot</u> go back during any of the four parts and listen again, and you cannot go back between the parts or at the end.

Part 1: Photographs	10 questions
Part 2: Question-Response	30 questions
Part 3: Conversations	30 questions (10 conversations with 3 questions each)
Part 4: Talks	30 questions (10 talks with 3 questions each)

Reading Section

The Reading Test is second on the TOEIC paper and pencil test. The Reading Test consists of three parts and 100 questions total. The Reading Test lasts 75 minutes. Because the reading material is in the test booklet, you <u>can</u> go back to check or adjust your answers during the Reading Test.

Part 5: Incomplete Sentences	40 questions
Part 6: Text Completion	12 questions
Part 7: Reading Comprehension	
Single Passages	28 questions (7–10 passages with 2–5 questions each)
Double Passages	20 questions (4 pairs of passages with 5 questions per pair)

Scoring for the Listening and Reading Test

You will receive a score for each section of the Listening and Reading Test. A raw score—the actual number of correct answers—is converted to a scaled score by the testing center using statistical analysis. The scores for the Listening and Reading Test are all done by computer. The raw score ranges per section are as follows.

Listening	0–100
Reading	0–100

General Test Information

On the day of the test, you must present an original, valid photo ID with a signature. The ID must be current, and the photo must be a recent one. Other types of ID may be required as well.

You may <u>not</u> bring any personal items, food, cell phones, or other electronic devices into the testing room. You may <u>not</u> bring in any books or paper, either.

Score Report

All test takers receive a TOEIC Score Report, which lists the test taker's name, birth date, identification number, test date and location, individual scores and total score, score descriptions, abilities measured, and so on. It can also include a photo of the test taker, if requested.

If you take the test through an organization or employer, a report will be sent directly to that organization or employer, and it will report the score to you.

Certificate of Achievement

Test takers in some parts of the world can request a TOEIC Certificate of Achievement, which lists the test taker's name, test date and location, individual scores and total score, and administering organization. This certificate is suitable for framing.

Guide to the TOEIC® Speaking Test

About the Speaking Test

The Speaking Test consists of a total of 11 questions. Each question presents you with a different type of speaking task. You will read out loud, give a description, use information provided to answer questions, and talk about your own experiences and opinions.

QUICK GUIDE: Speaking Test

Definition	The Speaking Test evaluates your ability to speak clearly and correctly and to convey a variety of types of everyday information and ideas in a way that is easily comprehensible to the listener. You will demonstrate this by responding to a variety of question types and prompts.
Targeted Skills	In order to do well on the Speaking Test you must be able to: • speak with correct pronunciation and intonation. • use appropriate vocabulary when speaking. • use correct grammatical structures when speaking. • provide information in response to specific questions. • express and explain your opinion. • talk about your ideas.
Parts of the Speaking Test	**Questions 1–2:** You will read a text out loud. **Question 3:** You will describe a photo. **Questions 4–6:** You will answer questions about familiar topics. **Questions 7–9:** You will answer questions using information provided. **Question 10:** You will propose a solution to a problem. **Question 11:** You will talk about your opinion on a particular topic. (See below for more thorough descriptions of each part of the Speaking Test.)
Timing	The Speaking Test takes approximately 20 minutes to complete.

Parts of the TOEIC® Speaking Test

Questions 1–2: Read a Text Aloud

For Questions 1 and 2, you will read a text aloud. A short text will appear on the screen. You will then have 45 seconds to look it over and get ready to speak. After that, you will have 45 seconds to read the text aloud. Each text is written in common everyday language and is the type of thing that is normally spoken, such as:

- Announcements
- Advertisements
- Introductions
- News reports
- Phone messages

Texts may be about such topics as:

- Office issues
- News
- Cultural events
- Sales
- Shopping
- Housing issues
- Education
- Transportation

You will be evaluated on:

- Pronunciation
- Intonation and stress

Question 3: Describe a Picture

For Question 3, you will describe a photo with as much detail as possible. A photo will appear on the screen. You will have 30 seconds to look it over and get ready to respond. Then you will have 45 seconds to talk about the photo. You will describe the people, objects, and activities that you see. The photo for Question 3 will focus on some type of everyday activity in a common context, such as:

- Leisure time
- Dining and entertainment
- Shopping
- Travel
- Home
- Sports

You will be evaluated on:

- Pronunciation
- Intonation and stress
- Vocabulary
- Grammar
- Cohesion of ideas

Questions 4–6: Respond to Questions

For Questions 4–6, you will be asked to imagine that you are taking part in a survey. You will be asked a series of three related questions. The questions will appear on the screen, and you will also hear them spoken. After each question is spoken, you will hear a beep. You will then need to begin speaking right away. There will be no preparation time. You will have 15 seconds to respond to Questions 4 and 5 and 30 seconds to respond to Question 6. Questions 4–6 will be about familiar topics, such as:

- Holidays and travel
- Dining and entertainment
- Friends and family
- Shopping
- News
- Health and sports
- Housing

You will be evaluated on:

- Pronunciation
- Intonation and stress
- Vocabulary
- Grammar
- Cohesion of ideas
- Completeness of content
- Relevance of content

Questions 7–9: Respond to Questions Using Information Provided

For Questions 7–9, you will answer three questions about information that will be provided to you. The information will be in the form of a schedule, agenda, or travel itinerary. The information will appear on the screen, and you will have 30 seconds to look it over. Then you will hear the questions. The questions will only be spoken. They will not appear on the screen. After each question, you will hear a beep and you will need to begin speaking right away. You will have 15 seconds to respond to Questions 7 and 8 and 30 seconds to respond to Question 9. Questions 7 and 8 ask for specific details on the schedule. They may be in the form of embedded questions, such as:

- *Can you tell me where the event will be?*
- *Do you know how many speakers there are?*
- *I was wondering if I could buy my ticket later.*
- *I don't remember what time the event begins.*

Question 9 asks you to connect pieces of information from different parts of the schedule. For example:

- *What topics do the workshops cover?*
- *Who will the speakers be?*
- *Will there be any special events in the afternoon?*
- *What special exhibits will be on display?*

The information provided will be about topics such as:

- Conferences
- Travel
- Theater
- Business meetings
- Tours

You will be evaluated on the same criteria as Questions 4–6.

Question 10: Propose a Solution

For Question 10, you will hear a voicemail message about a problem and you will be asked to propose a solution in a voicemail reply. You will only hear the problem; it will not appear on the screen. After you hear the problem, you will have 30 seconds to get ready, and then you will have 60 seconds to respond. You will have to understand the problem the speaker is describing, come up with a reasonable solution, and then describe your solution out loud. The problem will usually be in the form of a complaint or request. It will deal with familiar topics, such as:

- Travel and transportation
- Health
- Purchases
- Housing
- Office issues
- Dining

You will be evaluated on the same criteria as Questions 4–9.

Question 11: Express an Opinion

For Question 11, you will be asked to express your opinion about a particular topic. The question will appear on the screen, and you will also hear it spoken. After you hear the question, you will have 15 seconds to get ready, and then you will have 60 seconds to speak. You will need to make a clear statement of your opinion about the topic and provide details and examples to support your opinion. Question 11 will include a brief description of a situation or commonly held opinion. Then you will be asked about your thoughts and feelings on the issue, your preferences, or whether or not you agree. The question may be presented in one of these ways:

- *Which do you prefer?*
- *Are you in favor of this plan?*
- *What is your preference / opinion?*
- *Do you agree or disagree with this statement?*
- *Do you support or oppose this plan?*
- *What do you think about this issue?*

Question 11 will be about familiar topics, such as:

- Money and work
- Personal relationships
- Sports
- Shopping
- Transportation
- Education and community

You will be evaluated on the same criteria as Questions 4–10.

Speaking Test Challenges and Solutions

» CHALLENGE 1: "I have problems with things like stress, rhythm, pacing, and vocabulary in the speaking tasks."

SOLUTION: English can be difficult because it gives stress to some words and not others. Here are some simple stress rules to remember.

Stress content words. Content words are the words that carry meaning in a sentence. Content words can be:

- Nouns
- Main verbs
- Negative auxiliary verbs
- Adjectives
- Adverbs

Don't stress function words. Function words help form the grammatical structure of a sentence. Even though they are necessary, they are not normally stressed. Function words can be:

- Prepositions
- Pronouns
- Articles
- Conjunctions
- Auxiliary verbs

Stress words to give emphasis. A speaker may want to emphasize a word for a particular reason. For example, the speaker may want to contrast two things.

> **This** one is easy, but **that** one is not.

Stress can also be used to emphasize words when correcting misinformation.

> **A:** They both contributed to the report.
> **B:** Yes, but **he** did most of the work.

SOLUTION: Practice paying attention to the way English speakers use stress. You can use the audio and scripts in this book to do that. Follow along in the script as you listen to the audio. Notice which words are stressed and which words are not. Mark them in the script. Then practice reading aloud. Record yourself. Compare your stress to the audio. Do this as many times as possible.

SOLUTION: In one part of the Speaking Test, you will have to read short texts aloud. It is very easy to practice this using short newspaper and magazine articles or paragraphs from books. Record yourself as you read. Then listen to the recording. Practice reading at least one short text a day.

SOLUTION: Try singing along with English music to improve your rhythm and pacing. Singing along can often help non-English speakers get used to the rhythm of natural English.

SOLUTION: If you can't remember a word you want to use, explain around it using vocabulary you know and are comfortable using. There are several possible ways to do this. You can quickly explain your meaning by classifying things, saying how something is used, or comparing it to something else.

- **It's a type of** tool.
- **It's used for** fixing things.
- **It's similar to** a knife.

SOLUTION: Build your speaking vocabulary through practice. The tasks on the Speaking Test deal with common everyday activities and ideas. As you go through your day, try speaking to yourself in English about what you are doing and thinking. Practice describing photos in books and magazines. Note where you have difficulty finding the right words. Then look up those words in a bilingual dictionary and learn them.

» CHALLENGE 2: "I don't have a chance to speak to native speakers of English, so I get nervous."

SOLUTION: Look for opportunities to make English-speaking friends. There may be English speakers in your city who are studying your language, and you could offer to help them in return for helping you with English. You can sometimes meet English speakers at language schools, universities, and tourist areas.

SOLUTION: Practice recording yourself. Then play back your recording to evaluate your speaking style. This will also help you get used to the TOEIC test style of being recorded while speaking so you won't be so nervous.

» **CHALLENGE 3: "My pronunciation is bad. I'm afraid that the test graders won't even understand me!"**

SOLUTION: A good place to start is by recording your voice using the scripts at the back of this book. You can then listen to the audio program and compare your recordings to the recorded passages. That way, you can compare your pronunciation with the pronunciation of a native speaker.

SOLUTION: Four (or more) ears are better than two. Play your recordings from the tasks in this book for a friend who is studying English or for a teacher. What about your speaking do they have difficulty understanding? Ask them to help you determine which sounds or combinations of sounds are especially problematic for you. Practice those parts until your speech becomes more easily understandable.

SOLUTION: Don't try to hide the problem by speaking too softly. You can't get a good score if the grader can't hear you. Practice speaking English at the same volume you speak your own language.

SOLUTION: Listen to English as much as you can. Listening to English-speaker pronunciation will help you become accustomed to the way the language sounds. Look on the Internet for movies, videos, radio programs, news broadcasts, and podcasts in English. Listen and repeat after the speakers.

SOLUTION: When you learn a new word, learn its pronunciation. Learn to read dictionary symbols used to show pronunciation and stress. Be aware that stress makes a big difference in some words. Certain words become a different part of speech depending which syllable is stressed. Here are some common ones.

First syllable stressed = noun   Second syllable stressed = verb

Noun	Verb	Noun	Verb
address	*address*	*protest*	*protest*
combat	*combat*	*rebel*	*rebel*
conduct	*conduct*	*record*	*record*
contrast	*contrast*	*refund*	*refund*
convert	*convert*	*reject*	*reject*
insult	*insult*	*survey*	*survey*
permit	*permit*	*suspect*	*suspect*

First syllable stressed = adjective   Second syllable stressed = verb

Adjective	Verb
absent	*absent*
frequent	*frequent*
perfect	*perfect*

» **CHALLENGE 4: "I know some of the responses in the Speaking Test are timed. I'm afraid I'll still have time left after I've run out of things to say!"**

SOLUTION: You will naturally speak at a pace that is slower than an English speaker. It is better to be clear and evenly paced than to speak quickly and make errors. This will also help you use more time.

SOLUTION: Learn common English expressions to introduce ideas and transition from one idea to the next. These help you expand your answers. You will find lists of expressions for adding information, giving examples, offering details, and so on throughout this book. Here are some expressions that are commonly used in spoken English.

To Give Examples	To Add Information	To Explain	To Express an Opinion
For example,	*As well as*	*In fact,*	*To be honest,*
As an example,	*In addition,*	*As a matter of fact,*	*Honestly,*
For instance,	*Additionally,*	*The fact of the matter is*	*To tell the truth,*
	Furthermore,	*Actually,*	*Truthfully,*
	too / also		*As I see it,*

SOLUTION: Practice speaking with a timer. This will help you get used to the amount of time you need to speak. Make a chart like the one below and practice giving responses to questions. That way you can track your progress.

Question #	Time (first try)	Time (second try)	Time (third try)

» **CHALLENGE 5: "I know that the Speaking Test also requires good reading and listening skills. What can I do to help improve my understanding?"**

SOLUTION: You'll need to read quickly, or scan, texts to find specific information during the test. Practice scanning schedules, menus, price lists, advertisements, invoices, and similar things in English for specific information. You can switch your Internet search engine to the English version. Then do searches for texts like these. Scanning the search results for links in English is also good practice. Then time yourself as you scan to find specific types of information. Go back and check your answers by reading more slowly and carefully. This will help you learn how to find information quickly and report it accurately. Here's a list of things to find to help get you started.

1. For a restaurant menu, find:
   - the most expensive item on the menu.
   - the least expensive item.
   - two kinds of dessert.
   - a seafood dish.
   - the restaurant's opening and closing times.

2. For a train schedule, find:
   - the departure time of the earliest train.
   - the departure time of the latest train.
   - the names of three cities on a route.
   - information about how to purchase tickets.

3. For a theater schedule, find:
   - the times for performances on a particular date.
   - the types of performances scheduled.
   - the name of the star performer.
   - information about how to purchase tickets.

4. For a conference schedule, find:
   - the titles of the workshops to be given at a particular time.
   - the dates of the conference.
   - the cost to attend the conference.
   - information about exhibits.

SOLUTION: In one part of the Speaking Test, you will need to listen to a phone message in English, then briefly summarize and respond to it. Practice for this by looking on the Internet for short podcasts, radio programs, or news programs. Listen and summarize what you heard aloud. Record it if possible. Then listen to the original piece again to see if you forgot or misunderstood any parts of it.

SOLUTION: A good way to practice listening skills is to listen to songs in English. As you listen, try to write down the words. Listen as many times as you need to. You can find the lyrics to most popular songs online, so it is easy to check your work.

TOEIC® Test Speaking Questions 1–2

For Questions 1 and 2 of the Speaking Test, you will read a short text aloud. The text will be written in common everyday language and will deal with familiar topics, such as travel, shopping, work, and so on. When you see the text, you will have 45 seconds to prepare and 45 seconds to read the text aloud.

Possible topics may include:

» *Advertisements, announcements, and news broadcasts*

» *Tour information, traffic reports, and weather reports*

» *Entertainment, health, housing, shopping, and travel*

QUICK GUIDE: Read a Text Aloud

Definition	Questions 1 and 2 test your ability to pronounce words clearly and speak English in a comprehensible way. You will read a short text aloud, and your reading of the text will be recorded for scoring.
Targeted Skills	In order to do well on Questions 1 and 2, you must be able to: • pronounce common words correctly. • use correct intonation when reading sentences. • use correct stress on syllables and words.
Text Types	The length of each text is approximately 100 words. The texts represent something that would normally be read aloud, such as an announcement, a radio or television advertisement, or the introduction of a speaker.
A Good Response	A good response will: • reflect an accurate pronunciation of the words. • contain smooth connections between words. • contain accurate phrasing of groups of words and "chunks" of language. • include correct stress for emphasis, new information, and contrast. • include appropriate intonation to indicate the attitude or tone of the text.
Things to Remember	**1.** Scan the entire text before reading so you have an idea of the content. **2.** Read clearly and in a voice that can be easily heard. **3.** Remember to pause for commas and periods. **4.** Be sure to use intonation that matches the meaning of the sentences. **5.** Be careful to pronounce the words correctly.

WALK THROUGH: Read a Text Aloud

A What You'll See and Hear

For Questions 1 and 2, you will see and hear the directions, and you will see a text that you
will read aloud. Listen to the directions as you read along. Then quickly scan the text to get an
idea of its content.   🎧 Track 01-02.01

Speaking Test   VOLUME 🔊

Question 1 (or 2) of 11

Questions 1–2: Read a text aloud

Directions: In this part, you will read a text aloud. You will have 45 seconds to prepare and 45 seconds
to read the text aloud.

The city's annual summer festival will take place next Saturday and Sunday. There will be
activities that are fun for the whole family. You can try a variety of food, hear different
kinds of music, and enjoy games for all ages. Tickets cost fifteen dollars at the gate.
However, if you buy your ticket in advance, you will get a ten percent discount. Tickets are
available at many local stores, as well as at City Hall. Don't miss this fun event!

Preparation Time: 45 seconds

Response Time: 45 seconds

B What You'll Do

For Questions 1 and 2, you will read a text aloud. Time yourself while you read the text
above. Read clearly and in a voice that can be easily heard. Try to read the text in no more
than 45 seconds. Then listen to the model text on the audio. Listen carefully to the speaker's
pronunciation, intonation, and stress. Then try reading aloud along with the model.
🎧 Track 01-02.02

QUICK TIP

While you prepare your
response, scan the
reading for important
words. They may
be nouns, verbs, or
adverbs. These words
will require accurate
pronunciation and
stress. Pronouncing
them correctly will help
make your reading be
more understandable.

GET IT RIGHT: Tips and Tasks for Answering Correctly

Questions 1 and 2 on the Speaking Test are scored on a scale from 0–3. Your
recorded responses will be graded based on pronunciation, stress, and intonation.

- **Pronunciation** refers to how we produce the sounds of words. In the dictionary, you
  will see the correct pronunciation of a word using a modified version of the International
  Phonetic Alphabet (IPA). The dictionary gives examples of the general or standard
  pronunciations of a word. Listen to two correct ways to pronounce the word *pronunciation*.
  In the first one, you hear just the *n* in the middle of the word. In the second one, you hear *nt*.
  The dictionary shows the *t* in parentheses because it is optional.   🎧 Track 01-02.03

  pro·nun·ci·a·tion (noun) prə-ˌnən(t)-sē-ˈā-shən

- **Stress** is how we emphasize certain syllables when we pronounce a word. For example, we stress the first syllable of the word *syllable* (*SYLL-able*). We also use stress in our sentences to help us link phrases together and put emphasis on important focus words. Listen to the way the speaker stresses key words in the sentence below to show their importance.
  🎧 Track 01-02.04

  > The <u>meeting</u> will be in the <u>conference</u> room.

- **Intonation** refers to the pitch level—the rising and falling—of speech. There are two kinds of intonation in spoken English sentences: rising-falling and rising. We use rising-falling in most statements and information questions. We use rising intonation to form *yes-no* questions. 🎧 Track 01-02.05

  Rising-Falling: *We have a meeting on Tuesday.*
  We'll be talking about sales, earnings, and future plans.
  What time is the meeting?

  Rising: *Is the meeting at 2:00?*

Read and listen to an example of an effective reading of a text from Questions 1–2 of the Speaking Test. As you listen, pay special attention to the highlighted words and phrases. These are stressed words and phrases or especially tricky words. Then listen again and read aloud with the audio.   🎧 Track 01-02.06

> Could we have your attention, please? We'd like to take this time to thank you for attending this athletic banquet. This has been a fantastic year for our team and our athletes. We now hold a new record for most wins in our state's division. Your support has allowed us to purchase new uniforms and a new scoreboard for our field. To show our appreciation for the coaches, the staff, and our fans, we'd like to invite you to view the new scoreboard, enjoy some refreshments, and meet the team. Let's give a round of applause for the three candidates for player of the year.

PRONUNCIATION

» **TIP 1 Practice correct pronunciation and learn to recognize "tricky" sounds.** One of the main points for Questions 1 and 2 is to test your ability to correctly pronounce both known and unknown words. Learn to recognize the most commonly mispronounced sounds, and practice them as much as possible.

Look at the chart of commonly mispronounced words and sounds. The sounds and problem combinations are **boldfaced** in the words. Listen to the correct pronunciations of the words and sounds. Then play the audio again and repeat each word and sound.   🎧 Track 01-02.07

Commonly Mispronounced Words and Sounds					
Words	Sounds	Why They Are Tricky	Words	Sounds	Why They Are Tricky
thing *athlete* *throw* *months*	/θ/ or /th/* /θl/ /θr/ /θs/	The /θ/ sound alone or with other sounds is difficult for many speakers because of the tongue-teeth movement needed.	*zero* *wisdom* *wins*	/ʒ/ or /z/*	The /ʒ/ sound is similar to the /s/ sound, but /z/ is voiced, which means the vocal cords are vibrating.
then *clothes*	/ð/	The /ð/ sound is similar to /θ/, but /ð/ is voiced, which means the vocal cords are vibrating.	*window* *wagon*	/w/	The /w/ sound requires a strong lip movement that can be troublesome for some speakers.
clear *create*	/kl/ /kr/	The combination of /k/ with /l/ or /r/ can be difficult to say.	*shield* *motion* *wish*	/ʃ/ or /sh/*	The /sh/ sound uses the tongue, lips, and teeth, which can make it difficult.
like *whole* *shelf* *flake* *place* *blend*	/l/	The /l/ sound requires a movement between the tongue and teeth that can make it difficult at the start or end of words or in consonant combinations.	*child* *lunch* *watch*	/tʃ/ or /ch/*	The /tʃ/ sound uses the tongue, lips, and teeth, which can make it difficult.
repair *server* *trip* *prescribe* *clerk* *course*	/r/	The /r/ sound requires an entire mouth movement at the start or end of words or in consonant combinations. The actual sound varies considerably depending on its position.	*jump* *dodge* *lounge*	/dʒ/ or /j/*	Like /tʃ/, the /dʒ/ sound uses the tongue, lips, and teeth, but /dʒ/ is voiced, which means the vocal cords are vibrating.
silence *ceremony* *study* *streets* *script*	/s/	The /s/ sound is made by blowing air lightly through the teeth. It appears in many clusters with no vowel sound before it.	*volume* *curve* *shelves*	/v/	The /v/ sound requires the same movement as /f/—placing the teeth on the lower lip—but /v/ is voiced, which means the vocal cords are vibrating.

*modified IPA as used in many dictionaries

TASK 1 Listen to each consonant sound and word. Circle the word that you hear. Then listen to the audio again and repeat all of the words. 🎧 Track 01-02.08

1. thin	then	**8.** Esther	stare
2. laughed	raft	**9.** she'll	zeal
3. sip	zip	**10.** watch	wash
4. clothes	close	**11.** fans	vans
5. junk	chunk	**12.** veer	we're
6. lunch	lunge	**13.** zinc	sink
7. blight	bright	**14.** tan	than

TASK 2 Listen and number the words in the order you hear them. Then play the audio again and repeat the words. Repeat as many times as needed until you can match the pronunciation in the audio.

🎧 Track 01-02.09

___ though	___ light	___ den
___ then	___ clean	___ vend
___ right	___ cream	___ think
___ sink	___ tow	___ wind

» **TIP 2 When you look up the pronunciation of a word, also learn the number of syllables.** The dictionary uses special punctuation to mark each syllable in a word. Look for a dot (•) or bar (|) in the main entry and a hyphen (-) or period (.) in the pronunciation. It is important to learn the number of syllables for every new word because many English words have more or fewer syllables than they seem to. Say the word aloud several times to reinforce the correct syllable use.

QUICK TIP

⋮ Some words have
⋮ more than one way to
⋮ pronounce the syllables.
⋮ *Corporate* can have two
⋮ or three syllables, and
⋮ *invaluable* can have
⋮ four or five. A dictionary
⋮ shows the most com-
⋮ mon pronunciation first.

TASK 1 Look at the words. How many syllables do you think each word has? Write the number for your guess for each word in the first column. Then listen and write the number of syllables you hear on the audio in the second column. Was your first guess correct? 🎧 Track 01-02.10

1. corporate			6. frequently		
2. invaluable			7. cooperation		
3. February			8. athletics		
4. automatically			9. librarian		
5. candidate			10. unfortunately		

TASK 2 Look at the words. Draw lines to divide each word into syllables. Then listen to the audio to check your answers. While you listen, repeat the pronunciation of the word. 🎧 Track 01-02.11

Example: *calendar*   *cal/en/dar*

1. career	7. asked
2. carrier	8. intelligent
3. advertisement	9. dependability
4. improbable	10. acquisition
5. corporation	11. regional
6. clothes	12. liability

STRESS

Stress is important in words and sentences. Knowing whether a syllable is stressed or unstressed is an important part of pronouncing a word correctly. For example, *re-CORD* and *REC-ord* have two very different meanings, but they have the same spelling, *record*. Correctly stressing words and phrases gives rhythm to a sentence, and it signals the importance of some information.

» TIP 1 Learn stress in order to pronounce words correctly. All words with more than one syllable have stressed and unstressed syllables. Knowing which syllables are stressed will help you pronounce words correctly and convey the correct meaning.

In nouns and adjectives with <u>two</u> syllables, the stress usually falls on the first syllable. For verbs with two syllables, the stress usually falls on the second syllable. Listen and read the words in the chart. Then listen again and practice saying them with the audio. 🎧 Track 01-02.12

Nouns / Adjectives	Verbs	Nouns / Adjectives	Verbs
CONduct	*conDUCT*	*PERmit*	*perMIT*
CONtest	*conTEST*	*PROduce*	*proDUCE*
EXport	*exPORT*	*OBject*	*obJECT*
IMport	*imPORT*	*SUBject*	*subJECT*
INcrease	*inCREASE*	*SURvey*	*surVEY*
PROject	*proJECT*	*REfund*	*reFUND*

TASK 1 Write down whether each underlined word is used as a verb or a noun. Try to pronounce the word. Then listen to check your answers. 🎧 Track 01-02.13

1. You really need to learn how to <u>conduct</u> yourself in a meeting. _____

2. There are several important <u>projects</u> coming up. _____

3. We have to <u>address</u> the problems to avoid issues later. _____

4. They <u>import</u> most of their auto parts. _____

5. He set a new sales <u>record</u> last month. _____

6. We've made most of our money in <u>produce</u>. _____

7. Business is set to <u>increase</u> next year. _____

8. She decided to <u>contest</u> the decision to fire the people. _____

Knowing **suffixes** (the small parts that come <u>after</u> the root of the word) can help you predict the stress pattern of a word.

- For nouns that end in -*ion*, -*sion*, -*tion*, or -*ic*, the stress will be on the syllable right before the suffix: **na**tion, con**ver**sion, gradu**a**tion.

- For verbs with -*ize* or -*ate* suffixes, the stress will be on the first syllable of a three-syllable word or the second syllable of a four-syllable word: **spe**cialize, an**ti**cipate.

- For words ending with -*cy*, -*ty*, -*phy*, -*gy*, or -*al*, the stress will be on the third syllable from the end: de**moc**racy, pho**to**graphy, uni**ver**sity, ge**og**raphy, **prin**ciple.

TASK 2 Look at the words and analyze the suffixes. Underline the syllables that you think are stressed. Then listen to the audio to check your answers. Listen to the audio again and repeat the words.
🎧 Track 01-02.14

1. authorize	**8.** appreciate	**15.** cooperate
2. interruption	**9.** accommodations	**16.** direction
3. recreation	**10.** estimate	**17.** evaluate
4. validate	**11.** interpretation	**18.** recognize
5. version	**12.** notarize	**19.** suspension
6. geography	**13.** policy	**20.** charity
7. geographic	**14.** location	**21.** democracy

Knowing **prefixes** (the small parts that come <u>before</u> the root of the word) can also help you predict the stress pattern of a word. When the word is a verb or has more than two syllables, the stress is usually on the second syllable of the word. Here are examples of some common prefixes.

Prefixes	Examples	Prefixes	Examples
con- / com-	conTRACT comPARE	in- / im-	inSPIRE imPROVE
de-	deCIDE	pro-	proTECT
dis-	disAble	re-	reMODel
ex-	exPECT	pre-	preVENT
be-	beCOME	re-	reDO
over-	overLOAD	out-	outLAST
under-	underSTATE	un-	unSTAble

TASK 3 Look at the words and analyze the prefixes. Underline the syllables that you think are stressed. Then listen to the audio to check your answers. Listen to the audio again and repeat the words.

🎧 Track 01-02.15

1. descendent	7. dislocate	13. redundant
2. underestimate	8. extract	14. inspect
3. overuse	9. outstanding	15. unusable
4. belated	10. completely	16. contented
5. renew	11. unable	17. reduction
6. extensive	12. respectable	18. complaint

TASK 4 Read the sentences and notice the **boldfaced** words. Circle the boldfaced words that are nouns, and underline the boldfaced words that are verbs. Then double-underline (⎵) the stressed syllables in the boldfaced words. Listen to check your answers, and repeat the sentences to practice.

🎧 Track 01-02.16

1. Please use this software to **record** the day's sales.

2. All employees are expected to follow the company code of **conduct**.

3. Let's not **overestimate** the amount of work we can do.

4. Before we create our business plan for the month, let's **coordinate** our schedules.

5. **Prosperity** is the goal of all **nations**.

6. After you receive your pass code, you will have **authorization**.

7. This year, we decided to **recognize** our supervisor for his 10 years of service.

8. We **project** that our product sales will **increase** over the next two years.

9. It was a great **comfort** to **receive** your letter.

10. She studied **biology** at the **university**.

11. As we **progress** with this **project**, we will give everyone a monthly **report**.

12. The marketing team really **outdid** themselves with this **detailed explanation**.

QUICK TIP

Sometimes words have both a prefix and a suffix. In these cases, the word may have a primary and secondary stress, but whichever syllable is later in the word is usually stronger. For example,

comPATible –

compatiBILity

decision – indeCIsion

» **TIP 2 Stress words in sentences to emphasize or contrast information.** Use stress within a sentence to show that certain information is new or important. You can also use stress to contrast information. For example, listen and read the conversation below. Notice how Speaker B uses stress to (1) add new and important information, and (2) contrast information. ⌂ Track 01-02.17

> **A:** *Would you like some tea?*
>
> **B:** *I'd like some black (1) tea.*
>
> **A:** *Sure, here you are.*
>
> **B:** *Sorry, but this is green (2) tea. I asked for black (2) tea.*

You should also use stress to give more emphasis to the words that naturally carry meaning in sentences—the content words. Function words, or the words in a sentence that are used to give grammatical structure, don't usually receive as much stress unless the speaker wants to give some sort of contrast or emphasis. Listen and notice the stressed content words below. ⌂ Track 01-02.18

> *The **employees** are the ones to **thank**.*
>
> *There's really not a lot to **say** about that.*

Finally, adverbs are frequently stressed to add emphasis. Listen and notice the stressed adverbs below. ⌂ Track 01-02.19

> *We **really** don't have much time.*
>
> *I **completely** forgot the conference.*

TASK 1 Listen to the sentences as you read along. Underline the words that receive the most stress. Then listen and practice. ⌂ Track 01-02.20

1. The correct numbers are 13 and 17, not 30 and 70.

2. We strongly suggest that you back up your computer files at the end of the day.

3. Our genealogists will conduct a very thorough search of your family tree.

4. On the new schedule, you will see that the bus departs on Tuesday at 1 p.m.

5. Your estimated wait time to speak to a representative is ten minutes.

6. The parking spaces are clearly marked "visitor."

TASK 2 Read the sentences. Which boldfaced words do you think should be stressed? Underline your choices. Then listen and check your answers. ⌂ Track 01-02.21

1. The real estate office **is located** in the **green** house **on the** left.

2. You will receive **a credit** card within **ten days** after receipt **of** your application.

3. **The** message **said to** phone their office between **9 and 5**, Monday to Friday.

4. We are **currently** reviewing your request **and will** respond **within 30** days.

5. Please **turn down** the volume **on** the **TV**, not up.

INTONATION AND PAUSING

Sentence intonation helps the listener understand the speaker's meaning, in addition to the speaker's attitude or mood. The most common intonation patterns are **rising-falling** for statements and information questions and **rising** for *yes-no* questions.

» **TIP 1 Use correct intonation for phrasing in statements.** Statements typically have falling intonation, meaning the speaker's voice lowers slightly at the end of the sentence. Listen to the statements below and notice the intonation.   ⌒ Track 01-02.22

We've had a lot of success with the new plan.

There are a multitude of reasons for the problem.

She really hasn't done much in her new position.

However, within a sentence, speakers may use rising or higher intonation in different situations. When giving a series of numbers or a list of three or more items, the speaker will often use rising intonation to let the listener know there is more to come. The speaker will then usually use falling intonation on the last item to indicate the list is complete. Listen to the examples below and notice the intonation.
⌒ Track 01-02.23

The key points here are time, expense, and quality.

Hotel management, health care, accounting, and education are all good career options.

Our new number is 218-555-3675.

Speakers will also use rising or higher intonation when there are clauses in a statement to show that more information is to come. Listen to the examples below. Notice the underlined clauses, the **boldfaced** signpost words used to introduce them, and how the clauses affect intonation.
⌒ Track 01-02.24

Because <u>*we don't have the reports yet*</u>, *we can't have the meeting.*

We really wanted to leave at 5:00; ***however,*** <u>*the plane was delayed.*</u>

I really wanted to go to the conference, ***until*** <u>*I saw the huge entry fees.*</u>

Although <u>*I usually enjoy my job,*</u> *this past month has been tough.*

TASK Listen and mark the phrasing of each sentence with rising ⬈ or falling ⬊ intonation marks. Then listen again and repeat to practice. Be careful to model the phrasing you hear.   ⌒ Track 01-02.25

1. We will need ushers, ticket takers, and box office staff at the theater this weekend.

2. At this time, there is no one available to take your call. Please leave a message after the beep.

3. Our number is 202-555-4567. Please call if you have any problems.

4. Because the application forms were late, we'll need to adjust the start date.

5. Please turn off all cell phones and pagers before the movie begins.

6. In conclusion, we'd like to thank all of our guests for their participation.

QUICK TIP

These common words and phrases are often used as signposts to join sentences and paragraphs together:

Additionally, As a result of this, In comparison, For example, In other words, Finally, First / Next / Then

The word or phrase will usually have rising intonation. The sentence or clause that follows usually ends with falling intonation.

» **TIP 2 Use correct intonation for questions.** Information questions usually start with the word *Who, What, Where, When, Why,* or *How.* These types of questions have falling intonation at the end of the sentence. Listen to the information questions below and notice the intonation. 🎧 Track 01-02.26

What did you do last weekend?	*When do we need to be there?*
Where is the meeting?	*How many people are coming?*
Why didn't he call?	*How much does it cost?*

Yes-No questions usually start with some form of an auxiliary verb, such as *do, have, can,* or *be.* These types of questions, including tag questions at the ends of sentences, have an up intonation. Listen to the *yes-no* questions below and notice the intonation. 🎧 Track 01-02.27

Do you want to join the call?	*Those are my files, aren't they?*
Have you seen the report?	*Could you open that file?*

TASK Do these questions have rising or falling intonation? Write ➚ for rising intonation or ➘ for falling intonation. Then listen to check your answers and practice. 🎧 Track 01-02.28

1. What do you think?

2. If Friday is not a good day, can we meet on Saturday?

3. I'm sorry, could you repeat that, please?

4. We didn't hear that. What did he say?

5. What did John bring to the party?

6. How can I help you today?

7. Is this your first day here?

8. Have you sent the latest market reports?

» **TIP 3 Punctuation indicates where to pause.** Commas and periods are used to show where a writer would like to break a sentence or a thought. Be sure to include a slight pause between sentences and after commas, colons, and semicolons. Listen to the sentences below and notice how the written punctuation is reflected in the audio pauses. 🎧 Track 01-02.29

> *According to the monthly report, our production has increased 300% over the past five years. There's only one group to thank for this: you. Our support staff and team members have done so much to help over the past year; we couldn't have done it without you. Our thanks go out to everyone. We really appreciate it.*

You should also pause after transitions and prepositional phrases that introduce a sentence. Notice that the comma gives a second clue to the pause. Listen to the sentences below and notice the underlined transitions and prepositional phrases. 🎧 Track 01-02.30

<u>Nonetheless</u>, he got the promotion.

<u>Unfortunately</u>, there's nothing more we can do.

<u>By the time we got to the airport</u>, the plane had gone.

<u>As a result of the sale</u>, we all got raises.

TASK Listen to the audio as you read the sentences. Mark the rising intonation with ➚. Mark the falling intonation with ➘. 🎧 Track 01-02.31

1. They have not yet determined what the problem was.

2. Would you like the three-month or the six-month plan?

3. Do you know what time it is?

4. You wouldn't have an extra pencil, would you?

5. Would you mind closing the window?

6. When you need a reliable copy service, Tip Top Copy Shop has everything you need.

QUICK TIP

When you make a polite request by asking a rhetorical question, or one that people don't really need to answer, intonation will fall.

Can you please listen ➘ *carefully?*

PROGRESSIVE PRACTICE: Get Ready

A Read the texts. Notice the markings and notes for pronunciation, intonation, and stress.* Think about how the words should sound. Then listen to the audio. Listen again and read aloud with the speaker.

🎧 Track 01-02.32

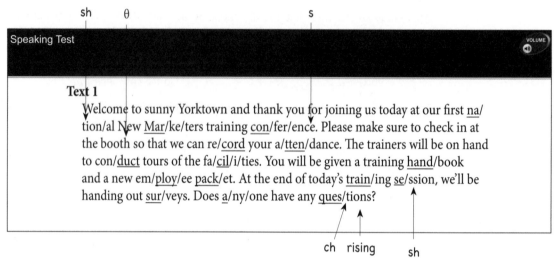

Text 1

Welcome to sunny Yorktown and thank you for joining us today at our first na/tion/al New Mar/ke/ters training con/fer/ence. Please make sure to check in at the booth so that we can re/cord your a/tten/dance. The trainers will be on hand to con/duct tours of the fa/cil/i/ties. You will be given a training hand/book and a new em/ploy/ee pack/et. At the end of today's train/ing se/ssion, we'll be handing out sur/veys. Does a/ny/one have any ques/tions?

🎧 Track 01-02.33

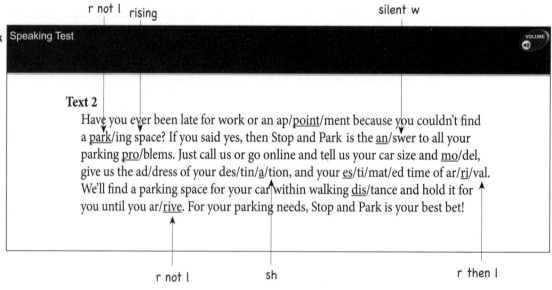

Text 2

Have you ever been late for work or an ap/point/ment because you couldn't find a park/ing space? If you said yes, then Stop and Park is the an/swer to all your parking pro/blems. Just call us or go online and tell us your car size and mo/del, give us the ad/dress of your des/tin/a/tion, and your es/ti/mat/ed time of ar/ri/val. We'll find a parking space for your car within walking dis/tance and hold it for you until you ar/rive. For your parking needs, Stop and Park is your best bet!

* key
/ = syllable break
___ = stress

B Listen to the model answers and read the texts in Part A again. Notice how the parts with markings and the problem words sound when read. Then listen to the pronunciation of the words and phrases below. Repeat and practice.

Text 1   Track 01-02.34

1. thank you	**7.** record	**13.** training session
2. national	**8.** attendance	**14.** surveys
3. marketers	**9.** conduct	**15.** anyone
4. conference	**10.** facilities	**16.** questions
5. sure	**11.** handbook	
6. both	**12.** employee packet	

Text 2   Track 01-02.35

1. late	**6.** problems	**11.** arrival
2. appointment	**7.** model	**12.** within
3. parking	**8.** address	**13.** distance
4. park	**9.** destination	**14.** for you
5. answer	**10.** estimated	**15.** arrive

C Read the texts in Part A aloud and record yourself. Compare your recordings with the models and note any mispronunciations or incorrectly stressed words in your recordings. Record your responses again if needed.

D Now listen to your recordings. Then read the statements below. How well did your responses meet the scoring criteria? Check (✓) *Yes* or *No*. Keep practicing until all of your answers are *Yes*.

Response Checklist: Questions 1 and 2	Yes	No
1. I spoke clearly and evenly, without hesitating.	☐	☐
2. I used correct pronunciation and syllable stress.	☐	☐
3. I used rising intonation and falling intonation where needed.	☐	☐
4. I stressed words for emphasis where needed.	☐	☐
5. I paused at the correct points in the text.	☐	☐

PROGRESSIVE PRACTICE: Get Set

A Pre-read the texts and notice the underlined words that might be challenging. To help you prepare to read the texts aloud, make notes about pronunciation, word and sentence stress, and intonation.

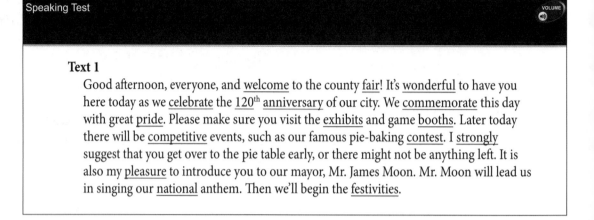

Speaking Test

Text 1

Good afternoon, everyone, and <u>welcome</u> to the county <u>fair</u>! It's <u>wonderful</u> to have you here today as we <u>celebrate</u> the 120th <u>anniversary</u> of our city. We <u>commemorate</u> this day with great <u>pride</u>. Please make sure you visit the <u>exhibits</u> and game <u>booths</u>. Later today there will be <u>competitive</u> events, such as our famous pie-baking <u>contest</u>. I <u>strongly</u> suggest that you get over to the pie table early, or there might not be anything left. It is also my <u>pleasure</u> to introduce you to our mayor, Mr. James Moon. Mr. Moon will lead us in singing our <u>national</u> anthem. Then we'll begin the <u>festivities</u>.

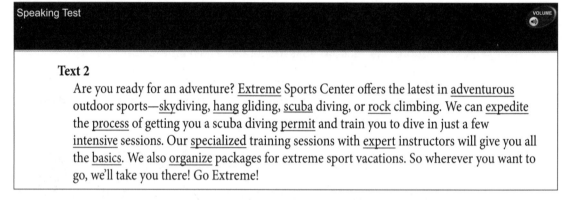

Speaking Test

Text 2

Are you ready for an adventure? <u>Extreme</u> Sports Center offers the latest in <u>adventurous</u> outdoor sports—<u>sky</u>diving, <u>hang</u> gliding, <u>scuba</u> diving, or <u>rock</u> climbing. We can <u>expedite</u> the <u>process</u> of getting you a scuba diving <u>permit</u> and train you to dive in just a few <u>intensive</u> sessions. Our <u>specialized</u> training sessions with <u>expert</u> instructors will give you all the <u>basics</u>. We also <u>organize</u> packages for extreme sport vacations. So wherever you want to go, we'll take you there! Go Extreme!

B Listen to the model answers and read the texts in Part A again. Then read the texts in Part A aloud and record yourself. Compare your recordings with the models and note any mispronunciations or incorrectly stressed words in your recordings.

🎧 Track 01-02.36 and 01-02.37

C Now listen to your recording. Then read the statements below. How well did your responses meet the scoring criteria? Check (✓) *Yes* or *No*. Keep practicing until all of your answers are *Yes*.

Response Checklist: Questions 1 and 2	Yes	No
1. I spoke clearly and evenly, without hesitating.	☐	☐
2. I used correct pronunciation and syllable stress.	☐	☐
3. I used rising intonation and falling intonation where needed.	☐	☐
4. I stressed words for emphasis where needed.	☐	☐
5. I paused at the correct points in the text.	☐	☐

PROGRESSIVE PRACTICE: Go for the TOEIC® Test

Time yourself as you prepare. Then time yourself as you record your responses.

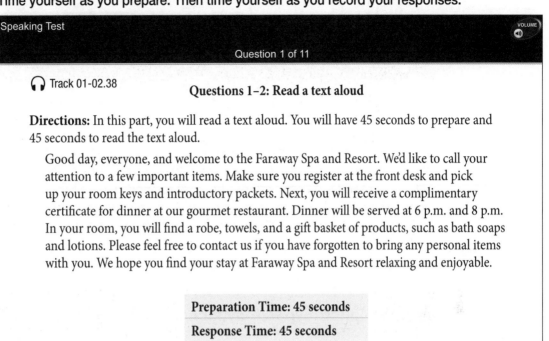

Speaking Test

Question 1 of 11

🎧 Track 01-02.38

Questions 1–2: Read a text aloud

Directions: In this part, you will read a text aloud. You will have 45 seconds to prepare and 45 seconds to read the text aloud.

Good day, everyone, and welcome to the Faraway Spa and Resort. We'd like to call your attention to a few important items. Make sure you register at the front desk and pick up your room keys and introductory packets. Next, you will receive a complimentary certificate for dinner at our gourmet restaurant. Dinner will be served at 6 p.m. and 8 p.m. In your room, you will find a robe, towels, and a gift basket of products, such as bath soaps and lotions. Please feel free to contact us if you have forgotten to bring any personal items with you. We hope you find your stay at Faraway Spa and Resort relaxing and enjoyable.

| Preparation Time: 45 seconds |
| Response Time: 45 seconds |

Preparation Time Used: _____ seconds   **Speaking Time Used:** _____ seconds

To hear a sample response, listen to Track **01-02.40.**

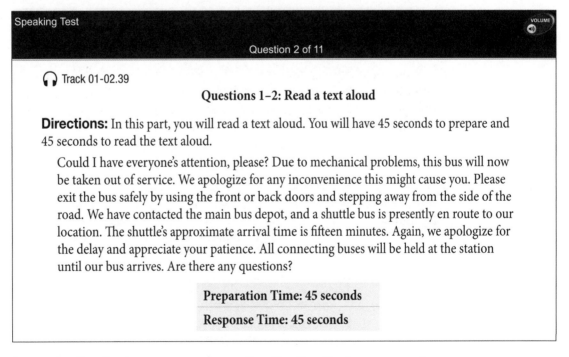

Speaking Test

Question 2 of 11

🎧 Track 01-02.39

Questions 1–2: Read a text aloud

Directions: In this part, you will read a text aloud. You will have 45 seconds to prepare and 45 seconds to read the text aloud.

Could I have everyone's attention, please? Due to mechanical problems, this bus will now be taken out of service. We apologize for any inconvenience this might cause you. Please exit the bus safely by using the front or back doors and stepping away from the side of the road. We have contacted the main bus depot, and a shuttle bus is presently en route to our location. The shuttle's approximate arrival time is fifteen minutes. Again, we apologize for the delay and appreciate your patience. All connecting buses will be held at the station until our bus arrives. Are there any questions?

| Preparation Time: 45 seconds |
| Response Time: 45 seconds |

Preparation Time Used: _____ seconds   **Speaking Time Used:** _____ seconds

To hear a sample response, listen to Track **01-02.41.**

TOEIC® Test Speaking Question 3

On Question 3 of the Speaking Test, you will see a photo and describe it. The photo will show a person or people involved in a common everyday activity in a familiar setting. When you see the photo, you will have 30 seconds to prepare. Then you will have 45 seconds to give your response. The photo will remain on the screen as you prepare and give your response. As in Questions 1 and 2, you will be evaluated on pronunciation, intonation, and stress. In addition, you will be evaluated based on your use of appropriate vocabulary, correct sentence structure, and the cohesion of your response. Photos will show common everyday situations.

Possible photo types may include:

» *Dining out and shopping*

» *Health care settings*

» *Household chores*

» *Entertainment and leisure activities*

» *Outdoor and street scenes*

» *Travel*

QUICK GUIDE: Describe a Picture

Definition	Question 3 tests your ability to speak about everyday situations in a clear and comprehensible way. You will describe a photo, and your description will be recorded.
Targeted Skills	In Question 3, you should be able to: • pronounce common words correctly. • use correct stress on syllables and words. • identify the important features of a photo. • describe a photo using appropriate vocabulary. • describe a photo using correct sentence structure.
A Good Response	You will be scored based on your ability to describe the photo accurately and comprehensibly. In order to do well, you need to speak clearly. You also need to accurately describe the people, activities, and objects in the photo. To achieve a good response, you should use vocabulary that accurately describes the photo, as well as correct grammar and sentence structure.
Things to Remember	**1.** First, scan the photo. What information will you need in your response? Brainstorm quickly when you see the image. **2.** Next, think about what you want to talk about and how you want to say it. You have 30 seconds to prepare and 45 seconds to respond. **3.** You will hear a beep signaling when to start. Begin your answer with a sentence starter, such as *In this photograph, there are . . .* or *In this picture, I see . . . .*

WALK THROUGH: Describe a Picture

A What You'll See and Hear

For Question 3, you will see a photo with one or more people. As soon as you see the photo, try to identify the main subject. What are the important details in this photo?

🎧 Track 03.01

Speaking Test

VOLUME 🔊

Question 3: Describe a picture

Directions: In this part, you will describe the photo on the screen with as much detail as possible. You will have 30 seconds to prepare. You will have 45 seconds to describe the photo.

Preparation Time: 30 seconds

Response Time: 45 seconds

> **QUICK TIP**
>
> While you prepare your response, ask yourself about the people in the photo and think of possible nouns, adjectives, verbs, and adverbs to describe the photo.

B What You'll Do

For Question 3, you will have 30 seconds to prepare your response. Time yourself while you brainstorm ideas. Look closely at the photo and identify the people. Look at the photo in Part A. Think about what the people are doing. Listen and notice how the speaker organizes his response. Listen carefully to the speaker's pronunciation, intonation, and stress. 🎧 Track 03.02

SAMPLE RESPONSE ▶

Well, there are two people inside a bakery in this photo. The woman who is facing us is probably a baker because she's wearing a white uniform and a black hat to cover her hair. And she's coming out of the kitchen carrying bread. It looks like she has just taken the hot bread out of the oven, and she's carrying the tray to the counter. We can see the oven behind her. The bakery looks very modern. I'd guess that the baker is going to put the bread on some kind of bread rack or a shelf to cool so that people can buy it. She's smiling at the customer. Um, next, she's probably going to help the man in the blue shirt, who's waiting in front of the counter. His back is to us. He's probably hoping to buy some of that delicious fresh bread.

Glossary:

⚡ POWERED BY COBUILD

rack: a frame or shelf, usually with bars or hooks, that is used for holding things or hanging things on

tray: a flat piece of wood, plastic, or metal, which usually has raised edges and which is used for carrying things, especially food and drinks

GET IT RIGHT: Tips and Tasks for Answering Correctly

Question 3 on the Speaking Test is scored on a scale from 0–3. Your response will be graded based on the same criteria as for Questions 1 and 2—pronunciation, intonation, and stress. You will also be graded on grammar, vocabulary, and cohesion.

- **Grammar** is the way that words can be put together in order to make correct English sentences. In this section of the test, your score will be based partly on how well you use the correct forms of words and correct sentence structures to make a clear and accurate description of the photo. You should also try to use a variety of different grammatical structures.

- **Vocabulary** refers to the number of words and the kinds of words you use to describe the photo. You will be expected to use a variety of vocabulary to accurately talk about what is in the photo.

- **Cohesion** is how well the information in your description fits together in a clear and easy-to-understand manner. A cohesive response uses conjunctions, references, and other language tools to make a well-organized description.

Look at the photo again as you listen to another good response below. As you listen, circle the nouns and underline the verbs. How many different nouns for people or objects did you find? 🎧 Track 03.03

QUICK TIP

Organize your thoughts around a main idea. Images usually have a main subject. So focus first on the main subject of the image. Is it a person? An object? A location? Then fill in what you know about that subject. Begin speaking first about that main point. Then add details.

A Good Response: *I see two people in this picture. I think this must be a bakery. There's a man on the right with his back to the camera. He's wearing a blue shirt. He must be a customer because he seems to be at the counter waiting to buy something. There's also a woman in the center of the picture. She's facing the camera. She's wearing a white jacket or uniform and a black cap to cover her hair. She's also carrying a large tray of rolls, so I think she must be a baker. It looks like she just took the tray of bread out of the oven. The oven is behind her. The bread probably smells delicious. Maybe the customer was waiting to buy some of the delicious fresh rolls, or maybe he's going to buy something else at the bakery.*

GRAMMAR AND VOCABULARY

To answer Question 3 effectively, you will need to know basic vocabulary (nouns, adjectives, prepositions, verbs, and adverbs) and demonstrate the ability to use correct grammar by structuring your sentences in a logical and coherent way.

» **TIP 1 Be sure to use the correct noun or pronoun and the correct verb form.** You can organize your response by asking yourself: Who or what is the main subject in the photo? Be sure to vary your response by using pronouns as well as different nouns to refer to the people and things in the photo.

QUICK TIP

Practice thinking of several different words to identify specific people and objects. The woman in the sample photo can be referred to as *woman, baker, she,* or *her,* depending on context and grammar. The man in the photo can be referred to as *man, customer, he,* or *him.* You can practice describing magazine photos.

	If there is one person:	**If there are two or more people:**
The first time you mention the person, people, or thing, use a noun:	*the man, the woman, the boy, the girl, the street*	*the men, the women, the people, the boys, the girls, the children, the streets*
The second time, you can use a pronoun:	*he, she, it (him, her, it; his, her, its)*	*they (them; their)*

TASK Look at the photo on page 18 again. Read each sentence below and fill in the blank with a correct noun or pronoun from the box. Some sentences have more than one answer. Write <u>all</u> possible correct answers, but be careful—your choices must logically fit the context and sentence structures for the photo.

baker	bread	customer	man	woman	he	it	she

1. The _____ is standing in the kitchen. _____ is probably a baker.

2. The baker is going to put the _____ on the rack. _____ is still hot.

3. The _____ is waiting to buy something. _____ is standing in front of the counter.

4. The woman is carrying a tray of fresh bread. _____ is probably hot.

5. There is a _____ standing behind the counter. _____ is holding a tray.

6. The _____ is wearing a casual shirt. _____ is waiting to buy some bread.

7. The _____ probably goes to the bakery every morning before _____ goes to work.

8. The woman is a baker. _____ works at the bakery every day.

» **TIP 2 Use specific verb tenses and structures for basic descriptions.** Make sure you are comfortable with these tenses: simple present, simple past, and present and past continuous. Also, make sure you can use *There is / There are . . . .*

QUICK TIP

Remember that we use **simple present** for actions that take place every day. Use **present continuous** for actions that are <u>not</u> complete and are happening at the moment.

The woman in the photo works in a bakery. (simple present)

She is carrying a tray of bread. (present continuous)

	Simple Present	**Simple Past +** *maybe/ probably*	**Present and Past Continuous**
Uses	For repeated actions that exist now or occur daily, usually, or in general	To make guesses about actions that may explain a condition in the picture	For actions that are happening at the moment, or **now**, or to make guesses about what happened before the picture was taken
Singular *he / she / it*	*is; She is in the living room.*	*was; Maybe it was rainy.*	*is + verb + -ing; He's talking to a friend. Perhaps he was running late.*
Plural *they*	*are; They are teachers.*	*were; They were probably busy earlier.*	*are + verb + -ing; They are waving good-bye. Maybe they were coming home.*

There is / There are			
There	is	a	man / woman.
There	are	two	people.

TASK Read the sentences and fill in the blanks with the correct forms of the verbs in parentheses. Use the simple present, present continuous, or *There is / There are*.

1. The woman _____ (stand) in the kitchen.

2. The man _____ (walk) to work every day.

3. He _____ (wait) for the baker to bring the bread.

4. _____ (be) two people in this photo.

5. The woman _____ (wear) a white coat and a black hat.

6. _____ (be) a man standing at the counter.

» **TIP 3 Use prepositions and adverbs to talk about location and how things move.** Remember that prepositions and adverbs help specify location and direction.

Location (Prepositions)	Direction (Adverbs)
at the front; in the back	forward; backward; toward; away from
in front of; behind	ahead; behind; toward the front / back
on the left / right; in the center (middle)	to the left / right; toward the center
below; above; at the top / bottom; underneath	from above / below; under; over
next to; in the corner; at the corner; on the side	next to; toward the corner; to the side

on top of / above

to the left

←

to the right

→

at the top

in the center /
in the middle

in the
corner

at the bottom

under / beneath / underneath / below

TASK Look at the photo on page 18. Read each sentence and fill in the blank with the correct preposition from the box.

at the back of	behind	on	in	in front of

1. The baker is _____ the counter.

2. The man is _____ the counter.

3. The bread is _____ the tray.

4. The baker has a tray _____ her hands.

5. The ovens are _____ the kitchen.

QUICK TIP

Make sure your subjects and verbs agree. If your subject is singular (*a man, a woman*), the present form of the verb needs *-s*. If the subject is plural (*men, women, people*), no *-s* is needed.

QUICK TIP

Words and phrases like *a lot of, a few, some,* and *many,* as well as numbers (*one of the loaves, two people*), can help you make your response more detailed and specific.

» **TIP 4 Use adjectives to give more information about people and objects.** Adjectives describe nouns, and more than one adjective can be used with a noun. Strings of adjectives follow a specific order in English. In normal speech, English speakers rarely use more than two or three adjectives to describe a noun. This chart will help you figure out the correct order, even if you use only two adjectives together.

Typical Order of Adjectives in English					
[1] Numbers and Quantifiers	[2] Size, Age, or Quality*	[3] Color	[4] Material or Type	[5] Origin or Type	[6] Noun
two	heavy	red	knit	wool	sweaters
several	small	white	wooden	colonial	houses
a few	enormous	blue	oil	paint	stains
a lot of	interesting	—	—	international	friends
a	short	blue-eyed	—	American	man

*Adjectives within categories have their own ordering as well.

TASK Put each noun and group of adjectives in the correct order.

1. (big / three / cars / black) _____

2. (customer / dark-haired / tall / a) _____

3. (some / French / bread / fresh) _____

4. (shirt / blue / cotton / nice) _____

» **TIP 5 Use adverbs to give more information about verbs.** Adverbs ending with *-ly* can specify how something happens (*quickly, slowly*). Other adverbs are used to describe how often something happens (*sometimes, usually, frequently*) or the level of certainty someone feels about something happening (*probably, possibly, supposedly*).

TASK Circle the correct adverb in each sentence.

1. They are sitting (quickly / quietly / sometimes) on a green blanket near the lake.

2. The man is (probably / often / frequently) going to make a photocopy.

3. The customer is waiting (usually / patiently / supposedly) to buy some fresh bread.

4. The man in the white shirt is from technology support. He's working (frequently / quickly / usually) to fix the computer.

5. The baker has on a black cap that she (probably / seldom / slowly) wears every day.

COHESION AND STRUCTURING A RESPONSE

» **TIP 1 Organize your response in a clear way.** For Question 3, refer to the photo, and focus on the main subject. Describe what the person or people are doing or the condition of the main thing in the image. Then describe how the action is taking place, where the person or thing is, and the focus of the action or attention. Remember to use adjectives to describe the nouns and adverbs to describe the verbs when possible.

You can follow a template like this to help you organize your response.

> – Refer to the photo.
> – Say <u>who</u> is in the photo.
> – Say <u>where</u> the person or people are.
> – Say <u>what</u> the person or people are doing.

TASK Look at the photo. Then read the sentences. Number the sentences from 1–6 to put them in the correct order.

____ So, finally, I'd say that they might be colleagues at the same company.

____ The young woman is on the left, and she's wearing a blouse and black pants. She's holding a document.

____ The man and the woman are standing in a mail room or a copy room, in front of a photocopy machine and near some mailboxes.

____ And it looks like they have just made copies, which they're looking over.

____ Next to the woman is a young man wearing a white shirt and casual slacks.

____ Well, there are two people in the picture, a man and a woman.

QUICK TIP

Don't forget to use signposts and sentence starters, such as *First, Next, Well, It appears that, I see,* and *There is / There are.*

» **TIP 2 Keep your responses coherent and easy to understand.** Make your responses flow smoothly. Use transitions and conjunctions like *However, Apparently, and, but, although,* and *because,* and use phrases like *It seems to me that, It seems like,* and *It appears that.*

TASK Look at the photo above. Listen to a sample response for the photo. Then write the answers to the questions. 🎧 Track 03.04

1. Who is in the photo? _____

2. Where are the people? _____

3. What are they doing? _____

4. Other details? _____

» **TIP 3 If you are not sure, make guesses.** You can use adverbs or adjectives to express certainty or uncertainty. You can also use modals of certainty. Look at the chart for examples.

Expressing Certainty / Uncertainty with Adjectives and Adverbs		
←Uncertain	Somewhat Sure	Very Sure→
I'm not positive . . .	*possibly*	*It's certain (that) . . .*
It's not likely (that) . . .	*probably*	*It's likely (that) . . .*
I'm not sure, but . . .	*perhaps*	*surely*
I'm doubtful about . . .	*maybe*	*undoubtedly*
might be	*most likely*	*definitely*
could be	*may be*	*must be*
		should be

QUICK TIP

Remember to keep your responses relevant and to focus on main ideas. Don't get lost in small details or talk about insignificant things in the image.

TASK Make these sentences less certain by adding adverbs or changing the underlined words. There is more than one possible answer for each sentence.

1. I think that the woman <u>is</u> the man's boss.

2. I'm <u>sure</u> the man is waiting for a document.

3. The woman <u>must be</u> the children's mother.

4. <u>It's likely that</u> the man is there to repair the computer.

5. The man and woman <u>are definitely</u> running in a race.

6. <u>Undoubtedly,</u> the man is a new employee at the company.

PROGRESSIVE PRACTICE: Get Ready

A Look at the photo. Write the number of the correct object next to each word.

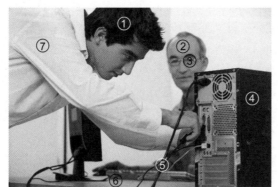

shirt _____

desk _____

glasses _____

computer _____

cables _____

older man _____

younger man _____

B Listen to the sample response. As you listen, number the sentences from 1–6 in the order that you hear them. 🎧 Track 03.05

_____ On the left, there is a young man with a white shirt leaning over a desk. He's probably a technology expert.

_____ An older man is sitting behind the desk. He's wearing glasses.

_____ There is a computer unit on the right side of the table.

_____ The older man is watching the younger man fix his computer.

_____ The computer cables are at the back of the computer unit, where the young man is working.

_____ The younger man is connecting the computer cables.

C Create your own response using the template. Record your response if possible.

> There _____ .
>
> The younger man _____ .
>
> He _____ .
>
> The older man is _____ .
>
> The younger man is probably _____ .

D Think about your response or listen to your recording. Read the statements. How well did your response meet the scoring criteria? Check (✓) *Yes* or *No*. Keep practicing until all of your answers are *Yes*.

Response Checklist: Question 3	Yes	No
1. I used correct pronunciation, intonation, and stress.	☐	☐
2. I used correct grammar and vocabulary.	☐	☐
3. My response was easily understood.	☐	☐
4. I included details about the photo and described the main subject thoroughly.	☐	☐

PROGRESSIVE PRACTICE: Get Set

A Look at the photo. Think about how you would describe it. Then listen to the sample response. 🎧 Track 03.06

B Now listen to the sample response in Part A again for the answers to these questions. Number the questions from 1–8 to put them in the same order as answers are mentioned in the sample response. 🎧 Track 03.06

_____ What are these people doing?   _____ What's the weather like?

_____ How many people are in the picture?   _____ What are the two people in the center holding?

_____ Where are the people?   _____ What is the woman on the right doing?

_____ What things do they have with them?   _____ Who might the people in the picture be?

C Now create your own response using answers to these questions. Record your response if possible.

Who is in the photo? _____

Where are they? _____

What are they doing? _____

What's the weather like? _____

What do they have with them? _____

D Think about your response or listen to your recording. Read the statements. How well did your response meet the scoring criteria? Check (✓) Yes or No. Keep practicing until all of your answers are Yes.

Response Checklist: Question 3	Yes	No
1. I used correct pronunciation, intonation, and stress.	☐	☐
2. I used correct grammar and vocabulary.	☐	☐
3. My response was easily understood.	☐	☐
4. I included details about the photo and described the main subject thoroughly.	☐	☐

PROGRESSIVE PRACTICE: Go for the TOEIC® Test

Speaking Test

Question 3 of 11

🎧 Track 03.07

Question 3: Describe a picture

Directions: In this part, you will describe the photo on the screen with as much detail as possible. You will have 30 seconds to prepare. You will have 45 seconds to describe the photo.

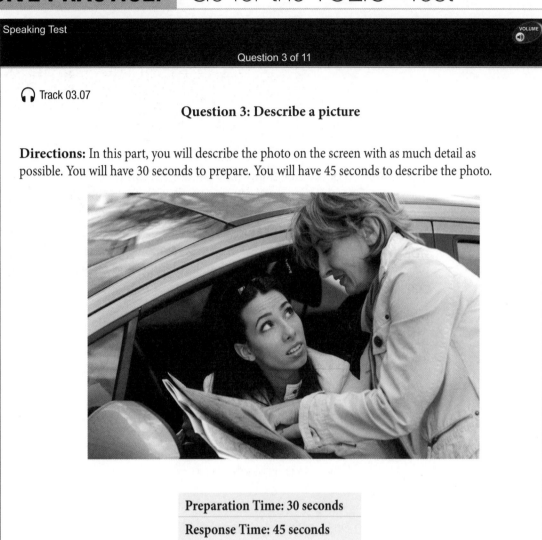

Preparation Time: 30 seconds
Response Time: 45 seconds

Preparation Time Used: _____ seconds

Speaking Time Used: _____ seconds

TO SEE AND HEAR SAMPLE RESPONSES, LOOK AT THE AUDIOSCRIPT AT THE END OF THE BOOK AND LISTEN TO TRACK 03.08.

TOEIC® Test Speaking Questions 4–6

Questions 4–6 of the Speaking Test feature a short prompt followed by three related questions. The questions will appear on-screen and will be read by a narrator. There is no preparation time allowed. You will be tested on your ability to comprehend the questions and respond. For Questions 4 and 5, you will have 15 seconds to answer each question. You will have 30 seconds to answer Question 6. Your responses will be evaluated based on pronunciation, intonation and stress, grammar, vocabulary, cohesion, and relevance and completeness of content.

Possible topics may include:

» *Personal and social interests (entertainment, travel, hobbies)*

» *Community life (environment, banking, housing)*

» *Marketing research and consumer practices*

QUICK GUIDE: Respond to Questions

Definition	Questions 4–6 test your speaking skills about personal experiences and familiar topics. The questions require you to respond with two short personal answers and one longer opinion or description. You will state a preference, use descriptive language, offer reasons and explanations, state an opinion, and support your answers with details.
Targeted Skills	In Questions 4–6, you should be able to: • express your opinion clearly, supporting it with details. • understand the main topic and identify key words. • select and use appropriate vocabulary. • describe frequency or duration of events or activities. • provide details and explanations about your opinion.
Question Types	Here are examples of questions you might find on the test. • **Personal and Social Interests:** *What kinds of sports do you like?* • **Community Life:** *What type of transportation do you use every day?* • **Marketing Research:** *What's your favorite food? Why?*
A Good Response	A good response will accurately and fluently address everything asked about in the prompt within the time provided. It will also demonstrate organizational skills, answer the question fully, and include supporting details.
Things to Remember	1. First, quickly analyze the prompt and questions. What key words are in the prompt? What do the questions ask for? What information do you need in your responses? 2. Next, think about what you want to talk about. You should immediately think of key words that will help you answer quickly. 3. You will hear a beep signaling when to start. Begin your answer with a topic sentence that restates the prompt and adds your own information. 4. Be sure to explain the main reason for your answer and provide personal details to support this reason.

WALK THROUGH: Respond to Questions

A What You'll See and Hear

In Questions 4-6, you will hear an introductory statement. Then you will respond to three questions. Read along as you listen to the sample introductory statement and questions below. What types of information are the questions asking for? 🎧 Track 04-06.01

Speaking Test   VOLUME 🔊

Questions 4–6: Respond to questions

Directions: In this part, you will answer three questions. Begin responding as soon as you hear the beep for each question. You will have 15 seconds for Questions 4 and 5 and 30 seconds for Question 6. There is no preparation time.

Imagine that an American marketing firm is doing research in your country. You have agreed to participate in a telephone survey about food shopping.

Question 4: What types of food stores are there in your neighborhood?

Question 5: How often do you go food shopping and when do you usually go?

Question 6: Describe what you buy and why you make those purchases.

B What You'll Do

Below are sample responses for the questions in Part A. Listen and notice how the speaker organizes his response to each question. Then try to answer the questions in Part A using your own information. 🎧 Track 04-06.02

SAMPLE RESPONSES ▶

Question 4: *Well, there are a lot of small general stores and some specialty meat shops in my neighborhood, but I usually like to go to a big supermarket that's not far from where I live.*

Question 5: *I usually go food shopping once or twice a week, and most of the time, I go on Thursday evening. I try to get there between 8 and 9 p.m., when it's not so busy.*

Question 6: *Well, there are so many things—mostly, I like to buy fresh fruit and vegetables and organic foods. I like to eat healthy food, so I think it's really important to shop for natural products. That's what I usually buy. I also like to purchase things on sale, so sometimes I stock up on canned goods and frozen foods.*

Glossary:

ℇ POWERED BY COBUILD

organic: methods of farming and gardening that use only natural animal and plant products, rather than chemicals, to help the plants or animals grow and be healthy

stock up: buy a lot of something in case you cannot get it later

GET IT RIGHT: Tips and Tasks for Answering Correctly

Questions 4–6 on the Speaking Test are scored on a scale from 0–3. Your responses will be graded based on the same criteria as Questions 1–3—pronunciation, intonation and stress, grammar, vocabulary, and cohesion. You will also be graded on relevance of content and completeness of content.

- **Relevance of content** is how well you connect your response to the topic. If the question asks, "What's your favorite kind of museum and why do you like it?," you must explain what kind of museum it is (for example, a museum of modern art, natural history, aerospace, film, sports, or photography). You must also say what you like about that museum (for example, its large collection, architecture, or sports trophies). You must avoid talking about unrelated topics, as that can negatively affect your score.

- **Completeness of content** is how fully you answer the question. Some questions may have more than one part. For example, for the question "What's your favorite kind of museum and why do you like it?," you must talk about two things in order to answer the question completely: (1) <u>what</u> your favorite museum is, and (2) <u>why</u> you feel that way.

Read along as you listen to this sample response. Track 04-06.03

> **A Good Response:** *My favorite kind of museum to visit is a natural history museum. I really enjoy seeing exhibits related to Earth, dinosaurs, different animals, and things like geology. For me, those are the most interesting exhibits. I usually spend hours looking around in that kind of museum.*
>
> **Analysis:** The speaker's answer is completely related to the question. The speaker also remembers to answer the second part of the question, "why do you like it?"

QUICK TIP

It is always best to speak from your own point of view. If you don't feel you have enough personal experience with a topic, use your imagination.

UNDERSTANDING THE QUESTIONS

Questions 4–6 ask you about your preferences and habits, or they ask for a description or an opinion about a topic. Questions 4 and 5 are usually *Wh-* questions that ask you *who, what, where, why,* or *how often / much.* Question 6 may ask you to offer a longer description of something or give a more detailed opinion.

Possible Questions

Stating and describing preferences:
- *Where do you usually watch TV?*
- *What kinds of TV shows do you like and why?*

Duration and frequency:
- *How much time do you get for vacation?*
- *How often do you go to the gym?*
- *How long have you been living in your neighborhood?*

Extended description / defend an opinion:
- *Describe your favorite vacation spot.*
- *Describe what you like best about . . .*

Opinion:
- *How important is it to buy things on sale?*
- *What do you think is the best way to travel?*

» **TIP 1 Become familiar with the types of prompts.** The introductory statements that you hear before the questions, called prompts, are often about a survey. You should imagine that a marketing firm is asking you for information about yourself and your preferences. As you read and listen to the introductory statement, notice what topic the survey is about, such as films, sports, or television programs. Then focus on keeping your responses directly related to that topic.

TASK Practice identifying content that is relevant to a topic. Look at the chart. Read the topic in **bold** on the left. Then circle the word or phrase that is NOT relevant to the topic.

1. sports	soccer	swimming	tennis	gardening
2. movies	drama	comedy	photography	horror
3. emergency services	ambulance	limousine	fire station	police station
4. public parks	school playground	national park	state park	community park
5. materials to read for enjoyment	novels	newspapers	magazines	employee handbooks

» **TIP 2 Become familiar with the types of questions you might hear.** There are several different question types that you may hear in this part of the TOEIC test. Look at the chart for some examples of the types of questions you may encounter, what they are asking for, possible structures to use, and ways to answer them.

QUICK TIP

Remember to scan the questions immediately. Look for the type of *Wh-* question asked in Questions 4 and 5 so you will know how to approach your response.

Question Types	What They're Asking For	Possible Structures for Responding	Sample Responses
What kinds of [movies] **do you like?**	a type, description, or preference	*I like* + nouns or adjectives with nouns: *comedies, classic horror films, dramas, romantic movies*	*I like mysteries and thrillers.*
Why do you [like that kind of movie]?	a reason	subordinating clauses, transition words: *because, since, however*	*I watch mysteries and thrillers* **because** *I enjoy getting scared.* **However,** *sometimes I have bad dreams.*
How often do you [watch movies]?	frequency	adverbs of frequency, time expressions: *usually, on the weekends, once a week, every day*	*I like to go to the movies about* **once every two months**.
How long have you [been interested in movies]?	duration	time expressions: *for X years, for a long time, for a short time, since*	*I've been interested in movies* **for many years**.
What do you think about [the price of movies in your neighborhood]?	opinion	opinion verbs: *think (that), believe (that), feel (that)*	*I* **think that** *movies have become too expensive.*

TASK Complete each question with the best *Wh-* phrase from the box. Then decide how you would answer each question. Write down your key ideas.

What kind of	What is	What do you	Where do you	Why do you

1. _____ go to get exercise? _____
2. _____ your favorite type of exercise? _____
3. _____ usually do for exercise? _____
4. _____ enjoy this type of exercise? _____
5. _____ exercise do you usually do? _____

» **TIP 3** Question 5 often asks you to talk about how long something lasts (duration) or how often something happens (frequency). To answer, you will need to think about numbers, times of day, or details relating to days of the week or dates. These types of questions can also ask you about how much time or how many hours or days you spend doing something.

TASK Complete the questions about duration, frequency, or amount of time. Use the correct phrases from the box. Then decide how you would answer each question. Write down your key ideas.

How long	How many	How much	How often	When

1. _____ do you go to sports events? _____
2. _____ time do you spend at the grocery store? _____
3. _____ hours a week do you exercise? _____
4. _____ do you usually shop for clothes? _____
5. _____ have you lived in your neighborhood? _____

» **TIP 4 Learn to recognize questions that ask for extra information.** Some questions may ask you to expand on a description of something. You may also be asked to give your opinion about a topic, defend your choice about why one thing is better than another, or state how you can improve something.

TASK Complete the sentences about describing something or defending an opinion. Use any appropriate phrase from the box. More than one answer may be possible. What types of information are they asking for?

Do you believe it	Describe	How important is it	What kind of
What do you think		How do you think	

1. _____ community center would you like to see built in your neighborhood?
2. _____ to buy clothes at a bargain price?
3. _____ one way that you think education could be improved.
4. _____ your neighborhood could be improved?
5. _____ about public transportation in your city?
6. _____ is a good idea for children to participate in after-school activities?

STRUCTURING YOUR RESPONSE

Structuring your response correctly is important to your score. A good way to do this is to follow a template, or a set of structured ideas. This will help you answer the question completely and in a clear way. For *Wh-* questions, the following template can help you give a clear and complete answer.

QUICK TIP

Sometimes there are two parts to one of the questions. Be sure to address both parts so that your response is complete. For example: *What's your favorite TV show and why?* *Where and when did you last go shopping?*

> – Restate the question
> – Give supporting information – idea 1
> – Add details – detail 1
> – Give supporting information – idea 2
> – Add details – detail 2

Notice how this response fits the template. Read along as you listen to this sample question and response. 🎧 Track 04-06.04

> **Sample Question:** *What's your favorite place to buy clothing?*
> **Sample Response:** *My favorite place to buy clothing is Del's Department Store. I like it because the prices are good and the selection is nice. Last year, I got a new winter coat for only $30. I also like it because the clerks there are very friendly. They always say hello and are really helpful.*

For questions that ask for a description or opinion, the following template can help you give a clear and complete answer.

> – Restate the topic with an opinion or general description
> – Give supporting information – idea 1
> – Add details – detail 1
> – Give supporting information – idea 2
> – Add details – detail 2

Notice how this response fits the template. Read along as you listen to this sample question and response. 🎧 Track 04-06.05

> **Sample Question:** *Describe your favorite restaurant.*
> **Sample Response:** *My favorite restaurant is really cozy and nice. It's in an old building, so the atmosphere is really "old-style." The walls are made of brick, and the restaurant is lit with candles. The restaurant serves excellent Italian food. The lasagna is my favorite.*

Remember to add more supporting information and details for Question 6 and for questions with two parts.

» **TIP 1 Start your response by restating the question.** Begin your response by restating or rephrasing the question. For example, if the question asks, "How often do you play sports?," your answer should start with a restatement of the prompt. For example, "I usually play sports about [three times a week]."

Questions	Restated Responses
What type of music do you like?	*I like [rock and roll] music.*
How long does it take you to get to your job?	*It usually takes me [five minutes] to get to my job.*
Describe your favorite restaurant.	*My favorite restaurant is [a small Italian restaurant called Piccolo].*

TASK Read each question. Then write the first sentence of your response by restating the question.

1. What is your preferred method of transportation?

_____

2. Where do you usually do your food shopping?

_____

3. Describe the kind of music you usually listen to.

_____

4. How long have you lived in your current residence?

_____

QUICK TIP

You will hear key words and phrases in Question 6. For example, "Describe one way emergency **services** in your **neighborhood** could be **improved**." Immediately restate the question and think of noun phrases that support your opinion. For example, "**Emergency services in my neighborhood** could be **improved** by **speeding up their response time**."

» **TIP 2 Learn set phrases to answer, give supporting information, and add information.** Learn common phrases that you can use to state preferences, offer opinions, and answer questions about duration, frequency, or quantity. Other expressions are helpful for adding information. Providing information to support your answer and adding personal or additional details make your answer more complete. This chart gives examples to help you state your preferences or likes.

Stating Preferences or Likes in Responses to *Wh-* Questions	
Stating Preferences	**Expressing Likes**
I really like . . .	*I enjoy . . .*
I prefer X over Y.	*For me, the best kind of X is . . .*
My favorite kind of X is . . .	*When it comes to X, Y is my favorite.*

The vocabulary and expressions in this chart may be useful when you respond to questions about duration, frequency, or quantity.

Common Expressions for Duration, Frequency, or Quantity		
Duration (*How long . . . ?*)	**Frequency** (*How often . . . ?*)	**Quantity** (*How many . . . ?*)
since I was young, since four o'clock, for several hours, for a long time, for six months, for a year	*all the time, always, regularly, usually, often, very often, from time to time, several times a week, hardly ever, rarely, never*	*several, a lot, many, some, a few, a couple, not many, hardly any, none*

QUICK TIP

Write out a 30- to 35-word response to a question like, *What is your favorite TV show? Why?* Then set a timer for 15 seconds. Record yourself and make sure you can respond in 15 seconds. Keep practicing until you can answer completely in the right amount of time.

The following sentence starters may be useful for offering or supporting opinions and giving reasons in response to Question 6 or for defending *Why* questions in Questions 4, 5, or 6.

Common Sentence Starters for Offering or Supporting Opinions and Giving Reasons	
Offering Opinions (*What is your opinion of X? What do you think about X?*)	**Supporting Opinions / Giving Reasons** (*Why do you like X? Why do you think X is important?*)
I think . . .	*The reason I say this is . . .*
In my opinion . . .	*This is necessary because . . .*
I would say that . . .	*Due to the fact that . . .*
I really believe that . . .	*Because of the . . .*
The best way to . . .	*By [doing X], we could improve . . .*
It seems to me that . . .	*X is important because . . .*

Finally, you can use expressions like these to add information or expand your answer.

Common Phrases for Adding Information and Expanding On Your Answer	
Also . . . / . . . , too.	*Another thing is . . .*
In addition . . .	*Finally . . .* (for adding the last piece of information)
Plus . . .	

TASK 1 Read each question and write numbers to put the sentences into the best order for a response.

Question 4: What's your favorite restaurant? Why?	Question 5: How often do you eat at this restaurant?	Question 6: What do you think about the service at this restaurant, and how could it be improved?
☐ I think they have the best cannoli in town. ☐ I would have to say my favorite restaurant is Piccolo restaurant. ☐ Another thing is that the food is really delicious. ☐ I like it because I enjoy the relaxing atmosphere.	☐ That's because it has become very popular. ☐ I usually eat at this restaurant once a week. ☐ So now I go only if I can get a reservation. ☐ I would go more often, but it's difficult to get a table.	☐ If they want to maintain the restaurant's popularity, they should make those changes. ☐ But sometimes the service is slow because the restaurant is so crowded. ☐ One thing I think they could do to improve the restaurant is to hire more servers. ☐ Most of the time, I think the service there is excellent. ☐ Another suggestion is that the servers could bring more bread while you wait for your meal.

TASK 2 Read each question and create a two-sentence answer that gives one piece of supporting information and adds one detail. Use the vocabulary given.

Example: What kinds of movies do you like? [science-fiction films / interesting / *Avatar*]

I like science-fiction films because they're so interesting. One of my favorites is *Avatar*.

1. What kind of music do you like?   [rock / great lyrics / sing along]

_____

_____

2. What is your favorite place to go on vacation?   [beach / Australia / swimming]

_____

_____

3. What is a popular place to meet friends in your neighborhood?   [neighborhood café / great atmosphere / good food]

_____

_____

QUICK TIP

Write out a 50- to 60-word response to a question like, *Do you think learning a second language is important? Why do you think so?* Set a timer for 30 seconds. Try recording yourself, and make sure you can respond in 30 seconds. Keep practicing until you can answer completely in the right amount of time.

» **TIP 3 Answer completely and keep your response relevant.** Stay focused on the topic, but give as many details as you can. Going off topic can negatively affect your score. If you don't answer all parts of the question, you will lose points on your score as well.

TASK 1 Read each question and circle the response that is NOT connected to the topic.

1. **What's your favorite type of literature?**

   a. I like historical novels.

   b. My favorite type of literature is fiction.

   c. I would have to say that biographies are my favorite type of literature.

   d. I like to read sports statistics in the newspaper.

2. **What kind of dessert do you like best?**

   a. My favorite kind of dessert is chocolate ice cream.

   b. I think that vanilla cake with chocolate frosting is my all-time favorite dessert.

   c. I like to eat potato chips for a snack right after dinner.

   d. The kind of dessert I like best is apple pie. It is really delicious with ice cream on top.

3. **What is your favorite season? Why?**

   a. My birthday is my favorite day because I love to have a big party.

   b. I would say that fall is my favorite season because I enjoy the colors of the leaves.

   c. My favorite time of year is winter because I enjoy winter sports, like skiing and ice-skating.

   d. I like summertime the best of all. I love to be near the ocean and spend my day on the beach.

TASK 2 Read each question and its possible responses. Write "correct" under the best response to the question. Then decide why the other two answers are not as effective. Is the answer off topic, or is it not complete? Write "off topic" or "not complete" under the ineffective answers.

Question 4: Do you think it is important to have a park in your community? Why?	Question 5: How often do you visit a park in your community?	Question 6: What could be done to improve the park in your community?
A I think parks are very important because they keep the air fresh and they are good for the animals.	**A** I like to go to the park at least once a week, but sometimes I go more often.	**A** I think that a park would improve my community. It would give kids a place to play and be a pretty place.
B I think it is important to have a park in my area.	**B** A lot of people like to go to the park in my community. My community is very active, and the people are nice.	**B** If my community wanted to improve the park, they could put benches in the shade, add picnic tables, and have more drinking fountains.
C I would have to say that I like parks because I can be around nature, have picnics, and get exercise.	**C** If I have time, I take a walk downtown every day in the morning before I go to work.	**C** I think the park needs improvement. It's really dirty now, and there's no playground. I don't like to go there at all.

PROGRESSIVE PRACTICE: Get Ready

A Read along as you listen to the speaking prompt and three questions. Then, for each question, check (✓) <u>one</u> response that restates the prompt and <u>two</u> supporting details that could be included in the response. 🎧 Track 04-06.06

Imagine that a Canadian market research company is conducting a survey about preferred methods of public transportation.

Question 4: What kind of transportation do you take most often? Why?	Question 5: How long is your commute to work every day?	Question 6: Describe one method of public transportation in your city and why it is the best way to travel.
☐ I don't take public transportation. ☐ I usually take the subway. ☐ The subway is very inexpensive. ☐ And it is not far from my house, which makes it very convenient.	☐ The city has a lot of problems with the buses being late. ☐ It usually takes me 45 minutes to get to work every day. ☐ It takes a long time for me to get to work because I live outside of the city. ☐ My commute to work is really long.	☐ The subway is the fastest and easiest method of travel. ☐ I think this because there are many lines, and every stop is close to major city areas. ☐ The city needs to invest more money in transportation. ☐ The subway is the quickest way to get around, especially when there is a lot of traffic.

B Listen to the sample responses for Questions 4, 5, and 6. Notice the words and phrases the speaker uses to introduce her response, give reasons, and give supporting details. Then listen again. Write the number of the correct purpose for each sentence in the sample responses. Use the purposes in the box. 🎧 Track 04-06.07

1. Restates the question or topic	**3.** Detail 1	**5.** Detail 2
2. Supporting information 1	**4.** Supporting information 2	**6.** Additional details

---

Question 4: What kind of transportation do you take most often? Why?

_1_ *The kind of transportation I take most often is the subway.* ___ *For me, the subway is a convenient and inexpensive way to travel.* ___ *I saved a lot of money last year when I stopped driving to work.* ___ *I also like the subway because I can read while I travel.* ___ *Reading helps me relax on the way to work.*

Question 5: How long is your commute to work every day?

___ *My commute to work only takes me 30 minutes in total every day.* ___ *It's a short walk from my house to the subway stop.* ___ *So I think it's very convenient and the best way for me to travel.* ___ *In addition, the subway stop where I get off is close to my job.* ___ *I'd have to walk farther to my office if I drove because the nearest parking lot is several blocks away.*

Question 6: Describe one method of public transportation in your city and why it is the best way to travel.

___ *I think the best method of public transportation in my city is the subway.* ___ *The subway is much faster than driving.* ___ *Because of the heavy traffic downtown, it can take twice as long to get anywhere with a car or in a taxi or bus.* ___ *Also, the subway operates 24 hours a day, seven days a week, so that makes it really convenient.* ___ *The buses stop running at midnight most nights, so you would have to pay for a taxi instead.* ___ *Plus, the subway stops are close to all the major places in the city.* ___ *If you look at a map, you don't have to walk more than a few blocks to catch the subway in most areas.*

C Now use your own words to complete the templates or use another piece of paper. Then practice your responses aloud. Record your responses if you can.

Question 4: What kind of transportation do you take most often? Why?

[Restate the question] The kind of transportation I take most often is _____

_____.

[Give supporting information – idea 1] For me, it's _____

_____.

[Add details – detail 1] The reason I say this is because _____

_____.

[Give supporting information – idea 2] I also think that taking the _____

_____

is good because _____.

[Add details – detail 2] This is due to the fact that _____

_____.

Question 5: How long is your commute to work every day?

[Restate the question] My commute to work every day is about _____

_____.

[Give supporting information – idea 1] It takes me this long because _____

_____.

[Add details – detail 1] I usually _____

during my commute. It makes the commute _____.

[Give supporting information – idea 2] I think my commute is _____

because _____

[Add details – detail 2] The reason I say this is _____

_____

Question 6: Describe one method of public transportation in your city and why it is the best way to travel.

[Restate the topic] I think the best method of public transportation in my city is _____

_____ because _____

_____.

[Give supporting information – idea 1] For me, it's _____

_____.

[Add details – detail 1] The reason I say this is because _____

_____.

[Give supporting information – idea 2] I also think that _____

is good because _____.

[Add details – detail 2] In addition, I feel that _____

is the best method of transportation because _____

_____.

[Add more details] And finally, _____

because _____.

D Now think about your responses or listen to them again if they were recorded. Then read the statements below. How well did your responses meet the question scoring criteria? Check (✓) *Yes* or *No*. Keep practicing until all of your answers are *Yes*.

Response Checklist: Questions 4–6		
	Yes	**No**
1. I used correct pronunciation, intonation, and stress. My responses were easily understood.	☐	☐
2. I used correct grammar and vocabulary.	☐	☐
3. My responses were well paced. They were neither too fast nor too slow, and I spoke for the full amount of time.	☐	☐
4. My responses were thorough, complete, and appropriate for the questions. I answered the prompt directly and did not include unnecessary information.	☐	☐
5. I included reasons, examples, opinions, and supporting details in my responses.	☐	☐

PROGRESSIVE PRACTICE: Get Set

A Read along as you listen to the speaking prompt and questions. Think about what you might say. Next, listen to the sample responses. Write the letters of the correct sample responses in the boxes. Last, check your answers by listening to the sample responses in order. 🎧 Track 04-06.08 to 04-06.10

Imagine that a European marketing firm is doing research in your country. You have agreed to participate in a phone survey about how people spend their free time.

Question 4: What is your favorite thing to do when you have free time?	Question 5: How much free time do you have during the week, and where do you spend your free time?	Question 6: How do you think the quality of your activities during your free time could be improved?
☐	☐	☐

B Now plan your own responses to the same prompt and questions. The bulleted questions below each question can guide you. Then use the templates and your own words to create a response to each question. Practice giving your responses to Questions 4 and 5 in 15 seconds and to Question 6 in 30 seconds. Record your responses if you can.

Imagine that a European marketing firm is doing research in your country. You have agreed to participate in a phone survey about how people spend their free time.

Question 4: What is your favorite thing to do when you have free time?	Question 5: How much free time do you have during the week, and where do you spend your free time?	Question 6: How do you think the quality of your activities during your free time could be improved?
• What is the activity? • How often do you do the activity? • Do you do it alone or with friends?	• Do you have a lot of free time or a little? • When is your free time? • Is it the same every week or does it change?	• What kinds of things could you do to better use your free time? • Where would it be better for you to spend your free time?

[Restate the topic] _____

_____

[Give supporting information – idea 1] _____

_____

[Add details – detail 1] _____

_____

[Give supporting information – idea 2] _____

_____

[Add details – detail 2] _____

_____

[Add more details to Question 6] _____

_____

[Restate the topic] _____

_____

[Give supporting information – idea 1] _____

_____

[Add details – detail 1] _____

_____

[Give supporting information – idea 2] _____

_____

[Add details – detail 2] _____

_____

[Add more details to Question 6] _____

_____

[Restate the topic] _____

_____

[Give supporting information – idea 1] _____

_____

[Add details – detail 1] _____

_____

[Give supporting information – idea 2] _____

_____

[Add details – detail 2] _____

_____

[Add more details to Question 6] _____

_____

C Now think about your responses or listen to them again if they were recorded. Then read the statements below. How well did your responses meet the question scoring criteria? Check (✓) *Yes* or *No*. Keep practicing until all of your answers are *Yes*.

Response Checklist: Questions 4–6		
	Yes	**No**
1. I used correct pronunciation, intonation, and stress. My responses were easily understood.	☐	☐
2. I used correct grammar and vocabulary.	☐	☐
3. My responses were well paced. They were neither too fast nor too slow, and I spoke for the full amount of time.	☐	☐
4. My responses were thorough, complete, and appropriate for the questions. I answered the prompt directly and did not include unnecessary information.	☐	☐
5. I included reasons, examples, opinions, and supporting details in my responses.	☐	☐

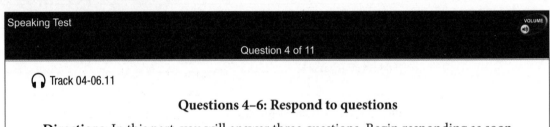

Speaking Test

VOLUME

Question 4 of 11

🎧 Track 04-06.11

Questions 4–6: Respond to questions

Directions: In this part, you will answer three questions. Begin responding as soon as you hear the beep for each question. You will have 15 seconds for Questions 4 and 5 and 30 seconds for Question 6. There is no preparation time.

Imagine that a marketing firm is doing research in your country. You have agreed to participate in a survey about live music and concerts.

Question 4: What kinds of concerts or live music performances do you attend?

Question 5: How often do you listen to live music?

Question 6: Describe where you go to listen to live music and why you like it there.

To see and hear sample responses, look at the audioscript at the end of the book and listen to track **04-06.12.**

TOEIC® Test Speaking Questions 7–9

This part of the Speaking Test provides information in the form of a schedule or an agenda followed by three questions. You will have 30 seconds to read the information. Then you will hear each question and respond. You will hear each question only once, and you will <u>not</u> be able to read the questions. You will have 15 seconds to respond to Questions 7 and 8 and 30 seconds to respond to Question 9. Your responses will be evaluated on pronunciation, intonation and stress, grammar, vocabulary, cohesion, and completeness and relevance of content.

Possible topics may include:

- » *Meeting agendas*
- » *Travel itineraries*
- » *Conference schedules*
- » *Tour schedules*

QUICK GUIDE: Respond to Questions Using Information Provided

Definition	Questions 7–9 test your ability to understand and convey information in a clear and cohesive manner. You will explain concrete details and summarize information in response to questions about information provided.
Targeted Skills	In order to correctly answer Questions 7–9, you should be able to: • locate relevant information on a written schedule or agenda. • summarize several connected pieces of information. • understand embedded questions. • use appropriate vocabulary and correct grammatical forms. • convey requested information clearly and coherently.
Question Types	**Detail:** *Could you tell me the cost of the tickets?* **Confirmation:** *I heard that the play begins at 8:00. Is that correct?* **Open-ended:** *What other kinds of workshops will there be?*
A Good Response	A good response will give accurate and complete information in a clear and cohesive manner. It will also use appropriate language for the situation.
Things to Remember	**1.** Read the title to identify the type of information provided. **2.** Scan the information for the main idea and to get a general sense of how the information is organized. **3.** As you listen to each question, skim the information for the answer. Start speaking as soon as you hear the beep. **4.** When you are speaking, use expressions like *Let's see* to give yourself time to find the information you need to provide.

WALK THROUGH: Respond to Questions Using Information Provided

A What You'll See

For Questions 7–9, you will see the directions and a schedule or an agenda. Read the directions and sample schedule below. What is the schedule for? What activities does it include?

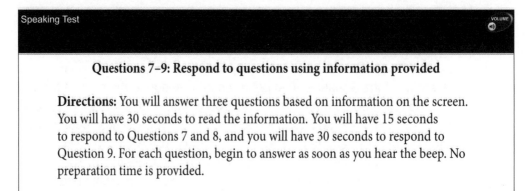

Speaking Test   VOLUME

Questions 7–9: Respond to questions using information provided

Directions: You will answer three questions based on information on the screen. You will have 30 seconds to read the information. You will have 15 seconds to respond to Questions 7 and 8, and you will have 30 seconds to respond to Question 9. For each question, begin to answer as soon as you hear the beep. No preparation time is provided.

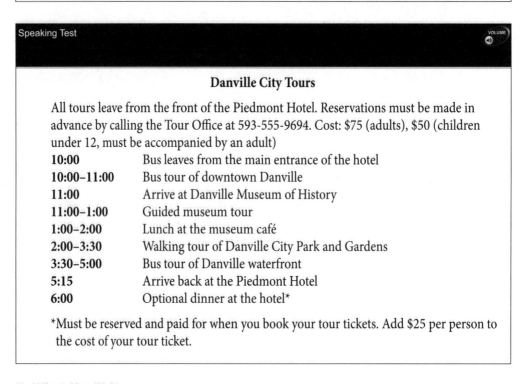

Speaking Test   VOLUME

Danville City Tours

All tours leave from the front of the Piedmont Hotel. Reservations must be made in advance by calling the Tour Office at 593-555-9694. Cost: $75 (adults), $50 (children under 12, must be accompanied by an adult)

10:00	Bus leaves from the main entrance of the hotel
10:00–11:00	Bus tour of downtown Danville
11:00	Arrive at Danville Museum of History
11:00–1:00	Guided museum tour
1:00–2:00	Lunch at the museum café
2:00–3:30	Walking tour of Danville City Park and Gardens
3:30–5:00	Bus tour of Danville waterfront
5:15	Arrive back at the Piedmont Hotel
6:00	Optional dinner at the hotel*

*Must be reserved and paid for when you book your tour tickets. Add $25 per person to the cost of your tour ticket.

B What You'll Hear

QUICK TIP

Pay attention to asterisks (*). These symbols point to footnotes with information that may be needed to answer a question.

For Questions 7–9, you will hear someone calling to ask for information about an event. The event is related to the schedule or agenda on the screen. You will then hear three questions from the caller. Your answers will be based on the information you see on the screen. Listen to the audio as you read along in the sample script. 🎧 Track 07-09.01

SAMPLE SCRIPT ▶
(script not available in test)

Hello. I'm interested in taking a tour of Danville, but I'm afraid it might be a bit too expensive.

Question 7: *Can you tell me how much it costs to take the tour?*

Question 8: *I heard that the tour includes dinner as well as lunch. Is that correct?*

Question 9: *Does the tour take place mostly in the morning, or will we also visit some places after lunch?*

C What You'll Do

You will use the information provided to answer each question. Listen to the sample responses to the three questions. Then use the information in Part A to answer the three questions in your own words. 🎧 Track 07-09.02

SAMPLE RESPONSES ▶

Glossary:

ⓒ POWERED BY COBUILD

over and above: more than the normal amount or to offer something in addition to it

get back: to return to the state someone was in before

Question 7: *Sure. Let me check the information on the schedule. The tour costs 75 dollars for adults, and for children under 12, the cost is 50 dollars.*

Question 8: *Let's see. According to the schedule, there's an optional dinner at the end of the tour. This costs an extra 25 dollars over and above the cost of your tour ticket.*

Question 9: *Yes, the tour includes visits to several places after lunch. First, there's a walking tour of Danville City Park and Gardens, which begins at two o'clock. Then after that, at three thirty, the tour goes by bus to the Danville waterfront. Then you'll get back to the hotel by five fifteen.*

GET IT RIGHT: Tips and Tasks for Answering Correctly

Questions 7–9 on the Speaking Test are scored on a scale from 0–3. Your responses will be graded based on the same criteria as Questions 1–6—pronunciation, intonation and stress, grammar, vocabulary, cohesion, relevance of content, and completeness of content. You will also be graded on your ability to politely convey accurate information.

Conveying information accurately and politely is very important for Questions 7–9. For these questions, you are expected to speak politely to a person calling to ask questions about an event or a plan. You should try to use language that is appropriate for speaking with someone you don't know and avoid speaking too informally or being impolite. More importantly, you need to be sure your information is correct and is what the caller is asking for. Giving the wrong information or information that is not relevant to the caller's question will negatively affect your score. To do well, you must quickly find the information needed. You must then effectively change the information from written to spoken language that is appropriate and easily understood. Listen to the audio as you read an example of a good response. Then read the analysis of the response. 🎧 Track 07-09.03

A Good Response: *Just a moment, sir. Let me check that for you. I'm really sorry, but the 3:00 presentation has been canceled. There's a similar presentation at 2:00. It covers increasing sales, motivating employees, and improving your work environment. I can give you more information on that, if you'd like.*

Analysis: Here, the speaker answers very politely and apologizes for the change to the presentation schedule. The response also offers a possible solution with accurate information to help solve the caller's problem.

UNDERSTANDING THE INFORMATION TEXTS AND QUESTIONS

Questions 7–9 are usually questions from a caller. The questions ask for more information about events, schedules, or agendas that you see on the screen. Questions 7 and 8 are often more basic questions asking for specific or detailed information. Question 9 may ask you to offer a longer description or explanation of something or to give more detailed information.

Possible Basic or Simple Detail Questions:

- *What time does the media presentation start, and what does it cover?*
- *I heard that the conference includes a question and answer session with the CEO. Is that true?*
- *Could you please confirm a couple of details for me? What airport do we fly into, and what time does the flight leave?*

Possible Extended Description / Explanation / Detail Questions:

- *I can attend only the morning session. What kinds of presentations will there be then?*
- *Other than the daytime tours, what other types of activities are offered?*
- *We have meetings all day on the third, but I'd like to know what's planned for the fourth.*

» **TIP 1 Familiarize yourself with the types of information texts you may find on the test.** The types of information texts you see before the questions are usually some sort of schedule, agenda, announcement, invitation, advertisement, or itinerary. See below for examples of the types of information texts you may see.

Text 1

<table>
<tr><td colspan="2" align="center">**Drilling Site Tour**</td></tr>
<tr><td colspan="2" align="center">Daily at 11:00 a.m. No tours on weekends.</td></tr>
<tr><td colspan="2" align="center">Safety equipment required for all participants!</td></tr>
<tr><td>10:45 a.m.</td><td>Meet at tunnel entrance</td></tr>
<tr><td>11:00–12:00</td><td>Walking tour (with guide) of finished part of the tunnel</td></tr>
<tr><td>12:00–1:00</td><td>Lunch in underground break room</td></tr>
<tr><td>1:00–1:30</td><td>Talk about drill site safety</td></tr>
<tr><td>1:30–2:30</td><td>Open viewing of drill area (guide available)</td></tr>
<tr><td>3:00</td><td>Return to base camp</td></tr>
</table>

Text 2

<table>
<tr><td colspan="2" align="center">**International Writers Conference**</td></tr>
<tr><td>**Date:**</td><td>Tuesday, March 15, 10:00 a.m. to 6:00 p.m.</td></tr>
<tr><td>**Location:**</td><td>Carver Hall, Thorpe Center, West University Campus</td></tr>
<tr><td>**Guest Speakers:**</td><td>Jenny Hill, President, Freelance Writers League, 10:00 a.m., Room 17</td></tr>
<tr><td></td><td>Marlon Thomson, Publishing Manager, Horton Publishing, 1:00 p.m., Room 21</td></tr>
<tr><td></td><td>Angela Moeller, CEO, Editorial Advisory Group, 3:00 p.m., Room 12</td></tr>
<tr><td>**Activities and Events:**</td><td>**Publisher exhibits: 10:00 a.m. to 6:00 p.m., Carver Reception Hall.** Browse through our booths offering valuable information on how to get published, what's new in the field, and where to send your work.</td></tr>
<tr><td></td><td>**Open forum with guest speakers: 4:00 p.m. to 6:00 p.m., Room 2.** Have a chance to ask questions and gain from the expertise of our guest speakers.</td></tr>
<tr><td>**Registration Cost:**</td><td>$26 per person; fees must be received by March 13</td></tr>
</table>

Text 3

Itinerary for Southeast Delegation

7:00 a.m.	Arrive at New York La Guardia Airport on Flight 681; Pick-up by Secretary Sullivan
8:15 a.m.	Arrive at Hotel Compton for check-in; One hour free
9:15 a.m.	Leave for Government Center
9:45 a.m.	Arrive Government Center
10:00 a.m.	Meet and greet with team members, Webber Room
10:30 a.m.	Presentation, "Global Environmental Issues: The Way Forward"
11:30 a.m.	Taxi to North Surfside restaurant
12:00 p.m.	Lunch with CEO, HCG Inc.*
1:45 p.m.	Taxi to Government Center
2:30 p.m.	Presentation, "Solar Energy and Why We Need It"
4:00 p.m.	Depart for New York La Guardia Airport with Secretary Sullivan
7:00 p.m.	Depart New York on Flight 682 for Los Angeles

*Lunch may be shortened if presentation runs over.

TASK 1 Read the definitions of text types below. Then write the number of the correct information text example in TIP 1 next to each text type.

a. An **itinerary** is a plan for a trip, including the travel and hotel arrangements and the places that will be visited. _____

b. An **announcement, invitation,** or **advertisement** gives details about an event. _____

c. A **schedule** or **agenda** is a list of things that will happen and when. _____

TASK 2 Look at the three information texts in TIP 1. What is the main focus of each text? Circle the correct focus.

Text 1: a conference schedule / a self-guided tour / a tour of a work site

Text 2: a gathering of professional writers / a party for a publisher / an exhibition of books

Text 3: a meeting at Government Center / a presentation schedule / travel plans for a speaker

» **TIP 2 Practice scanning for detailed information.** You have 30 seconds to scan the text before answering the questions. During this time, you should scan for the kinds of important information you may need to answer the questions. For example, you should locate or note any prices, dates, times, activities, or other information the caller might ask about. This way you will be prepared to find information quickly when answering questions.

TASK Look at the information texts in TIP 1 and answer the questions below.

Text 1

1. When can someone take the tour? _____

2. How long does the tour last, and what do you see? _____

Text 2

1. Who are the main speakers at the conference? _____

2. What things can a person do in the afternoon? _____

Text 3

1. What time does the delegation arrive, and who's picking them up? _____

2. How long does the delegation have for lunch? _____

» **TIP 3 Get to know the types of introductions and questions you might hear.** You will usually hear a short introductory statement by the caller before you hear the questions. This often gives general information about the situation. As you listen to the statement, think about the types of related information that the caller might ask for. After that, you will hear the first question.

There are several types of questions you might hear, but the most important thing to do is listen for the key words. These tell you the main information to find so you can scan the information text in more detail. Remember, you will only <u>hear</u> the questions—you will <u>not</u> see them on-screen. Therefore, it is important to listen carefully and not get distracted by looking at the information text! Here are some common question types you may hear.

Question Types	Examples
Information Questions	• *When does the flight arrive?* • *I'm getting in late. **Who**'s picking me up?* • ***Where** are we having lunch?*
Yes-No Questions	• ***Can** I get an earlier train?* • ***Are** there any fees involved?* • *I'd like to stay with friends. **Do** we have to stay at the hotel?* • ***Will** we have a break for coffee?*
Embedded Questions	• ***Could you please** let me know what time it starts?* • *I'd like to meet other attendees. **Do you have any idea** what there is to do in the evenings?* • ***Would you be able to tell me** if there are any seats left?*
Tag Questions	• *There are supposed to be speakers all day long, **aren't there?*** • *There won't be a problem with coming early, **will there?***

QUICK TIP

You may hear additional polite questions that use phrasal expressions. These are often answered with *Yes* or *No*.

Would it be possible to . . .

Would I be able to . . .

Does anyone mind if I . . .

May I ask if . . .

TASK Look at the questions in the chart in TIP 3. Circle two or three key words or phrases in each question that may help you find the answer. Then listen to some more questions. Write down two or three key words for each. 🎧 Track 07-09.04

1. _____

2. _____

3. _____

4. _____

5. _____

6. _____

7. _____

8. _____

9. _____

10. _____

STRUCTURING YOUR RESPONSES

There are a variety of possible responses to Questions 7–9, depending on the information text. However, there are some templates that might help you structure your responses. For Questions 7 and 8, which require a shorter response length (15 seconds), try the following template format.

> – Politely acknowledge the question.
> – Use a phrase for getting time to find the answer (if needed).
> – Answer the question.
>   – Explain or give a reason (if needed).

Listen to the audio as you read the sample question and response.   Track 07-09.05

> **Sample Question 7 or 8:** *Can you tell me how much it costs to attend the conference?*
> **Sample Response:** *Certainly, sir. Let me check for more information on that. Let's see, it looks like one-day registration will cost $235.*

Question 9 requires a longer response length (30 seconds) and often requires you to find more information or information in more than one place in the text. For Question 9, try the following template format.

> – Politely acknowledge the question.
> – Use a phrase for getting time to find the first answer (if needed).
> – Answer the first question.
>   – Give additional information or an explanation.
> – Use a phrase for getting time to find the second answer (if needed).
> – Answer the second question.
>   – Give additional information or an explanation.

Now listen to the audio as you read a sample question and response for Question 9.
 Track 07-09.06

> **Sample Question 9:** *What other events are happening in the evening, after the conference?*
> **Sample Response:** *Hmm . . . that's a good question. Let me see here. I've got a schedule in front of me. It looks like there's a reception for the attendees on Tuesday. That starts at 5:00 and goes until 7:00. It's in the lobby. Then on Wednesday evening there's a dinner in the main dining room. That starts at 7:30. I hope that answers your question.*

» **TIP 1 Learn useful phrases to acknowledge questions, get time to find the answers, and introduce responses.** Here are the steps you can follow: 1) When the caller is finished asking a question, acknowledge that you heard the question. You can do this by responding to the question directly, repeating a key word, or restating the question. 2) If needed, you can then follow with a general "filler" phrase to get time to find the answer. 3) Finally, start your actual response with an introductory phrase.

These steps are especially important if the answer to a request is no or if the information is different from what the caller is expecting (for example, if something has been canceled). The three charts that follow show ways to acknowledge caller questions, expressions to get time to look for answers, and ways to introduce your responses.

QUICK TIP

You can often restate basic information from the information text and add a subject and verb to make a complete, grammatically correct spoken response.

Information Text: $235 per person; advanced registration required

Response: *The fee is $235 per person, advanced registration required.*

Question Types and Examples	Strategies	Phrases to Acknowledge the Questions
Information Questions: *How much is the registration fee?*	Repeat the key word or phrase from the question—using either question intonation or statement intonation and a pause—and follow with a phrase to get more time.	*The registration fee? I'll have to check on that for you . . .* *The registration fee . . . let me find out how much that is.*
Yes-No Polite Questions: *Can you tell me what time my plane arrives and when the meeting starts?*	Respond politely and follow with a phrase to get more time.	*Of course I can, sir / ma'am. Let me see here . . .* *Sure, no problem. I'll just have a look . . .*
Statement with a Question: *I have some free time in the mornings. What else is happening then?*	Rephrase and repeat the comment and question to confirm understanding (best for Question 9) and follow with a phrase to get more time.	*I see. So you'd like some more information about morning events. Let's see what I can find . . .* *OK. Let's see what's happening in the morning. I'll take a look at the schedule . . .*

Phrases to Get Time to Find Information	
Um . . . let me check that for you. *Give me just a minute to look into that, sir / ma'am.* *Hmm . . . I'll need a moment to find that information for you.* *Let's see here. / Let me have a look . . .*	*I've got a schedule / agenda / itinerary right here.* *I have that information right here in front of me.* *Just a minute. I'd like to check something . . .* *I'm not certain. I'll have to look into that.*

Phrases for Introducing a General Response	Phrases for Introducing a *No* or an Unexpected Response
It looks like that's . . . *It appears that X is . . .* *According to the schedule / agenda / itinerary . . .*	*I'm really sorry, but . . .* *Unfortunately . . .* *I apologize, but . . .* *I'm afraid that . . .*

QUICK TIP

Remember, it is important to be polite at all times. Do not use slang or words that might offend anyone. Expressions like the ones below can also help you sound polite.

I see, sir/ma'am.

I'd be happy to help.

I hope that answers your question.

QUICK TIP

Sir is the polite way to address a man whose name you do not know. The polite way to address a woman is either *madam* or *ma'am*. *Madam* is correct but is often considered old-fashioned and too formal. *Ma'am* (pronounced /mæm/) is more common today and is the shortened form of *madam*.

TASK Listen to the questions again from the TIP 3 TASK on page 46. Then write the numbers of the questions next to the correct responses. Listen to the audio more than once if you need to. 🎧 Track 07-09.04

a. Yes, I have that information right here. It's $240. _____

b. No, they don't. Unfortunately, everyone is busy at that time. _____

c. On Thursday? Let me see here. I'm afraid she's busy that day. _____

d. So you need to keep up with your regular work. Let me look at the schedule. Yes, you'll have time. There's a break from 4:30 to 5:30. _____

e. In the afternoon? Let me check that for you. He has time at 3:45. _____

f. No, you don't. You can leave whenever you want. _____

g. In the morning session? Just a minute. Let me check for you. It's Dr. Williams. _____

h. Certainly. Just give me a minute to check. They're $65 each. _____

i. So you'd like to see Professor Hunter speak. Let me check that for you. He'll be speaking at 1:00 on Thursday and 8:00 on Friday. _____

j. I don't know. Let me check that for you. Yes. You can pay those when you arrive on the first day. _____

» **TIP 2 Practice talking about times, dates, locations, and costs.** Questions 7–9 are often about schedules and agendas, so you should become familiar with useful phrases for providing details shown in the text. You should also practice making full sentences from the shortened information you will see in agendas, schedules, itineraries, and so on. This chart shows some useful responses and alternatives for giving times, dates, locations, and costs.

Text Information	Information Needed	Sample Responses
Times		
6:00 a.m. Tour Start	Start time	The tour starts **at** six a.m. You should be there **by** six in the morning.
7:15–7:45 Meeting	Start and finish time	The meeting will begin **at** seven fifteen / a quarter past seven. It should be over **at** seven forty-five / a quarter to eight.
9:10–9:50 Presentation	Duration	The presentation will **last for** forty minutes. The presentation will **last from** 9:10 **to** 9:50. The presentation will **take** forty minutes.
6:30 a.m. to 11:15 a.m. / 12:01 p.m. to 5:00 p.m. / 5:01 p.m. to 7:00 p.m. 12:00 p.m. About 7:00 p.m. to 11:59 p.m. 12:00 a.m.*	Time of day	The conference takes place **in the** morning / afternoon / evening. The first event starts **at** noon. There are no meetings **at** night. You'll get home **at** midnight.
Days, Dates, Years		
Tuesday, October 1	Day and date	The event is **on** Tuesday. The event is **on** October first. It's **on** Tuesday, October first.
June 2014	Month and year	It's **in** June. It's **in** 2014. [twenty fourteen or two thousand fourteen] It's **in** June 2014.
Locations		
Evans Building, Room B	Place	The meeting will be held **at** the Evans Building **in** Room B. The meeting will be held **in** Room B **of** the Evans Building.
Costs and Fees		
Registration Fee: $26.90	Amount	The registration fee will be **twenty-six dollars and ninety cents**. The registration fee will be **twenty-six ninety**.

*Except for the military, the United States does not use a 24-hour clock.

As you can see, you will likely need certain grammatical forms to make your sentences. Here are some helpful grammatical forms to practice.

Grammar Forms	Sample Responses
Future Forms	You **will be leaving** at 3:00 p.m. on March 6th. They're **going to have a reception** at 6:00. They're **offering** a free lunch to all attendees on the 22nd.
There is / There are Statements	**There's** a lecture at 2:00. **There are** several people attending that day.
Modals	You **should call** the office no later than 2:00. There **may be** a slight delay because of rain.
Passive Forms	She's supposed **to be picked up by** Mr. Smith. The conference **will be held** in August of this year.

TASK Look at the three information texts on pages 44 and 45. Use the information in the texts to answer the questions below. Write complete sentences. Then practice saying your answers out loud.

Text 1

1. What time do we need to meet for the tour? _____

_____

2. What exactly will we do on the tour? _____

_____

Text 2

1. Can you please tell me who Angela Moeller is and where she will be speaking?

_____

_____

2. What can you do at the exhibits? _____

_____

Text 3

1. This is Mr. Gibson. Who's taking the Southeast delegation to the airport, and what time is the flight?

_____

_____

2. What is the delegation doing between presentations?

_____

_____

PROGRESSIVE PRACTICE: Get Ready

A Practice quickly finding the topic of the schedule. Scan the schedule. Then answer the question below.

Speaking Test   VOLUME ◀))

National Association of Business Professionals (NABP)
Annual Awards Banquet
December 12, 7:00 p.m. to 11:30 p.m.
Radford Hotel, Los Angeles

7:00	Beverages and appetizers served in the Green Room
8:00	Dinner served in the East Dining Room
9:00	Awards Ceremony
	– Welcome speech: Peter Harris, Association Membership Secretary
	– Presentation of award to Rose Smith
	– Slide show of highlights from last year's ceremony
10:00	Music and dancing with the Moonlight Swing Band
11:00	Closing speech: Arthur Cummings, Association President

What is this information mainly about?

(A) Dining room service hours

(B) A special dinner

(C) A business meeting

B Read each question. Scan the schedule above to find the information requested. Circle the information on the schedule. Then check (✓) the correct answer.

Question 7: Where will appetizers be served?

☐ Appetizers will be served in the Green Room.

☐ Appetizers will be served in the hotel lobby.

☐ Appetizers will be served in the East Dining Room.

Question 8: Will there be dancing immediately following dinner?

☐ Yes. Peter Harris will lead the band.

☐ No. There will be an awards ceremony first.

☐ No. There won't be any music or dancing.

Question 9: Will there be any speakers during the banquet?

☐ No. But there will be a slide show.

☐ Yes. There will be five speakers.

☐ Yes. Both the membership secretary and the president will speak.

Now listen to the questions and sample responses to check your answers. Notice how the speaker incorporates the information from these answers into the responses and adds more relevant information. 🎧 Track 07-09.07

C Read each question below and scan the schedule from Part A to find the information requested. Then complete the template to answer the questions. Practice your responses aloud and record them if you can. Be sure to check the amount of time you use!

Question 7: When will the main meal begin?

The _____? Just let me check that for you. OK.
_____ will be served in the East Dining Room at
_____.

Question 8: Will the Radford Orchestra provide the music?

No, I don't think so, but let's see here. There will be music and dancing, but the music will be played by
_____.

Question 9: What will happen during the awards ceremony itself?

So you'd like to know what will happen during the ceremony? OK. Well, let me take a look. There are several parts to the ceremony. First, there will be a _____
by _____. Then _____
will _____. Finally, everyone will enjoy a
_____. I hope that answers your question.

D Now think about your responses or listen to them again if they were recorded. Then read the statements below. How well did your responses meet the scoring criteria? Check (✓) *Yes* or *No*. Keep practicing until all of your answers are *Yes*.

Response Checklist: Questions 7–9	Yes	No
1. I used correct pronunciation, intonation, and stress. My responses were easily understood.	☐	☐
2. I used correct grammar and vocabulary.	☐	☐
3. My responses were well paced. They were neither too fast nor too slow, and I spoke for the full amount of time.	☐	☐
4. My responses were well organized, socially appropriate, and polite.	☐	☐
5. I accurately provided the information that was requested.	☐	☐

PROGRESSIVE PRACTICE: Get Set

A Scan the schedule. What is the information mostly about?

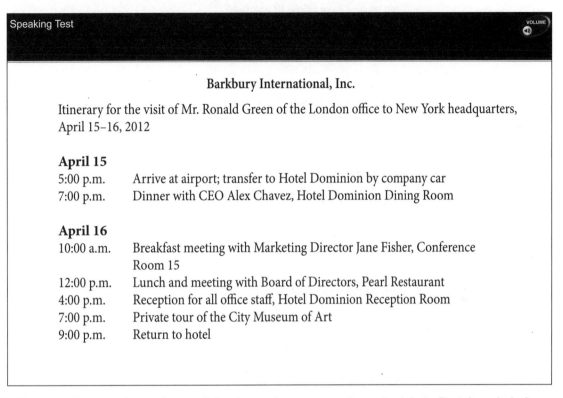

Speaking Test

Barkbury International, Inc.

Itinerary for the visit of Mr. Ronald Green of the London office to New York headquarters, April 15–16, 2012

April 15
5:00 p.m.   Arrive at airport; transfer to Hotel Dominion by company car
7:00 p.m.   Dinner with CEO Alex Chavez, Hotel Dominion Dining Room

April 16
10:00 a.m.   Breakfast meeting with Marketing Director Jane Fisher, Conference Room 15
12:00 p.m.   Lunch and meeting with Board of Directors, Pearl Restaurant
4:00 p.m.   Reception for all office staff, Hotel Dominion Reception Room
7:00 p.m.   Private tour of the City Museum of Art
9:00 p.m.   Return to hotel

B Listen to the questions. As you listen to each one, scan the schedule in Part A and circle the information you will need for your answer. Can you find all the information needed for each response? Listen to the model responses to check your answers. Track 07-09.08 and 07-09.09

C Listen to the questions in Part B again and complete the templates to answer the questions. Then practice your responses aloud and record them if you can. Be sure to check the amount of time you use! Track 07-09.08

Question 7:

[Acknowledge question] _____

_____

[Use phrase to get time (if needed)] _____

_____

[Answer question] _____

_____

[Give additional information (if needed)] _____

_____

Question 8:

[Acknowledge question] _____

_____

[Use phrase to get time (if needed)] _____

_____

[Answer question] _____

_____

[Give additional information (if needed)] _____

_____

Question 9:

[Acknowledge question] _____

_____

[Use phrase to get time (if needed)] _____

_____

[Answer first question] _____

_____

[Give additional information] _____

_____

[Use phrase to get time (if needed)] _____

_____

[Answer second question] _____

_____

[Give additional information] _____

_____

D Now think about your responses or listen to them again if they were recorded. Then read the statements below. How well did your responses meet the scoring criteria? Check (✓) *Yes* or *No*. Keep practicing until all of your answers are *Yes*.

Response Checklist: Questions 7–9		
	Yes	No
1. I used correct pronunciation, intonation, and stress. My responses were easily understood.	☐	☐
2. I used correct grammar and vocabulary.	☐	☐
3. My responses were well paced. They were neither too fast nor too slow, and I spoke for the full amount of time.	☐	☐
4. My responses were well organized, socially appropriate, and polite.	☐	☐
5. I accurately provided the information that was requested.	☐	☐

PROGRESSIVE PRACTICE: Go for the TOEIC® Test

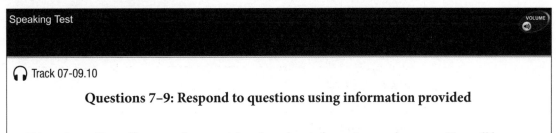

Speaking Test VOLUME

🎧 Track 07-09.10

Questions 7–9: Respond to questions using information provided

Directions: You will answer three questions based on information on the screen. You will have 30 seconds to read the information. You will have 15 seconds to respond to Questions 7 and 8, and you will have 30 seconds to respond to Question 9. For each question, begin to answer as soon as you hear the beep. No preparation time is provided.

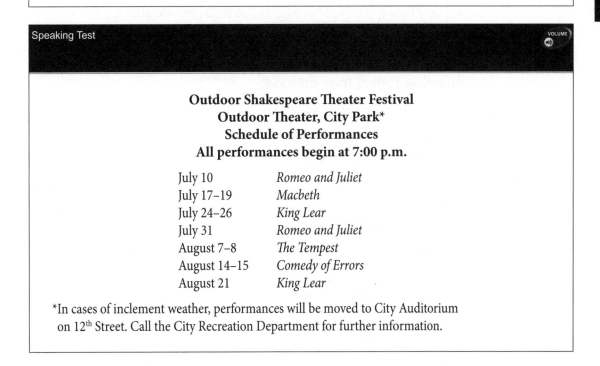

Speaking Test VOLUME

Outdoor Shakespeare Theater Festival
Outdoor Theater, City Park*
Schedule of Performances
All performances begin at 7:00 p.m.

July 10	*Romeo and Juliet*
July 17–19	*Macbeth*
July 24–26	*King Lear*
July 31	*Romeo and Juliet*
August 7–8	*The Tempest*
August 14–15	*Comedy of Errors*
August 21	*King Lear*

*In cases of inclement weather, performances will be moved to City Auditorium on 12th Street. Call the City Recreation Department for further information.

Question 7 of 11 *Response Time Needed: 15 seconds*

Speaking Time Used: _____ seconds

Question 8 of 11 *Response Time Needed: 15 seconds*

Speaking Time Used: _____ seconds

Question 9 of 11 *Response Time Needed: 30 seconds*

Speaking Time Used: _____ seconds

To see and hear sample responses, look at the audioscript at the end of the book and listen to track **07-09.11**.

TOEIC® Test Speaking Question 10

In Question 10 of the Speaking Test, you will hear a voicemail message that describes a problem and you will be asked to suggest a solution. The problem will be in the form of a complaint or a request. The message will not appear on the screen—you will only hear it. You will have 30 seconds to prepare your answer and 60 seconds to speak. Your response will be evaluated on pronunciation, intonation and stress, grammar, vocabulary, cohesion, and relevance and completeness of content.

Possible topics may include:

» *Problems with rental housing or office space*

» *Problems with deliveries*

» *Travel-related issues*

» *Customer service requests*

» *Requests for information about classes*

QUICK GUIDE: Propose a Solution

Definition	Question 10 tests your ability to restate a problem and present your ideas for a solution in an organized, coherent way. You will summarize the problem and offer a reasonable solution to it.
Targeted Skills	In order to answer Question 10 effectively, you should be able to: • understand what a speaker is asking for. • summarize a problem clearly and briefly. • come up with a solution to a problem. • organize your ideas while speaking. • select and use appropriate vocabulary and correct grammatical forms. • speak clearly.
Question Types	There are no specific question types for Question 10. You will be expected to simply restate the problem that you hear and suggest a solution.
A Good Response	A good response will demonstrate that you understand what the complaint or request is about and are able to propose a solution that is clear and well organized. Your response will have clear delivery, use an appropriate level of formality, be well paced, and be understood by the listener with little effort.
Things to Remember	**1.** First, listen carefully to the message to understand what the problem is and what the listener is asking for. **2.** Next, think of a reasonable solution. It doesn't have to be complicated. It just has to make sense and be something you can explain. **3.** Imagine you are leaving a voicemail. Include a greeting, and be sure to introduce yourself. **4.** Apologize for the problem, or show that you understand the reason for the request. **5.** Explain your solution step-by-step.

WALK THROUGH: Propose a Solution

A What You'll See

In Question 10, you will see directions and a sentence telling you what role to assume. You will also see a reminder about what to include in your response. Read the directions and sample voicemail below. What is the message about? What role are you told to play?

Speaking Test

VOLUME 🔊

Question 10: Propose a solution

Directions: In Question 10, you will hear a problem and you will propose a solution. You will have 30 seconds to prepare your response. You will have 60 seconds to speak.

Respond as if you are the building manager.

In your response, you should

- show that you understand the problem.
- propose a solution for the problem.

QUICK TIP

Listen carefully to the first two sentences of the voicemail message. The speaker will usually state the problem there.

ssary:

POWERED BY COBUILD

stration: something
t upsets or angers you
ause you are unable
to anything about the
blems it creates

asant: describing
ething that is nice,
yable, or attractive

B What You'll Hear

You will hear a voicemail message about a problem or a request. Listen to the audio as you read the sample message. What is the caller's complaint? In the script, underline the sentence where the caller first identifies the problem. 🎧 Track 10.01

SAMPLE MESSAGE ▶
(script not available in test)

Hi. This is Chris Robertson in Apartment 314. I'm calling about the elevator, which doesn't seem to be working again. This afternoon, when I got home, I pushed the button to call the elevator, but nothing happened. I waited and waited and pushed the button several times, but the elevator never arrived. I had a heavy bag of groceries with me, and I, you know, had to carry them all the way up the stairs to my apartment on the third floor. Can you let me know what's going to be done about this situation? Using the stairs isn't easy for me because I have a bad back—and it's especially hard when I'm carrying groceries or packages. It's really an inconvenience, and this is the third time this year that the elevator has broken down. I hope it can be repaired soon. Again, this is Chris Robertson from number 314. Thank you.

C What You'll Do

You will respond by showing you understand the problem and by proposing a solution. Below is a sample response to the message in Part B. Read along as you listen to the sample response. Notice how the speaker organizes her response. Then use the sample response to practice responding to the question with your own ideas. 🎧 Track 10.02

SAMPLE RESPONSE ▶

Hello, Mr. Robertson. This is Tara Conner from Rental Management. I understand you had a problem with the elevator this afternoon. I'm very sorry for the inconvenience. I know it's difficult for you because of your back. I also understand that it is frustrating because it has happened before. I think you'll be happy to know that we plan to replace the elevator. The new elevator will be installed early next week. After that, there won't be any problems with the elevator breaking down. In the meantime, I invite you to use the service elevator. It's near the entrance to the stairs. I know it's not as nice as the passenger elevator, but I think it will be easier for you than the stairs. Then next week you'll be able to use the new passenger elevator. Please let me know if you have any questions.

GET IT RIGHT: Tips and Tasks for Answering Correctly

Question 10 on the Speaking Test is scored on a scale from 0–5. Your response will be graded based on the same criteria as in Questions 1–9: pronunciation, intonation and stress, grammar, vocabulary, cohesion, relevance of content, and completeness of content. As in Questions 7–9, it is important that you speak politely and use language that is appropriate for the situation—in this case, leaving a message for someone you don't know. In your response, you must acknowledge the problem and propose a solution for dealing with it.

Look at this response to a problem about a late delivery of a package needed for a party. The person is responding as a customer service representative. 🎧 Track 10.03

A Good Response: *Hello, Ms. Jones. This is Marco with Sunco Products returning your call. We're very sorry to hear that your package is late. We understand how frustrating that is, especially because you want it for a party this weekend. I checked into the problem. It appears that the delivery person tried to deliver the package three times. Unfortunately, there was no one at home at the time. I'd like to suggest that we set up a time this week when you know you will be home. Then we can try to deliver the package again. That way, we should be able to get your delivery to you before the weekend. Let me know if this will be OK with you or if you have any questions. And again, we're very sorry about the delay.*

Analysis: The speaker's answer is well organized, and it completely addresses the task. First, the speaker greets the person, introduces himself, and says why he is calling. He also apologizes for the problem. He then gives an explanation for the problem and makes a clear, detailed suggestion about how to solve it. During the call, he uses polite language, speaks clearly, and uses appropriate and varied grammar and vocabulary.

UNDERSTANDING THE VOICEMAIL MESSAGES

Question 10 begins with a voicemail message from a caller who makes a complaint, makes a request, or does both. These voicemail messages are structured like real messages.

The messages usually start with a short greeting and introduction by the caller. This is followed by a statement about the complaint or the request. The caller then gives some details about what happened and what he or she would like done. This part often indicates why it is a problem or why the person has the request. Often, the caller mentions a deadline or an urgent need. The end of the voicemail usually includes a restatement of the person's name and, sometimes, the person's contact information.

» **TIP 1 Learn to recognize the basic types of voicemail messages you may hear.** The types of voicemail messages will vary, but the caller will have some fairly common problem or request. It is important to listen for key words that give you clues as to whether the caller has a complaint, a request, or both. The chart on the next page gives examples of some expressions that can give you clues about the reason for the call.

QUICK TIP

Remember, your solutions and explanations for problems don't have to be complicated. Propose something you know you can explain. Use grammatical structures you are comfortable with.

Expressions for Making Complaints	Expressions for Introducing Requests
I'm calling about a problem / issue that I have (with) . . .	*I'd like you to . . .*
There's something wrong with . . .	*Could I / you (please) . . . ?*
X isn't working.	*I want / need . . .*
I'm sorry to say (that) . . .	*I was wondering if you could . . .*
I have a complaint about . . .	*What I'd like you to do is . . .*
I'm very disappointed (with X. / that Y happened.)	*Is there any way that you could . . . ?*
There seems to be something wrong with . . .	*I'd appreciate it if you . . .*
I'm sorry to have to say this, but . . .	*Do you think you . . . ?*
I need X taken care of right away.	*Would you mind . . . ?*
X was supposed to be . . . , but it's . . .	*I'd like some help with . . .*
	I know you don't usually do this, but could you . . . ?

TASK Listen to each message. Does the caller have a complaint, a request, or both? Circle the correct answer. ⌒ Track 10.04

1. complaint   request   both

2. complaint   request   both

3. complaint   request   both

» **TIP 2 Listen carefully for key information about the person, situation, or request.** For an effective response, you will need to include some key information. Listen for these types of information.

• The name of the person calling

• Specific information about the problem

• What happened or what the person needs

• Any special requests or conditions

The chart includes some expressions that give clues to important information.

Giving Names and Information	Describing Complaints		Describing Requests
	Goods	Services	
My name is . . .	*not working*	*didn't do a good job / did a bad job*	*urgently*
This is . . .	*broken*		*right away*
I'm calling about . . .	*damaged / crushed / ruined / defective / imperfect*	*didn't fix / wasn't fixed properly*	*as soon as possible / ASAP*
I'd like to speak with . . .		*hasn't been fixed yet*	*a (special) favor / request*
I'm a customer / resident / tenant / guest / member / visitor, and . . .	*missing*	*did X incorrectly / wrong*	*If X happens again, then . . .*
	wrong color / type / size / package	*got X wrong*	*If X doesn't get fixed / resolved, then . . .*
I'm in Apartment / Room . . .	*delayed*	*came / arrived / got here late*	*I'd like . . .*
	something wrong with		*I'm hoping that . . .*
	unusable	*unacceptable*	*It's very important that . . .*

» **TASK** Listen again to the messages from the TIP 1 TASK on page 59. Use the templates below to take notes on key information.   🎧 Track 10.04

Message 1:

Name of the person: _____

Main problem: _____

What happened: _____

Why it is a problem: _____

Special requests (if any): _____

Message 2:

Name of the person: _____

Main problem: _____

What happened: _____

Why it is a problem: _____

Special requests (if any): _____

Message 3:

Name of the person: _____

Main problem: _____

What happened: _____

Why it is a problem: _____

Special requests (if any): _____

QUICK TIP

Sometimes the caller will give similar information or talk about information that is not related to the problem. Ignore information that is not relevant. Look at the example below. The information that is not needed is crossed out. Notice the boldfaced words that are similar to information you do need.

I'm missing the connector cable. ~~The plug, **battery**, and other parts are all here.~~

STRUCTURING YOUR RESPONSE

Structuring your response well is important because your message should be clear and easy to understand. It is also very important that you show you understand the problem well and offer a detailed solution to help the caller. For Question 10, the following templates will work for most messages, but you may need to adjust them to fit the situation.

QUICK TIP

Remember to respond in the role indicated on the screen in the line after the directions. For example, the line might tell you to answer as if you work at the bank. This tells you immediately that the problem is about something relating to a bank.

COMPLAINTS	REQUESTS
– Greeting and introduction	– Greeting and introduction
– Apologize / Show understanding	– Acknowledge request
– Possible explanation	– Respond to request
– Proposed solution 1	– Explain reasons or conditions
– Details 1	– Give solution or option 1
– Proposed solution 2 (where needed)	– Details 1
– Details 2	– Give solution or option 2 (where needed)
– Closing statement	– Details 2
	– Closing statement

Listen and read the sample message and response about a complaint. Notice the way the response follows the template for a complaint. 🎧 Track 10.05

SAMPLE MESSAGE: *Hi, this is Sarah Brown. I'd like to make a complaint about a problem I've been having with my new stove. We just bought it two weeks ago, but the last few times I've turned it on, nothing has happened. Then, when I try again, it works. I don't know what the issue is, but I need to get it fixed right away. I have people coming over for dinner on Friday night, and it's already Tuesday. I really need someone to come out and have a look at it. I'd prefer it if someone could come today or, at the latest, tomorrow. Please call me back as soon as possible. Sarah Brown at 906-555-7272. Thank you.*

SAMPLE RESPONSE: *Hello, Ms. Brown. My name is Brenden, and I'm with Miller Stoves. I'm returning your call from this morning. We're very sorry that you're having problems with your stove. I know you're worried about your dinner party, so we'll try to fix the stove right away. The problem could be that the stove was damaged in shipping, so we'll have to come and take a look at it. I need to check with our repair department first, but they might be able to come this evening. If they can't come today, we should be able to come tomorrow. I'll call back later this afternoon to check what times you are available. Thanks again for your call, and again, we're very sorry about the problem with the stove.*

» **TIP 1 Learn set phrases for greeting the person, introducing yourself, and apologizing for the problem or acknowledging the request.** After you hear the message, you will have 30 seconds to organize and prepare your response. The first parts of an effective response can include set or basic expressions. You can practice these in "chunks." Here are some basic expressions for greeting the caller and introducing yourself.

Greetings and Introductions
Hi, [**name of caller**]. *This is* [**your invented name**], *and I'm returning your call.*
Hello. I'm calling for [**name of caller**]. *I'm* [**your invented name**] *with* [**name of company**], *and we just got your message.*
Good morning, [**name of caller**]. *My name's* [**your invented name**]. *I just wanted to get back to you about your message.*
Hello. I would like to leave a message for [**name of caller**]. *I'm calling from* [**name of company**]. *My name is* [**your invented name**].

As part of your apology or to show you understand, you can just say, *I'm very sorry about the problem.* However, if possible, you should say something specific. To do this, you can use set phrases with more details added. Look at the examples in the chart.

Apologizing for Complaints		
Set Phrases*	**Detail Formats**	**Examples**
We're sorry to hear that . . . *I'm sorry to hear that . . .*	a complete sentence restating the problem	*We're sorry to hear that your stove is broken.* *I'm sorry to hear that you're unhappy with your purchase.*
We're very sorry for / about . . . *I'd like to apologize for / about . . .* *Please accept our apologies for / about . . .*	a noun or gerund phrase	*We're very sorry about the late delivery.* *I'd like to apologize for getting your reservation wrong.* *Please accept our apologies for the error.*

(continued)

QUICK TIP

If you want to add a company name, you can easily make one up by adding a last name before a product name.

For example:
Johnson Dishes
Lee Apartments
Cortez Construction

Acknowledging Requests		
Set Phrases*	**Detail Formats**	**Examples**
Thank you very much for asking about . . .	a noun or gerund phrase	***Thank you very much for asking about*** *our services.*
I understand that you're interested in . . .		***I understand that you're interested in*** *getting a delivery.*
So it seems the main thing you need is . . .	a noun phrase	***So it seems the main thing you need is*** *your home painted.*

*You can speak as an individual (*I / me / my*) or for the company (*we / us / our*).

You should also try to add to your response any information from the caller's description of the problem. This will help show you understand how the issue might affect the caller and help you give a more complete answer. See the examples in the chart.

Showing Understanding of the Problem		
Set Phrases*	**Detail Formats**	**Examples**
We know you need / want . . .	noun or infinitive phrase	***We know you need*** *to get up early for the meeting.* ***I know you want*** *the repairs done by Sunday.*
I know this is especially a problem because . . . *We know you're really worried about this, since . . .* *I understand that . . . , so we want to help.*	sentence giving a special condition mentioned in call	***I know this is especially a problem because*** *you're having a dinner party this weekend.* ***We know you're really worried about this, since*** *the broken vase is a gift.* ***I understand that*** *you have a bad back and can't carry things,* ***so we want to help.***

*You can speak as an individual (*I / me / my*) or for the company (*we / us / our*).

TASK 1 Listen to the partial responses to the problems from the TIP 1 TASK on page 59. Write the expressions used to greet and introduce, apologize for problems or acknowledge requests, and show understanding. 🎧 Track 10.06

Expressions to greet and introduce	Expressions to apologize or acknowledge requests	Expressions to show understanding (if any)
1.		
2.		
3.		

TASK 2 Now use the expressions from TASK 1 above to greet the caller and introduce yourself, apologize for a complaint, or acknowledge a request. Make notes and then practice aloud. Use the information given in parentheses.

1. Greeting and introduction (Susan Jones / your invented name) _____

2. Apologize for a complaint (missing computer part) _____

3. Acknowledge a request (wants to take a driving course) _____

» **TIP 2 Learn set phrases for explaining reasons and responding to difficult requests.** For complaints, after you introduce yourself and apologize, you should try to offer at least one possible reason for the problem. This will help expand your answer and show you understand what is wrong. It is fine to invent a reason, but your reason should be realistic.

QUICK TIP

- Remember that to be polite, your greeting should use the caller's full name or one of the following titles and the last name.
- *Mr.* (mis-ter) for a man
- *Ms.* (miz) for a woman
- If the caller gives a professional title (e.g., *Doctor, Professor*), use that title with the last name.
- Do not use *Mr., Mrs.,* or *Ms.* with a first name!
- Do not use *Mrs.* unless the caller has used *Mrs. Use Ms.* instead.

Question 10 requests will often be very urgent or difficult to do. Therefore, you should be prepared to give an apologetic response or say no to the caller and explain the reason why. Here are some expressions to explain reasons for problems and respond to difficult requests.

Giving Reasons for Problems		
Set Phrases	**Detail Formats**	**Examples**
It's / It was most likely / probably a problem with . . . *It could be / may be / might be . . .*	a person, place, thing, or event	***It's most likely a problem with** the connection.* ***It could be** a loose wire.*
It could / must / might / may have been . . .	past participle (passive verb); a person, place, thing, or event	***It could have been** sent to the wrong address.* ***It must have been** a bank error.*
There could / must / might / may have been . . .	noun phrase	***There could have been** a problem in shipping.* ***There must have been** something wrong with the phone system.*
It seems / appears that . . .	sentence explaining the problem	***It seems** that the booking didn't go through.*
Responding to Difficult Requests		
Set Phrases	**Detail Formats**	**Examples**
I'm afraid there's a problem with that because . . .	sentence explaining the problem	***I'm afraid there's a problem with that because** we don't offer that service.*
Unfortunately, it's not our policy to . . .	verb phrase	***Unfortunately, it's not our policy to** accept students without applications.*
As you mentioned / know, . . . , so we won't be able to . . .	sentence giving a condition stated in the message; verb phrase	***As you mentioned,** the morning course is full, **so we won't be able to** enroll you in that course.*

TASK 1 Listen to the full responses to the problems from TIP 1 TASK 1 on page 62. Circle the expression you hear each speaker use to give a reason for a problem or respond to a difficult request. 🎧 Track 10.07

1. a. As you know, we don't . . .   **b.** I'm afraid there's a problem with that.

2. a. It could have been . . .   **b.** It was probably a mistake with . . .

3. a. It must have been . . .   **b.** It seems that . . .

TASK 2 Read each complaint or request. Think of at least one reason why the problem could have happened or why the request is difficult. Then write sentences to explain the reason or respond to the difficult request. Use the expressions from the chart above. Then practice saying the responses aloud.

1. A woman's dress was ruined by a greasy elevator. _____

_____

2. A man wants to get a doctor's appointment today, but there isn't one available.

_____

3. A taxi that a man ordered is late. _____

_____

» **TIP 3 Learn set phrases for offering solutions, proposing options, and ending the call.** After you introduce yourself, apologize, and explain possible reasons for the problem or difficulties with the request, you should offer at least one detailed suggestion to resolve the problem or address the request. For complaints, this can include actions that you or the customer can take to solve the problem. It can also include options for solving the problem or meeting the request. This chart has useful expressions for offering solutions and options.

Offering Solutions		
Set Phrases	**Detail Formats**	**Examples**
I'd like to suggest that . . .	sentence offering solution	***I'd like to suggest that** you let us know a time when you'll be home.*
We're going to . . .	verb phrase offering solution	***We're going to** send another one out to you right away.*
I'll . . .		***I'll** check with our ordering department.*
We might / should be able to . . .		***We might be able to** resend the package today.*
I can arrange for . . .	noun phrase with a solution	***I can arrange for** another delivery.*
	noun + infinitive phrase and solution	***We can arrange for** the cleaning to be reimbursed.*
I can arrange to . . .	infinitive verb phrase	***I can arrange to** get you a new one.*
In order to . . . , let's / we can . . .	verb phrase explaining desired result; verb phrase offering solution	***In order to** get the book to you quickly, **let's** send another package through express mail.*
We just need to . . . , and then we can . . .	a requirement; verb phrase with solution	***I just need to** check with the order department, **and then we can** send a new one to you.*
Expressions for Offering Options		
Set Phrases	**Detail Formats**	**Examples**
If you can / could . . . , (then) we can / could . . .	cause with requirement; effect with solution	***If you can** be here at 2:00, **we can** see you today.*
		***If you could** tell us when you ordered the product, **then we could** check our delivery records.*
One thing we could do is . . .	verb phrase offering solution	***One thing we could do is** replace the damaged shirt.*
Another option would be to . . .		***Another option would be to** fix the shirt you have.*
If you'd prefer, we could . . .		***If you'd prefer, we could** send you another book.*
I / You / We could also try . . .	gerund or infinitive with option	***You could also try** washing it yourself.*
		***I could also try** to place the order again.*

For some complaints or requests, the response may need to make an exception. When a complaint can't be fixed, you could offer compensation, such as a discount, a free item, or an upgrade. You might also offer suggestions for avoiding the problem in the future. Finally, you should end your call with a closing statement that apologizes again for the situation or explains the next steps. See below for expressions for making exceptions, offering benefits, making suggestions for the future, and ending the call.

Expressions for Making Exceptions	Possible Benefits and Compensations	Possible Suggestions for the Future	Expressions for Ending the Call
Because you're an important customer, . . . *We really appreciate your business, so . . .* *Normally we don't do this, but . . .* *For your inconvenience, . . .*	*. . . we'd like to offer . . .* *a 20 percent discount.* *a free [room / package / etc.].* *a reduced rate.* *a replacement [stove / computer / etc.].* *reimbursement for your [cleaning costs / travel costs / etc.].* *to pay for your [cleaning costs / travel costs / etc.].*	*Next time, please remember to . . .* *call earlier.* *let us know as soon as possible.* *give more notice.* *allow more time.* *call customer service right away.* *check the website first for more information.*	*Thanks again for calling. We really appreciate your business.* *Please let us know if you have any questions. And again, we're very sorry for any inconvenience.* *Please contact me at [phone number] for more information.*

TASK 1 Listen again to the complete responses from TIP 2, TASK 1 on page 63. Circle the two expressions each speaker uses to offer solutions or options. 🎧 Track 10.07

1. a. I can arrange for . . .   **b.** One option would be . . .   **c.** If we did that, then . . .

2. a. I can arrange for . . .   **b.** We're going to . . .   **c.** In order to . . . , let's . . .

3. a. I just need to . . .   **b.** I'll give you . . .   **c.** We should be able to . . .

TASK 2 Read the complaint or request. Think of <u>one</u> possible solution for the problem or <u>one</u> possible way to deal with the request. Then think of <u>one</u> way to compensate the caller. Write sentences with your ideas. Practice saying them aloud.

1. A DVD someone ordered is a week late. _____

_____

_____

2. A person wants to reschedule a meeting for the next day. _____

_____

_____

3. A resident has a broken lock on her apartment door. _____

_____

_____

4. A woman received a repair bill, but the charges are much higher than she expected.

_____

_____

5. A man's Internet is off, and he needs to get it back on right away.

_____

_____

PROGRESSIVE PRACTICE: Get Ready

A Listen to the voicemail message as you read along in the script. Then answer the questions. 🎧 Track 10.08

SAMPLE MESSAGE ▶
(script not available in test)

Good morning. My name is Marty Jones. I signed up to take the advanced Spanish course that meets on Saturday mornings. However, I just found out that I'll be starting a new job this week, and my work schedule will include Saturday mornings. So I won't be able to take that class. Could I take it at another time? I'm free most evenings during the week and on Monday and Tuesday afternoons. If there's an advanced Spanish class that meets at one of these times, maybe I could transfer into it. Please let me know. I can be reached at 403-555-1212. Thanks.

1. This call is about

   a. a request.

   b. a complaint.

   c. both a request and a complaint.

2. What is the caller's main problem?

   a. He can't study, because he is too busy at work.

   b. He thinks the class level is too advanced.

   c. He can't go to class at the scheduled time.

3. What does the caller want?

   a. His money to be returned

   b. A transfer to a different class

   c. Extra help with his classwork

B Listen to the sample response as you read along in the script. Notice the words and expressions the speaker uses to recognize the problem and offer a solution. Then listen again. Write the numbers of the purposes next to the correct sentences in the sample response. Use the purposes in the box. 🎧 Track 10.09

Purposes

1. Proposed solution

2. ~~Greeting and introduction~~

3. Acknowledgement of request

4. Closing statement

5. Reasons or conditions

6. Response to request

Response:

_2_ *Hello, Mr. Jones. My name is Kim.* ___ *I understand that you can't take the Saturday morning Spanish class because of your new work schedule. I'm sorry that the class schedule doesn't work for you. I know that it can be complicated to try to study and work at the same time.* ___ *However, this problem is very easy to solve. We do have another advanced Spanish class. It meets on Tuesday afternoons, and there's still room for another student in it.* ___ *I'll put your name on the list for that class, so all you have to do is show up next Tuesday afternoon at two o'clock.* ___ *Please let me know if you have any problem with this.* ___ *Otherwise, we hope to see you next Tuesday.*

C Now complete the response template below or use another piece of paper to create a response to the message in Part A. Then practice your response aloud. Record your response if possible.

Response:

Thank you for calling, _____.

Your message said that you can't _____

_____ because of your _____

_____. I'm sorry to hear about this difficulty with your _____

_____, but I think this problem is easy to solve. You said that you're available

on _____ and _____

_____ afternoons. We have an advanced

Spanish class you can attend on either of those days. Please choose which day you want and let me

know. I hope this will work well for you.

D Now think about your response or listen to it again if it was recorded. Then read the statements below. How well did your response meet the scoring criteria? Check (✓) *Yes* or *No*. Keep practicing until all of your answers are *Yes*.

Response Checklist: Question 10	Yes	No
1. I used correct pronunciation, intonation, and stress. My response was easily understood.	☐	☐
2. I used correct and varied grammar and vocabulary.	☐	☐
3. My response was well paced. It was neither too fast nor too slow, and I spoke for the full amount of time.	☐	☐
4. My response was clear and well organized.	☐	☐
5. I gave a summary of the problem.	☐	☐
6. I apologized for the problem and expressed sympathy.	☐	☐
7. I provided at least one solution for the problem.	☐	☐
8. I spoke politely and used language appropriate to the situation.	☐	☐

PROGRESSIVE PRACTICE: Get Set

A Listen to the voicemail message and make notes about the content. 🎧 Track 10.10

> **Notes**
> **1.** Name of caller _____
> **2.** Is it a request or a complaint (or both)? _____
> **3.** Main problem _____
> _____
> **4.** What happened _____
> _____
> **5.** Why it is a problem _____
> _____
> **6.** Special requests (if any) _____
> _____

B Listen to the model response to the message in Part A. Notice how the person organizes the response. Then listen again and complete the sentences below. 🎧 Track 10.11

1. Apologize and show understanding of the problem.

I understand that you haven't been able to _____
_____. I realize how _____
_____ this must be.

2. Give a possible explanation.

There could be _____
_____
or _____.
_____

3. Summarize the two solutions in your own words.

a. _____
_____

b. _____
_____

4. Give a closing statement.

Thanks so much for _____,

and please accept our apologies for the _____
_____

C Listen to the message in Part A again. Then complete the template below to respond to the message. Use phrases from Part B or your own ideas. Practice your response aloud, and record it if possible. Be sure to check the amount of time you use!

Response:

[Greeting and introduction] _____

_____

[Apologize / Show understanding] _____

_____

[Possible explanation] _____

_____

_____

[Solution 1 / Details 1] _____

_____

_____

[Solution 2 / Details 2] _____

_____

_____

[Closing statement] _____

_____

D Now think about your response or listen to it again if it was recorded. Then read the statements below. How well did your response meet the scoring criteria? Check (✓) *Yes* or *No*. Keep practicing until all of your answers are *Yes*.

Response Checklist: Question 10	Yes	No
1. I used correct pronunciation, intonation, and stress. My response was easily understood.	☐	☐
2. I used correct and varied grammar and vocabulary.	☐	☐
3. My response was well paced. It was neither too fast nor too slow, and I spoke for the full amount of time.	☐	☐
4. My response was clear and well organized.	☐	☐
5. I gave a summary of the problem.	☐	☐
6. I apologized for the problem and expressed sympathy.	☐	☐
7. I provided at least one solution for the problem.	☐	☐
8. I spoke politely and used language appropriate to the situation.	☐	☐

PROGRESSIVE PRACTICE: Go for the TOEIC® Test

Listen to the message and then give your response. Time yourself as you speak, and record your response if possible.

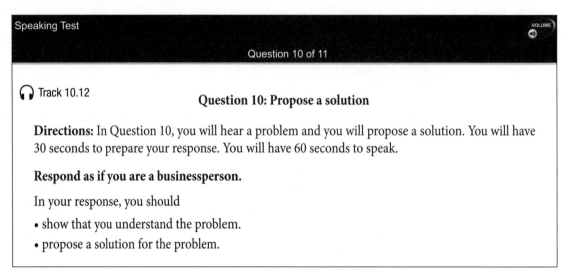

Speaking Test

VOLUME

Question 10 of 11

🎧 Track 10.12   **Question 10: Propose a solution**

Directions: In Question 10, you will hear a problem and you will propose a solution. You will have 30 seconds to prepare your response. You will have 60 seconds to speak.

Respond as if you are a businessperson.

In your response, you should

• show that you understand the problem.

• propose a solution for the problem.

Preparation Time Used: _____ seconds

Speaking Time Used: _____ seconds

TO SEE AND HEAR SAMPLE RESPONSES, LOOK AT THE AUDIOSCRIPT AT THE END OF THE BOOK AND LISTEN TO TRACK **10.13.**

QUICK TIP

Refer to the countdown clock from time to time while you are giving your response. Make sure you're not spending too much time on any one part of your response. Don't risk running out of time before you can give your solutions!

TOEIC® Test Speaking Question 11

In Question 11 of the Speaking Test, you will be asked to state your opinion about a topic. You will be asked to agree or disagree with a statement, explain a preference, or discuss your opinion of a situation. The question will appear on-screen and will be read by a narrator. You will have 15 seconds to prepare your response and 60 seconds to speak. You will be scored on your ability to respond appropriately to the task, state your opinion clearly, and support it with examples. In addition, you will be evaluated on pronunciation, intonation and stress, grammar, vocabulary, cohesion, and relevance and completeness of content.

You may be asked to express an opinion on such things as:

» *Transportation*	» *Friendships*
» *Housing*	» *Shopping*
» *Work*	» *Travel*

QUICK GUIDE: Express an Opinion

Definition	Question 11 tests your ability to express an opinion about common topics. You will state your opinion and support it with reasons and examples.
Targeted Skills	In order to answer Question 11 effectively, you should be able to: • express your opinion clearly. • support your opinion with reasons and examples. • select and use appropriate vocabulary. • use correct and varied grammatical structures. • speak clearly.
Question Types	**Preference:** *Which do you prefer and why?* **Agreement:** *Do you agree or disagree with this statement?* **Opinion:** *What is your opinion of this issue? Do you support or oppose this plan?*
A Good Response	A good response is well developed and expresses a clear opinion, supporting details, and clear relationships between ideas. Speaking is easily understandable, vocabulary is appropriate, and grammatical structures are correctly used.
Things to Remember	**1.** First, form an opinion statement. **2.** Next, think of three or four key points that support your opinion. **3.** Begin your answer by stating your opinion. **4.** Then list your supporting key points. **5.** After each key point, give additional details about it, including personal information, reasons, and examples.

WALK THROUGH: Express an Opinion

A What You'll See and Hear

In Question 11, you will see directions and a question asking you to give an opinion about something. Read and listen to the sample task and questions below. Circle the two main questions being asked. Then think about your own personal opinion on the topic and three or four reasons to support it. 🎧 Track 11.01

Speaking Test VOLUME

Question 11: Express an opinion

Directions: In Question 11, you will give your opinion about a topic. You will have 15 seconds to prepare your response. You will have 60 seconds to speak. Say as much as you can in the time you have.

Question:
Some people enjoy the excitement of city life. Other people prefer the peace and quiet of small-town living. Would you rather live in a big city or a small town? Why? Use specific examples to support your preference.

B What You'll Do

You will respond by showing you understand the question and by expressing your opinion about the matter. Below is a sample response to the question in Part A. As you listen to the audio, notice how the speaker organizes the response. 🎧 Track 11.02

SAMPLE RESPONSE ▶

Glossary:

⊜ POWERED BY COBUILD

restrictive: describing something that prevents people from what they want to do or from moving freely

come across: find something or someone or meet someone by chance

I would definitely prefer to live in a big city. I like the excitement of city life. There are always so many interesting activities to do, like different kinds of theater, concerts, classes you can take, and so on. You can also meet a lot of different kinds of people in your daily life—people from all different places with all different kinds of interests. In addition, it's much easier to find jobs in a city than it is in a small town. That's really important. You have to work, right? So you want to live in a place where you have a chance of finding a good job. I think life in a small town is very restrictive. There aren't many options for entertainment, and you don't come across many different kinds of people. I would be really bored if I lived in a small town.

GET IT RIGHT: Tips and Tasks for Answering Correctly

Question 11 on the Speaking Test is scored on a scale from 0–5. Your response will be graded based on the same criteria as Questions 1–10—pronunciation, intonation and stress, grammar, vocabulary, cohesion, relevance of content, and completeness of content. However, your response to Question 11 will be graded on two additional points: your ability to give a clear and relevant opinion, and your ability to support that opinion with reasons, details, and examples.

Read and listen to the question and a good response. Then read the analysis, which explains what makes the response a good one. 🎧 Track 11.03

Question: *Some people enjoy jobs in which they do the same work every day. Others enjoy jobs that involve changing from project to project. Which type of job would you prefer and why?*

A Good Response: *I would prefer a job that involves changing from project to project. I feel this way for a number of reasons. First of all, I don't really like doing the same thing every day. I like change and need some variety in my life. Second, I like to meet new people. Working on different projects would give me a chance to make a lot of new friends and contacts. Finally, I think doing the same thing all the time could be really boring. If I did the same thing every day, I might never learn new things. In my opinion, a job that involves changing from project to project would just be more exciting.*

Analysis: The speaker's answer is well organized, and it answers both parts of the question—what she prefers and why she prefers it. She then supports her opinion with three personal reasons. She also adds some additional explanation about why she feels that way. She then offers an example of what might happen if she worked in the other type of job. Finally, she restates her opinion.

QUICK TIP

Many of the questions begin with a scenario. A scenario is a statement that sets the scene for the question. This type of question often mentions *you* or *your*, but it doesn't really refer to you specifically. The scenario simply tells you what to imagine. Look at these two examples.

Your city plans to build a new stadium in your neighborhood.

Your boss asks you to choose more vacation time or a raise.

UNDERSTANDING THE TOPIC AND QUESTION

Question 11 will ask you for your opinion on a subject, if you agree or disagree with a statement, or if you have a preference between two or more things. It will most often be personal and designed to allow you to state your own ideas in a number of different areas. The question will remain on the screen as you respond, so you can refer to it as you speak.

» **TIP 1 Familiarize yourself with the question types.** There are three main types of questions that you can expect to see on the test: opinion, agreement, and preference. It is important to familiarize yourself with the types of questions you may encounter so that you can quickly prepare a response that is relevant and addresses the question correctly. Learn to watch for key questions, words, and phrases to tell you what the question is asking for.

Question Types	Examples of Typical Questions	Key Questions, Words, and Phrases
Opinion	Many people think that electric cars will solve the world's pollution problems. What is your opinion on this issue? Give reasons and details to support your answer. Some people think that living in an apartment is better than living in a house. What do you think? Give reasons for your choice.	*What do you think?* *What is your opinion?* *issue* *plan* *. . . people think that . . .*
Agreement	Do you agree or disagree with the following statement? "If you work hard, you will be successful." Give reasons and details to support your answer. Your company is planning to lay off several older employees. They want to do this so they can hire more new employees at lower salaries. Would you be in favor of this plan? Give reasons and examples to support your choice.	*Do you agree or disagree . . . ?* *Would you be in favor of . . . ?* *statement*
Preference	Some people want to work at home. Some people prefer to work in an office. Which type of job would you prefer and why? Would you rather work for a big corporation or in a small company? Give reasons and examples to support your answer.	*Which do you think is better and why?* *Which do you prefer and why?* *Would you rather X or Y?* *Do you prefer X or Y?* *Some . . . Some . . .*

TASK Read each question or statement and choose the letter of the next part.

1. Some people like working at home better than working in an office. _____
2. Do you agree or disagree with the following statement? _____
3. Would you rather shop online or go to a store? _____
4. There is a plan to offer free wireless service in your city, but there will be a slight tax increase as a result. _____
5. Many people feel that taking time to relax is the key to being productive at work and at home. _____
6. Some people think that all young people should be able to attend college for free. _____

a. "People should get a pay raise every year, even if they don't perform well."
b. Would you be in favor of the planned tax increase? Give reasons and details to support your answer.
c. What's your opinion about free education? Support your answer with reasons and details.
d. Give reasons and examples to support your shopping preference.
e. How do you feel about taking time to relax? Does it make people more productive? Use reasons and examples to support your opinion.
f. Which work environment do you prefer and why?

» **TIP 2 Think about what the question is mainly asking for and how you feel about it.** You have only 15 seconds to prepare your response, so you need to quickly form an opinion. Therefore, it is important to be able to understand exactly what the question is asking for as soon as possible. That way you will have time to think about key supporting points and how you will organize your response.

TASK Read the questions from the TIP 1 TASK above. As quickly as possible, circle the letter of the main information each question is asking for. Then think about your own opinion on the topic.

1. a. My opinion about working at home
   b. Would I like to work at home or in an office
   c. If I agree that working at home is better
2. a. Would I like a pay raise every year, even if I don't perform well
   b. My opinion about giving a pay raise every year
   c. If I agree or disagree that yearly pay raises should not be based on performance
3. a. If I like to shop at home or in stores
   b. If I agree or disagree that online shopping is more popular
   c. My opinion about online shopping
4. a. My opinion about free wireless services offered by cities
   b. Would I like free wireless in my city or a slight tax increase
   c. If I would agree or disagree to pay more taxes for free wireless Internet

5. a. Would I like having more time to relax at work
   b. Would I agree or disagree that relaxation at work is good
   c. My opinion about taking time to relax to increase productivity
6. a. My opinion about offering all young people a free college education
   b. Would I agree that young people want a free college education
   c. Would I like to attend college for free

QUICK TIP

Remember, for a good score, you must give reasons, examples, and details to support your opinion. As soon as you are sure you understand the question, start thinking of key points to express how you feel and how you will support your opinion.

STRUCTURING YOUR RESPONSE

Structuring your response correctly is important to be sure your answer is well organized and easily understood. It will also help ensure you address all points in the prompt. For Question 11, the following template will work for most messages.

> – State opinion
> – Introduce supporting information
>   – Key point 1
>   – Supporting details 1
>   – Key point 2
>   – Supporting details 2
>   – Key point 3
>   – Supporting details 3
> – Restate opinion

Read and listen to the question and sample response. Notice the way the response follows the template. 🎧 Track 11.04

Question: Do you agree or disagree with the following statement? "It's more important to eat a good diet than to exercise a lot." Support your choice with reasons and details.

Sample Response: *I disagree with the statement, "It's more important to eat a good diet than to exercise a lot." There are several reasons for this opinion. For one thing, exercise is a very important part of a healthy lifestyle. It's good for your heart, your muscles, and for controlling your weight. Another reason exercise is important is that it's fun. Playing sports and moving your body can make you feel happier and feel better. Finally, eating a good diet can be healthy, but if you don't move your body, it will become weak. Good nutrition will give you energy, but you should use that energy to move! In conclusion, I have to say exercise and diet are equally important.*

Analysis: The speaker's answer is well organized and clearly relates to the question. The speaker begins by clearly stating his opinion. He then introduces his reasons for feeling this way and includes several details and personal experiences to support them. After speaking for the required length of time, he then closes with a statement restating his opinion.

» **TIP 1 Start by giving a basic statement of your opinion and introducing your supporting statements.** You can start your answer by restating the question and then adding your opinion. You will often be able to use the same verb and many of the same words that are in the prompt. This helps make a strong opening statement and shows that you understand what the question is asking. Look at the sample questions and statements of opinion in the chart. Notice the expressions used to introduce the opinions and the changes to form to add an opinion.

Questions	Statements of Opinion
Many people think that electric cars will solve the world's pollution problems. What is your opinion on this issue? Give reasons and details to support your answer.	*I think that electric cars will **probably not** solve the world's pollution problems.* *I **don't believe** (that) electric cars will solve the world's pollution problems.*
Some people think that living in an apartment is better than living in a house. What do you think? Give reasons for your choice.	*In my opinion, living in a house **is better than** living in an apartment.*
Do you agree or disagree with the following statement? "If you work hard, you will be successful." Give reasons and details to support your answer.	*I **(strongly / kind of) disagree with the opinion** that if you work hard, you will be successful.* *I **don't agree with the statement,** "if you work hard, you will be successful."*

(continued)

Your company is planning to lay off several older employees. They want to do this so they can hire more new employees at lower salaries. Would you be in favor of this plan? Give reasons and examples to support your choice.	*I would **not** be in favor of this plan.* *I would **be against** laying off several older employees.*
Some people want to work at home. Some people prefer to work in offices. Which type of job do you prefer and why?	*I would **prefer** to work at home.* *I would **prefer** working at home **to** working in an office.*
Would you rather work for a big corporation or in a small company? Give reasons and examples to support your answer.	*I would **rather** work for a small company.*

TASK Change the questions into statements giving your opinion.

1. Your boss has said that all employees must attend a three-day company trip every year. How would you feel about this?

   _____

2. If you were planning a vacation, would you prefer to go to the beach or to the mountains?

   _____

3. Your company offers you the option to receive a raise in exchange for getting fewer vacation days. Which would you prefer, getting a pay raise or keeping your vacation days?

   _____

4. Some people think that young people should not be able to drive until they are 21. What do you think?

   _____

» **TIP 2 Follow up with a statement to introduce your main points.** When possible, you should follow your statement of opinion with a sentence that introduces the main points to support your opinion. This helps organize your response and gives you time to think. Use expressions like the ones in the chart to introduce what you will be talking about.

Introducing Support		
Opinion Questions	**Agreement Questions**	**Preference Questions**
I feel this way for several reasons.	*I agree with this statement because of the following reasons.*	*I prefer / don't prefer X for a few different reasons.*
I have this opinion for the following reasons.	*I disagree with this for several reasons.*	*I know that some people like X, but personally, I prefer Y.*
There are a number of reasons I feel this way.	*This would be a good / bad idea for a number of reasons.*	*Although some people may think X is better, I don't feel that way.*
		There are advantages and disadvantages for both, but I think X is better because . . .

TASK Write statements introducing support to go with your statements of opinion in the TIP 1 TASK above. Use expressions like those in the chart above.

1. _____

2. _____

3. _____

4. _____

» **TIP 3 Support your opinion with three key points with additional details.** In order to score well on Question 11, you must include support for your opinion. You can do this by giving key points that offer reasons for an opinion or arguments for or against a viewpoint. This chart gives some basic phrases for introducing key points.

Offering and Supporting Key Points		
General	**Giving Reasons**	**Giving Examples**
For one thing, . . . *For another thing, . . .* *First, . . . / First of all, . . .* *Second(ly), . . . / Third(ly), . . .* *To begin with, . . .* *Additionally, . . . / Also, . . .* *Next, . . .* *Furthermore, . . .* *Finally, . . .*	*The main reason is . . .* *Another reason that I think this is . . .* *My first / second / third reason for thinking this is (that) . . .* *My last / final reason for this view is . . .*	*For example, . . .* *Take X, for example.* *Let me give you an example of what I'm talking about.* *Here's one example.* *And here's another example of what I'm talking about.* *For example, in my country . . .*

After you state a key point, you should also give additional details about the key point to provide further explanation. You can do this by:

- adding personal details that relate to your experiences or why you feel a certain way.
- giving explanations of the key points.
- adding examples or other supporting details to reasons.

TASK Listen to the complete responses to the questions in the TIP 1 TASK on page 74. Write three key points used to support each opinion. Then think of three key points to support your own opinions for the questions. Write your notes on a separate sheet of paper.

1. *In my opinion, taking time to relax is the key to being productive.* 🎧 Track 11.05

   Key point 1: _____

   Key point 2: _____

   Key point 3: _____

2. *I guess I prefer to shop online rather than shop in the store.* 🎧 Track 11.06

   Key point 1: _____

   Key point 2: _____

   Key point 3: _____

3. *I strongly disagree with the statement, "People should get a pay raise every year, even if they don't perform well."* 🎧 Track 11.07

   Key point 1: _____

   Key point 2: _____

   Key point 3: _____

4. *I guess I would prefer to work at home.* 🎧 Track 11.08

   Key point 1: _____

   Key point 2: _____

   Key point 3: _____

QUICK TIP

You can also compare and contrast both sides of the issue to support your point. Use words like *but, however, on the other hand,* or *although.*

*Working at home may be a good idea for some people, **but** it's just not right for me.*

***Although** free Internet service may help some businesses, I don't want to have to pay for it.*

5. *In my opinion, all young people should be able to attend college for free.* 🎧 Track 11.09

Key point 1: _____

Key point 2: _____

Key point 3: _____

6. *I would not be in favor of the planned tax increase.* 🎧 Track 11.10

Key point 1: _____

Key point 2: _____

Key point 3: _____

QUICK TIP

: Remember to stay
: focused. Be sure not
: to move away from
: your opinion or include
: information that is not
: relevant to the ques-
: tion. This could use up
: time and make your
: answer unclear.

» **TIP 4 Close with a restatement of opinion.** If you have time left after giving your supporting information, bring your response to a conclusion. Restate your original opinion and recap the main key points. Use phrases like those in the chart.

Making Restatements of Opinion	
In general, I think that . . . *So basically, I would have to say that . . .* *In conclusion, . . .* *The main point / thing for me is . . .*	*As you can see, there are a lot of reasons why . . .* *Overall, I would say . . .* *All in all, I'd have to say . . .*

TASK 1 Write concluding statements for these opinions.

1. _____ I think that electric cars will not solve the world's pollution problems.

2. _____ I agree that if you work hard, you will be successful.

3. _____ I would rather work for a small company.

TASK 2 Listen to the audio for the completed questions and statements that go with the TIP 1 TASK on page 74 one at a time. Try to respond to the questions and statements completely yourself. Use your notes and previous answers to help you. Record your responses if possible. 🎧 Tracks 11.11 to 11.16

PROGRESSIVE PRACTICE: Get Ready

A Read and listen to the sample question. Then choose the correct answer to the question. 🎧 Track 11.17

> **Question:**
>
> Some people enjoy cooking and eating most of their meals at home. Other people would rather eat out at a restaurant most of the time. Which do you prefer? Use specific examples to support your answer.

The main thing this question asks about is

a. agreement with an idea

b. preferences about something

c. support or opposition to an idea

B Read and listen to the sample response. Notice the words and expressions the speaker uses to give an opinion and supporting details. Then listen again. Write the number of the correct purpose next to each sentence in the sample response. Use the purposes in the box. 🎧 Track 11.18

> **Purposes**
>
> **1.** Key point 1
>
> **2.** Supporting details 2
>
> **3.** ~~State opinion~~
>
> **4.** Supporting details 3
>
> **5.** Key point 2
>
> **6.** Supporting details 1
>
> **7.** Key point 3
>
> **8.** Introduce supporting information

> **Response:**
>
> __3__ I prefer to eat out at restaurants most of the time. ___ I feel this way for several reasons. ___ The main reason for this is that I don't know how to cook very well. ___ If I eat at a restaurant, the food always tastes better than food I cook myself. ___ I also eat more of a variety of food at restaurants. ___ This is because I only know how to cook a few things. ___ Finally, there are a lot of good restaurants in the neighborhood where I live. ___ I have lots of choices for places to eat, and the food at each one is delicious.

C Now complete the response template below or use another piece of paper to create a response to the question in Part A. Then practice your response aloud. Record your response if possible.

Response:

I think I would prefer to _____.

I have several reasons for this. First, I think the food tastes better at _____
_____.

This is because _____.

In addition to that, I think it is more enjoyable to eat at _____
_____ because _____.

Finally, I think _____.

The reason I feel this way is _____
_____.

D Now think about your response or listen to it again if it was recorded. Then read the statements below. How well did your response meet the scoring criteria? Check (✓) *Yes* or *No*. Keep practicing until all of your answers are *Yes*.

Response Checklist: Question 11		
	Yes	**No**
1. I used correct pronunciation, intonation, and stress. My response was easily understood.	☐	☐
2. I used correct and varied grammar and vocabulary.	☐	☐
3. My response was well paced. It was neither too fast nor too slow, and I spoke for the full amount of time.	☐	☐
4. My response was clear and well organized.	☐	☐
5. I stated my opinion clearly.	☐	☐
6. I gave reasons for my opinion.	☐	☐
7. I supported my reasons with details.	☐	☐

PROGRESSIVE PRACTICE: Get Set

A Read and listen to the sample question. Then answer the questions that follow to help prepare for your response. 🎧 Track 11.19

Question:

Do you agree or disagree with the following statement? "Young people should not be allowed to drive cars until they are twenty-one years old." Use specific reasons and examples to support your answer.

---

1. This question is asking for (preference / agreement / support or opposition).

2. I (agree / disagree) with the statement. I believe that young people should

_____

_____

_____

3. The main reasons, details, and examples to support my opinion are

_____

_____

_____

_____

B The sample response below is not in the correct order. Write numbers to order the sentences from 1–9. Then listen to check your answers. 🎧 Track 11.20

_____ In the first place, many young people are careless, but a car can be a dangerous machine.

_____ They should learn to use public transportation until they can afford a car of their own.

_____ I strongly agree with the statement that people should not be allowed to drive until they are 21.

_____ Another reason is that most young people don't have enough money to buy and maintain a car.

_____ Finally, many young people probably don't really need to drive a car.

_____ In my country, you can get a driver's license at age 18, but most people don't start driving regularly until they're married and have families of their own.

_____ It isn't safe to let someone have the responsibility of driving such a dangerous machine until they're mature enough to be serious and careful about it.

_____ I agree with this because of the following reasons.

_____ So basically, it isn't always safe for young people to drive cars, they can't afford it, and they usually don't need to, anyway.

C Read and listen to the question in Part A again. Then complete the template below to respond to the question. Use your notes from Part A, phrases from Part B, and your own ideas. Practice your response aloud and record it if possible. Be sure to check the amount of time you use! 🎧 Track 11.19

Response:

[State opinion] _____

_____

[Introduce supporting information] _____

_____

[Key point 1] _____

_____

[Supporting details 1] _____

_____

[Key point 2] _____

_____

[Supporting details 2] _____

_____

[Key point 3] _____

_____

[Supporting details 3] _____

_____

[Restate opinion] _____

_____

D Now think about your response or listen to it again if it was recorded. Then read the statements below. How well did your response meet the scoring criteria? Check (✓) **Yes** or **No**. Keep practicing until all of your answers are **Yes**.

Response Checklist: Question 11	Yes	No
1. I used correct pronunciation, intonation, and stress. My response was easily understood.	☐	☐
2. I used correct and varied grammar and vocabulary.	☐	☐
3. My response was well paced. It was neither too fast nor too slow, and I spoke for the full amount of time.	☐	☐
4. My response was clear and well organized.	☐	☐
5. I stated my opinion clearly.	☐	☐
6. I gave reasons for my opinion.	☐	☐
7. I supported my reasons with details.	☐	☐

PROGRESSIVE PRACTICE: Go for the TOEIC® Test

Listen to the question and then give your response. Time yourself as you speak, and record your response if possible.

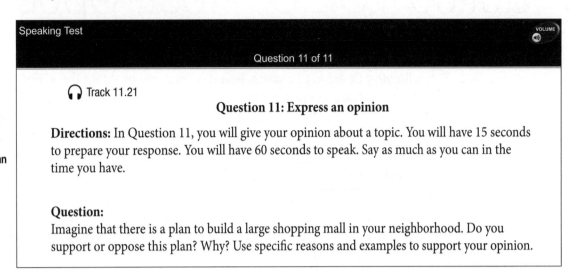

Speaking Test

Question 11 of 11

Track 11.21

Question 11: Express an opinion

Directions: In Question 11, you will give your opinion about a topic. You will have 15 seconds to prepare your response. You will have 60 seconds to speak. Say as much as you can in the time you have.

Question:
Imagine that there is a plan to build a large shopping mall in your neighborhood. Do you support or oppose this plan? Why? Use specific reasons and examples to support your opinion.

QUICK TIP

You don't always need to have three supporting statements; you can have two statements with more supporting details if you prefer.

Preparation Time Used: _____ seconds

Speaking Time Used: _____ seconds

To see and hear sample responses, look at the audioscript at the end of the book and listen to track **11.22.**

Practice TOEIC® Test: Speaking

TAKING THE PRACTICE TEST

The **following** Speaking Practice Test will help you evaluate the TOEIC test-taking skills that you have learned for the Speaking section of the test. The Speaking Practice Test is divided into six parts, just as on the actual test. The level of difficulty of the audio and the written material is like that of the TOEIC test. Your timing should be set like the actual test as well, so plan to complete the Speaking Practice Test questions in the time limits given.

We advise you to simulate the actual test when you take the Speaking Practice Test. Take the test in a quiet setting. Be sure to follow the directions exactly as instructed and record your responses if possible. **Don't replay the audio or go back to previous pages.**

SCORING THE TEST

For the actual test, your responses will be sent to graders who will assign a score for each question. Questions 1–2, Question 3, Questions 4–6, and Questions 7–9 are scored on a scale of 0–3. Questions 10 and 11 are scored on a scale of 0–5 and carry more weight in your overall score. The specific requirements for these scoring scales are available from any testing center. These scores are then translated into Speaking Proficiency Levels that give a detailed description of speaking ability. These Proficiency Level indicators are meant to assign a general speaking level to each test taker.

For this Speaking Practice Test, you or a qualified evaluator may want to check your responses against the checklists given for each question in the *Progressive Practice* sections of the book when you are finished. This will help you assess if you are meeting the main scoring criteria used to measure TOEIC test performance. If you answer *No* to any areas, you may want to practice more on those points by reviewing and taking the test again. In addition, a model response for each question has been provided in both audio and script form. Listen to audio tracks Track SPT-08 through SPT-14 to hear them or go to the script section at the back of this book to read them. Reviewing these model responses will give you a better idea of what you will need in order to be successful on the test.

SPEAKING PRACTICE TEST

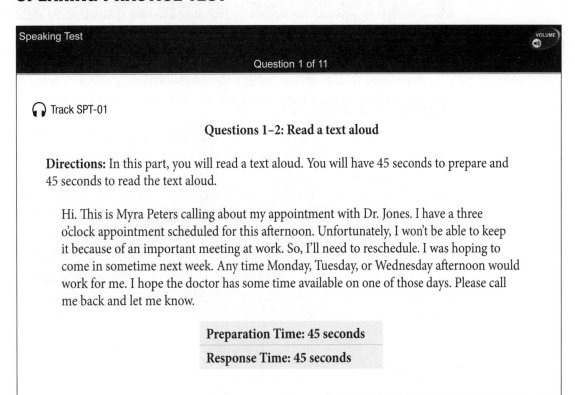

🎧 Track SPT-01

Questions 1–2: Read a text aloud

Directions: In this part, you will read a text aloud. You will have 45 seconds to prepare and 45 seconds to read the text aloud.

Hi. This is Myra Peters calling about my appointment with Dr. Jones. I have a three o'clock appointment scheduled for this afternoon. Unfortunately, I won't be able to keep it because of an important meeting at work. So, I'll need to reschedule. I was hoping to come in sometime next week. Any time Monday, Tuesday, or Wednesday afternoon would work for me. I hope the doctor has some time available on one of those days. Please call me back and let me know.

Preparation Time: 45 seconds

Response Time: 45 seconds

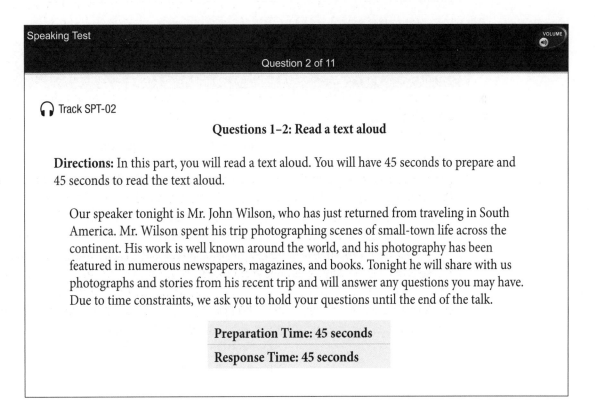

🎧 Track SPT-02

Questions 1–2: Read a text aloud

Directions: In this part, you will read a text aloud. You will have 45 seconds to prepare and 45 seconds to read the text aloud.

Our speaker tonight is Mr. John Wilson, who has just returned from traveling in South America. Mr. Wilson spent his trip photographing scenes of small-town life across the continent. His work is well known around the world, and his photography has been featured in numerous newspapers, magazines, and books. Tonight he will share with us photographs and stories from his recent trip and will answer any questions you may have. Due to time constraints, we ask you to hold your questions until the end of the talk.

Preparation Time: 45 seconds

Response Time: 45 seconds

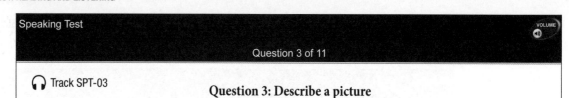

🎧 Track SPT-03

Question 3: Describe a picture

Directions: In this part, you will describe the photo on the screen with as much detail as possible. You will have 30 seconds to prepare. You will have 45 seconds to describe the photo.

Preparation Time: 30 seconds

Response Time: 45 seconds

🎧 Track SPT-04

Questions 4–6: Respond to questions

Directions: In this part, you will answer three questions. Begin responding as soon as you hear the beep for each question. You will have 15 seconds for Questions 4 and 5 and 30 seconds for Question 6. There is no preparation time.

Imagine that a research firm is doing a telephone survey of people in your city. You have agreed to answer some questions about sports.

Question 4: What sports do you enjoy playing?

Preparation Time: 0 seconds

Response Time: 15 seconds

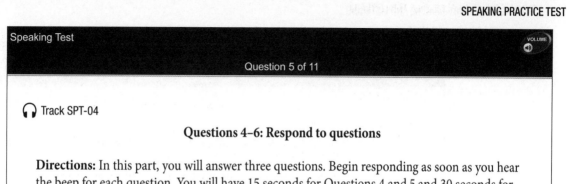

🎧 Track SPT-04

Questions 4–6: Respond to questions

Directions: In this part, you will answer three questions. Begin responding as soon as you hear the beep for each question. You will have 15 seconds for Questions 4 and 5 and 30 seconds for Question 6. There is no preparation time.

Imagine that a research firm is doing a telephone survey of people in your city. You have agreed to answer some questions about sports.

Question 5: How often do you usually play sports?

Preparation Time: 0 seconds
Response Time: 15 seconds

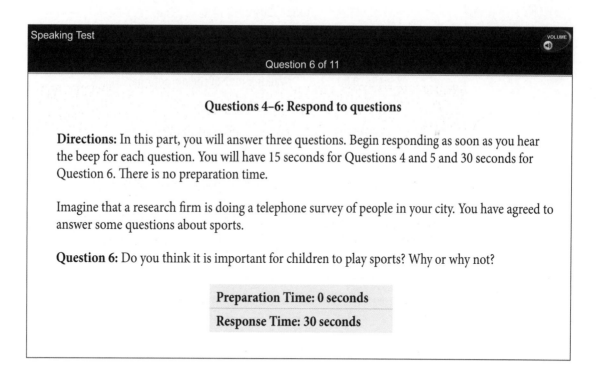

Questions 4–6: Respond to questions

Directions: In this part, you will answer three questions. Begin responding as soon as you hear the beep for each question. You will have 15 seconds for Questions 4 and 5 and 30 seconds for Question 6. There is no preparation time.

Imagine that a research firm is doing a telephone survey of people in your city. You have agreed to answer some questions about sports.

Question 6: Do you think it is important for children to play sports? Why or why not?

Preparation Time: 0 seconds
Response Time: 30 seconds

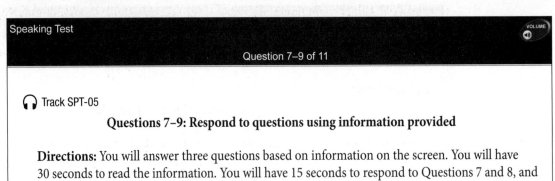

🎧 Track SPT-05

Questions 7–9: Respond to questions using information provided

Directions: You will answer three questions based on information on the screen. You will have 30 seconds to read the information. You will have 15 seconds to respond to Questions 7 and 8, and you will have 30 seconds to respond to Question 9. For each question, begin to answer as soon as you hear the beep. No preparation time is provided.

Preparation Time: 0 Seconds
Response Time: 15 Seconds
Response Time: 30 seconds

Botanical Gardens Tour
June 5, 20—
Tickets: $25 per person*

9:00 a.m.	Meet at the front entrance: 301 South Main Street
9:15–10:00	Walking tour of the outdoor gardens
10:00–11:00	Tour of the greenhouses
11:00–12:00	Lecture on flowers of the region
12:00–1:00 p.m.	Lunch in the Garden Café
1:00–3:00	View special exhibits on tropical plants
3:00–4:00	Tea and pastries in the outdoor garden

* Special discount: Buy your ticket by May 15 and pay $20.

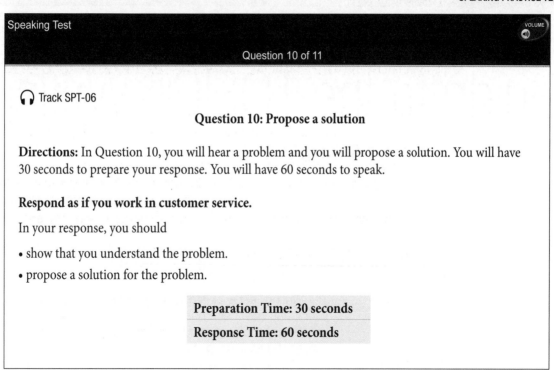

🎧 Track SPT-06

Question 10: Propose a solution

Directions: In Question 10, you will hear a problem and you will propose a solution. You will have 30 seconds to prepare your response. You will have 60 seconds to speak.

Respond as if you work in customer service.

In your response, you should

- show that you understand the problem.
- propose a solution for the problem.

Preparation Time: 30 seconds

Response Time: 60 seconds

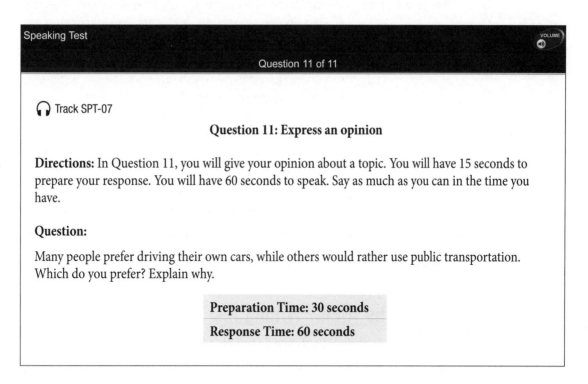

🎧 Track SPT-07

Question 11: Express an opinion

Directions: In Question 11, you will give your opinion about a topic. You will have 15 seconds to prepare your response. You will have 60 seconds to speak. Say as much as you can in the time you have.

Question:

Many people prefer driving their own cars, while others would rather use public transportation. Which do you prefer? Explain why.

Preparation Time: 30 seconds

Response Time: 60 seconds

Guide to the TOEIC® Writing Test

About the Writing Test

The Writing Test consists of a total of eight questions in which you are presented with different types of writing tasks. In response to various prompts, you will compose sentences using the words provided, respond to written requests, and write an essay.

QUICK GUIDE: Writing Test

Definition	The Writing Test evaluates your ability to convey information and to express your ideas in written English in a comprehensible manner using appropriate vocabulary and grammar forms. You will demonstrate this by responding to a variety of question types and prompts.
Targeted Skills	In order to do well on the Writing Test, you must be able to: • write simple, compound, and complex sentences. • use appropriate vocabulary. • use correct grammar. • respond to requests in writing. • explain problems and ask questions in writing. • express and explain your opinion in writing. • organize and write an essay.
Parts of the Writing Test	**Questions 1–5:** You will write sentences about photos. **Questions 6–7:** You will respond to e-mails. **Question 8:** You will write about your opinion on a particular topic. (See below for more thorough descriptions of each part of the Writing Test.)
Timing	The Writing Test takes approximately 60 minutes to complete.

Parts of the TOEIC® Writing Test

Questions 1–5: Write a Sentence Based on a Picture

For each of Questions 1–5, you will see a photo accompanied by two words or phrases. You will write a sentence about the photo using the two words or phrases provided. You will have a total of eight minutes to complete all of Questions 1–5. In this section, you <u>can</u> go back to previous questions by clicking the "Back" button. The photos show people involved in common everyday activities, such as:

- Meeting with colleagues
- Doing office work
- Cooking
- Eating at home or at a restaurant
- Using public transportation
- Traveling
- Enjoying leisure time
- Banking
- Shopping

Word combinations you may see in Questions 1–5 may include:

- Noun / noun
- Noun / verb
- Noun / preposition
- Verb / preposition
- Noun / coordinating conjunction

- Verb / coordinating conjunction
- Noun / adjective
- Noun / adverb
- Noun / subordinating conjunction
- Verb / subordinating conjunction

In Questions 4–5, one word or phrase of the pair will always be a subordinating conjunction. Therefore, to respond to these questions, you will have to write a sentence with a subordinate clause. Types of subordinating conjunctions you may see in Questions 4–5 include:

- Time: *when, while, after, before, until*
- Location: *where*
- Cause and effect: *because, as, since, so, so that*
- Contrast: *although, even though, though, in spite of the fact*
- Condition: *if, even if, unless*

For Questions 1–5, you will be evaluated on:

- Grammar
- Appropriate use of both provided words or phrases

- Relevancy of the sentence to the picture

Questions 6–7: Respond to a Written Request

For Questions 6–7, you will read an e-mail and write a response to it in which you address the tasks you are given. For each of the e-mails, you will be given two or more tasks to address in your response. You will have ten minutes to read each e-mail and write a response to it. The e-mails in Questions 6–7 deal with common scenarios in everyday business and personal life, such as:

- Making appointments
- Scheduling meetings
- Ordering supplies
- Explaining problems with shipments
- Requesting repairs

- Organizing events
- Solving office problems
- Making travel plans
- Applying for jobs
- Advertising employment opportunities

You will be asked to address tasks such as the following:

- Making suggestions
- Asking questions
- Making requests
- Giving information

- Explaining reasons for problems
- Describing problems
- Making statements about specific things

For Questions 6–7, you will be evaluated on:

- Organization and cohesion of ideas
- Appropriate tone

- Use of a variety of correct sentence structures
- Appropriate use of vocabulary

Question 8: Write an Opinion Essay

For Question 8, you will be asked a question and will respond with a written essay in which you explain and support your opinion. You will have a total of 30 minutes to read the question, plan your response, and write your essay. Question 8 asks your opinion on a topic such as:

- Workplace issues
- Family
- Friendships
- Career choices
- Education
- Transportation issues
- City issues
- Shopping
- Leisure time

You will be asked to state your opinion on the topic in one of the following ways:

- Agree or disagree with a statement
- State your preference for something
- Describe the advantages and disadvantages of a situation
- Explain the importance of something

You will be evaluated on:

- Organization and cohesion of ideas
- Use of reasons and examples to support your opinion
- Relevancy to the topic
- Appropriate use of vocabulary and grammar

Writing Test Challenges and Solutions

» **CHALLENGE 1: "I never write this type of material in English. I don't even know where to start."**

SOLUTION: Practice writing as often as you can. One way to do this is to keep a journal in English. You can write about your daily activities, thoughts, and plans. This will help you get used to expressing your ideas in written English.

SOLUTION: Expand your vocabulary by learning the English words and phrases for things you most commonly write about in your own language. You can practice by translating e-mails that you've recently written to friends, colleagues, or customers into English. This is another way to get used to expressing your ideas in written English.

SOLUTION: Become familiar with business English. Go online and look for companies with English-language websites. Many of these websites allow people to write in with questions. Write e-mails and notice the language of the responses. Some companies even have social networking sites where you can practice interacting personally with others in writing. This will help you get used to using written business English.

SOLUTION: Look for employment ads online and practice writing e-mails in response to them. This will help you develop the language you will need for responding to written requests on the test.

SOLUTION: Look for photos in magazines that show people in a variety of situations. Practice writing sentences that describe what is happening in the pictures. This will help you write sentences about photos on the test.

» CHALLENGE 2: "My grammar and spelling are weak, so I'm afraid I'll make a lot of mistakes."

SOLUTION: Review and practice useful grammatical structures. Pay attention to the grammar used in this book. What you see on the test will be very similar. Make a note of any grammatical structures that are difficult for you. Find a good English grammar book, and practice the things you find most problematic.

SOLUTION: Do practice activities to keep your grammar and spelling skills sharp. Check online sources for free grammar and spelling practice activities. There are dozens of tests online that have answer keys. Some also offer explanations about grammar or spelling. This will help you become familiar with correct grammar forms and spelling.

SOLUTION: Learn about different types of sentences, and practice writing different sentence types as often as possible. This will help you use correct sentence structure when you write during the test. It will also help you become more comfortable with a variety of sentence types—something that can improve your score on the test.

> **Sentence Types:** Sentences are made up of clauses. A clause is a part of a sentence that contains a subject and a verb. An independent clause can stand alone. A dependent clause must be part of a sentence with an independent clause.
>
> A **simple sentence** consists of one independent clause.
>
> > The clerk answered the phone.
>
> A **compound sentence** consists of two independent clauses joined by a coordinating conjunction, such as *and, but, or,* or *so.*
>
> > The man dropped the box, and the computer broke.
> > (independent clause)   (independent clause)
>
> A **complex sentence** consists of an independent clause and one or more dependent clauses. A dependent clause is one that begins with a subordinating conjunction, such as *because, after, before, although, if, while,* or *when.*
>
> > If we get the contract, we will need to hire some people.
> > (dependent clause)   (independent clause)
>
> A **compound-complex sentence** consists of three or more clauses. At least two are independent clauses, and one is a dependent clause.
>
> > The conference was interesting, but not many people attended because it was so expensive.
> > (independent clause)   (independent clause)   (dependent clause)

» CHALLENGE 3: "I can handle the short sentences, but I have a hard time writing a long essay."

SOLUTION: A long essay is basically just a lot of well-written sentences organized in a logical way. If you can write good sentences, you just need to learn to become comfortable combining them in interesting ways to produce paragraphs and longer essays.

SOLUTION: Learn how essays are developed by studying basic organizational structures used in the essays and templates in this book. Look on university websites for examples of student essays and study how the essays are organized. Looking at a lot of sample essays will help you understand different ways to organize your ideas in writing.

SOLUTION: Practice writing essays. The more you practice essay writing, the easier it will be for you. You can use the sample essay questions in this book. Write about each topic twice. Take a different point of view each time.

SOLUTION: Study other written pieces to see how other writers do it. Look online for editorials and other opinion pieces to see how writers present opinions. After you read an editorial, think about your own opinion on the topic, then write an essay expressing your opinion.

» **CHALLENGE 4: "I just can't think of anything to say when I have to answer a written request."**

SOLUTION: Begin by focusing on just one thing. Practice writing e-mails about a single topic. For example, write an e-mail apologizing for missing a meeting, an e-mail requesting a day off, an e-mail offering advice to a co-worker about a raise, or an e-mail explaining a problem.

SOLUTION: Practice brainstorming. This will help you come up with a lot of different ideas. When you come up with a lot of ideas, you can choose the best ones. This will make your writing much easier. Think about any topic, and brainstorm ideas. You can do this while riding on the bus, waiting for a doctor's appointment, or eating lunch by yourself. You can start with the e-mails in the exercises in this book. For each task, brainstorm a list of at least ten possible ways you could address the task. Some of the ideas you come up with may be silly, but it doesn't matter. The point is to loosen up your mind. If you have trouble coming up with ideas, think about different people you know and how they might respond to the situation presented in the e-mail. Practicing in this way will help you get used to coming up with ideas when you need them on the test.

» **CHALLENGE 5: "I never have a chance to write to native English speakers."**

SOLUTION: Join an online forum. Post your thoughts on different subjects that interest you. This will give you a chance to practice writing English in a situation of real communication.

SOLUTION: Take advantage of free online resources and read native speaker texts. Even if you don't have the chance to write to someone in English, you can learn a lot by reading correspondence in English. Look at how the responses are structured. Look at some of the words and phrases used. The more you read, the more examples you will see and the more accustomed you will become to the ways the language is used.

» **CHALLENGE 6: "By the time I think about what to write and then write it, I'm out of time."**

SOLUTION: For the Writing Test, you will need to be comfortable using a computer for writing. Practice typing on a computer using a word-processing program. Also, be sure to practice editing what you write because you will be able to change what you write during the test. You should be comfortable cutting and pasting text.

SOLUTION: You will also need to be very comfortable using an English keyboard. It is extremely important that you know where all of the letters are on the keyboard, how to make capital letters, and where the punctuation marks are. You do not want to waste time figuring these things out during the test. See page vii for more about typing practice needs.

SOLUTION: Practice working within a time limit. Use the timing suggestions in this book, and practice writing to meet time limits. Do this frequently. This will help you learn to use your time more efficiently.

SOLUTION: Write simply. Don't make things overly complex. A good simple piece will get a better grade than a poorly written complex one. It will also take less time.

SOLUTION: Don't spend a lot of time trying to figure out what your opinion really is or what the most interesting response to a task might be. Just think of something that you can write about and that is relevant to the given task. When you answer the questions, you must respond to the tasks, but other than that, the content is not as important as your ability to demonstrate good writing skills.

TOEIC® Test Writing Questions 1–5

The Writing Test is done on computer. For Questions 1–5, you will see five photos. For each photo, you will be given two words, and you will write a sentence about the photo using the two words. You will have eight minutes to complete this part of the test, and you will be able to move at your own pace. You click on "Next" to move to the next photo when you are ready, and you can also click on "Back" to go back to previous photos. You will be scored on your ability to write grammatically correct sentences that are relevant to the photos.

The photos will depict common everyday scenes in places such as:

» Offices

» Banks

» Stores

» Restaurants

» Parks

» Airports

QUICK GUIDE:	Write a Sentence Based on a Picture
Definition	Questions 1–5 test your ability to write meaningful sentences using correct grammar.
Targeted Skills	In order to correctly respond to Questions 1–5, you should be able to: • use correct word order. • write sentences with one clause. • write sentences with two clauses. • use adjectives, adverbs, and prepositions correctly. • use subordinating conjunctions correctly. • write sentences that are relevant to the photos.
Question Types	You will be given a pair of words for each photo. The two words will be some combination of the following: • Noun • Preposition • Verb • Coordinating conjunction • Adjective • Subordinating conjunction • Adverb
A Good Response	A good response uses the two provided words correctly in terms of both grammatical structure and word meaning and is relevant to the photo.
Things to Remember	1. Begin by thinking about how you can use the two words to describe something in the photo. 2. Decide what your subject and main verb will be. These may or may not be one or both of the words provided. 3. Nouns will always be provided in the singular form, and verbs will always be provided in the base form. You can change these forms if you want.

WALK THROUGH: Write a Sentence Based on a Picture

A What You'll See

For Questions 1–5, you will see the directions, and you will see a photo and two words on the screen. Look at the sample. Think about how you can use the words to describe something about the photos.

Writing Test   HELP   BACK   NEXT

Questions 1–5: Write a sentence based on a picture

Directions: You will write <u>one</u> sentence about a photo. You will be given <u>two</u> words or phrases. You must use them in your sentence. You can change the word forms, and you can use the words in a different order.

Your sentence will be scored on

- appropriate use of grammar.
- relevance of the sentence to the photo.

In this part, you can move to the next question by clicking on "Next." If you want to return to a previous question, click on "Back."

You will have eight minutes to complete this part of the test.

read/newspaper

B What You'll Do

For Questions 1–5, you will write a sentence about a photo using the pair of words provided. Now, write a sentence for the photo in Part A using the word pairs given. Then look at the sample response. Notice that the grammar is correct, the response is relevant to the photo, and it uses both of the words provided.

SAMPLE RESPONSE ▶ The man is reading the newspaper.

GET IT RIGHT: Tips and Tasks for Answering Correctly

GRAMMAR AND VOCABULARY

Writing Basic Sentences

In order to do well on Questions 1–5, you must be able to write sentences that are grammatical, coherent, and relevant to the photo. Study the following tips to familiarize yourself with the basic grammar and vocabulary points you will need to know when you write your sentences.

QUICK TIP

When one of the words is a noun, first decide whether it should be the subject or the object of your sentence.

» **TIP 1 Learn the basics of good sentence-writing in English.** Writing strong sentences in English requires you to follow sentence structure rules. These are the rules about the order of words in English sentences. The most common sentence structure in English is the S-V-O pattern (subject-verb-object).

By learning this pattern, you will have a useful starting point for writing easy-to-understand responses. Study the chart below for an explanation and examples of each of the sentence parts.

	S (Subject)	V (Verb)	O (Object or complement*)
Explanations	• Tells who or what is doing the action • Usually a noun or pronoun	• Describes an action, a state, or a feeling	• Receives the action of the verb • Examples show a noun, pronoun, adjective, adverb, and prepositional phrase following the verb.
Examples	*I*	*visit*	*Elisa.*
	He	*didn't ask*	*us.*
	My mother	*is*	*tall.*
	The car	*is turning*	*right.*
	Mike	*was waving*	*at the man.*

QUICK TIP

Remember that you must use <u>both</u> of the words on the screen in your sentence. If you forget to use one of the words, you will get a lower score. Also, you may write only <u>one</u> sentence. Do <u>not</u> write more than one sentence.

*For the purposes of this discussion, O is whatever may follow the verb.

TASK Write the sentence parts in the correct order.

1. [She] [a bike.] [rides] _____

2. [at the screen.] [Sally] [looks] _____

3. [The map] [folded.] [is] _____

4. [The book] [on the table.] [is] _____

5. [is] [empty.] [The refrigerator] _____

» **TIP 2 Use correct capitalization and punctuation.** To write a good sentence that is easy to understand, you need to use capitalization and punctuation correctly.

Capitalization refers to the use of capital letters. These large letters are also called uppercase letters. <u>All</u> sentences in English begin with a capital letter. The English language also uses capital letters to begin all <u>proper</u> nouns. Proper nouns include the names of people, companies, languages, and places. The English language also uses capital letters on months, days, and titles. Look at these examples.

- Mary Smith
- IBM

- Tuesday, June 3
- Dr. Evans (*Notice the period after the title.*)

- Fox Theater
- Miami, Florida (*Notice the comma between the city and state.*)

Punctuation refers to the symbols, such as periods (.), question marks (?), and commas (,), in the sentence. These marks are used to make written language easier to understand. <u>All</u> sentences in English end with some type of punctuation.

TASK These sentences need capital letters and punctuation. Rewrite the sentences with the correct capitalization and punctuation.

1. i need to order some pens _____

2. we went to new york in june _____

3. did mr smith call you _____

4. the spanish book is on the desk _____

5. has the flight from paris france arrived _____

» **TIP 3 Know the basic grammar features to use in your sentences.** When you write your responses for Questions 1–5, you must choose the right sentence structure and verb tense. In most cases, you will be able to use the basic S-V-O structure with the present continuous tense. However, in some cases, you will use *There is/are* + subject.

The verb tense that you use depends on the photo. Other than the two tenses shown in the chart, you will not usually have to use other verb tenses for Questions 1–5. This chart will help you choose the correct tense for your response.

Grammar for Basic Descriptions of Photos			
Photo Types	**Verb Tenses**	**Sentence Constructions**	**Examples**
Photos with people in them	Present continuous	Subject + verb + object	• <u>*The men* **are eating** *pancakes.*</u> • <u>*The woman* **is talking** *to the clerk.*</u>
Photos with <u>no</u> people in them	Simple present	*There is/are* + subject	• <u>*There is* **some milk** *in the glass.*</u> • <u>*There are* **several books** *on the table.*</u>

TASK Write the correct form of the verb in parentheses.

1. There _____ (be) several empty seats in the theater.

2. They _____ (make) a phone call.

3. There _____ (be) a lamp on the table.

4. The man _____ (write) a letter.

5. There _____ (be) a ladder against the house.

QUICK TIP

In Questions 1–5, you will be writing statements. not questions, so you must use a period at the end.

QUICK TIP

Be careful <u>not</u> to use capitals on general words. A word like *theater* does not have a capital letter unless it is part of the name of the theater or is the first word of a sentence.

Using Prepositions and Modifiers to Give Details

In addition to choosing the correct sentence construction and verb tense, you should also know how to use prepositions and modifiers in your responses to provide more details about the photograph.

» **TIP 1 Use prepositions to talk about where people or things are.** Prepositions are words that give information about the location of an object. By combining prepositions with nouns, pronouns, or clauses, you can create prepositional phrases that provide more information about the person or object. Look at these examples of prepositional phrases.

> *The woman <u>at the desk</u> is busy.* (indicates which woman and where she is)
>
> *The table <u>next to the door</u> is empty.* (indicates which table and where it is)

TASK Use the given words to write sentences about the location of items in the photograph.

1. photo frames / clock / in between

_____

2. laptop / table / on top of

_____

3. bottle / glass / phone / next to

_____

» **TIP 2 Use modifiers to describe other words and give details.** Modifiers are words, phrases, or clauses that provide more information about words in a sentence. **Adjectives** modify nouns and pronouns, while **adverbs** modify verbs, adjectives, and other adverbs.

For Questions 1–5, you may want to use **participles** as adjectives in your responses. Participles are verb forms that serve as adjectives in sentences. This chart has more information on participles.

Forms	Positions in Sentences	Usage	Examples
Present Participles: Regular verb + *-ing**	• Before the noun that it modifies • After a linking verb (*be, become, seem,* etc.)	• Modify a noun that is the cause of an experience	*The **tiring** <u>trip</u> takes over ten hours.* *The trip <u>is</u> **tiring**.*
Past Participles: Regular verb + *-ed*		• Modify a noun that is experiencing something	*The **tired** <u>man</u> is sleeping in his seat.* *The man <u>is</u> **tired**.*

*Note that the present participle has the same form as the present continuous verb form.

TASK Place a check mark (✓) where the modifier in parentheses should be added to the sentence.

1. (homemade)   The ☐ cookies ☐ were ☐.

2. (interesting)   The ☐ film ☐ starts ☐ at ☐ 8:00.

3. (bored)   The ☐ man ☐ looks ☐ at ☐ his ☐ watch ☐.

Using Function Words

» **TIP Familiarize yourself with function words.** Function words are words that don't have a lot of meaning on their own, but they express grammatical connections with other parts of the sentence. Prepositions, conjunctions, and some adverbs are examples of function words. You may need to use function words in your responses. See the chart below for more information about function words.

Function Word Types	Usage	Examples
Coordinating Conjunctions *and, but, or, yet, for, nor, so*	• Connect two clauses • Ideas connected by the conjunction receive equal emphasis	• *Teresa enjoys <u>watching movies,</u> **and** she enjoys <u>reading books.</u>* • *I'll order either <u>the soup</u> **or** <u>the salad.</u>*
Subordinating Conjunctions Time / location: *after, before, since, when, while, until, where, wherever* Cause / effect: *because, since, so that, why* Contrast: *whereas, although* Similarity: *like, just as* Condition: *if, unless, until, in case, as if, as though, provided that*	• Connect an independent clause and a dependent clause • Express the relationship between two clauses (e.g., of time, reason, place, etc.) • Idea in the first clause more important than the idea in the second clause	• ***After** <u>she bought the ticket,</u> <u>she boarded the train.</u>* (time) • *<u>Elisa studies</u> **because** <u>she wants a good grade.</u>* (cause) • ***Unless** <u>he takes his medicine,</u> <u>Jack will not feel better.</u>* (condition)
Correlative Conjunctions *both . . . and; not only . . . but also; not . . . but; either . . . or; neither . . . nor; whether . . . or; as . . . as*	• Connect two ideas • Ideas receive equal emphasis • Second noun must agree with the verb that follows	• ***Both** <u>Sally</u> **and** <u>James</u> work at the office.* • *It **not only** <u>takes a long time to open the file,</u> **but also** <u>it is very difficult to store.</u>*
Non-Location Prepositions	• Don't indicate location • Often part of phrasal verbs • Often idiomatic, so they must be memorized	• *He goes to work **by** bus.* • *Ellen must turn in the project **on** Monday.* • *They should pay **for** it at the register.*
Intensifiers *very, too much/many, quite, rather, so*	• Typically modify adverbs and adjectives • Make the meaning of the words they modify stronger	• *She is **very** <u>happy</u> with the results.* • *It is **quite** <u>cold</u> there.* • *The ferry is traveling **rather** <u>slowly.</u>*

QUICK TIP

On Questions 4 and 5, one of the words in the given word pair will be a subordinating conjunction. Since it is more challenging to create sentences with subordinating conjunctions, you should always leave yourself a few more minutes to work on these questions.

TASK Choose the correct function words to complete the sentences.

1. The dessert is flavorful (yet / for) light.

2. (Whereas / Just as) Sidney prefers warm weather, Sam prefers cold weather.

3. They only have enough money to visit (not only / either) Greece (but also / or) Spain.

4. There was a bit of confusion (about / for) the final bill.

WRITING YOUR RESPONSE

» **TIP 1 Understand the possible combinations of word pairs that you may see on the test.** On Questions 1–3, you may find any of the following combinations.

noun + noun	verb + noun
noun + preposition	verb + preposition
noun + function word	verb + function word

Questions 4 and 5 are typically more difficult, and you may find the following combinations.

noun + subordinating conjunction	adverb + subordinating conjunction
verb + subordinating conjunction	preposition + subordinating conjunction
adjective + subordinating conjunction	

By familiarizing yourself with types of word pairs you may see, you will be able to figure out what you need to do in order to write the sentence. Study the chart below for a review of the parts of speech and how they are typically used in sentences.

Parts of Speech in the Word Pairs			
Parts of Speech	**Explanations**	**Uses in Sentences**	**Examples**
Nouns	Refer to a person, place, or thing	• Can be the subject or object of the sentence	*The woman* (subj.) *is holding the bag* (obj.).
Verbs	Refer to an action, state, or feeling	• Should go after the subject in a statement	*He drinks from the big mug.*
Adjectives	Modify nouns or pronouns	• Usually come before nouns or pronouns • Can be part of the subject or object clause	*The old man is walking up the stairs.* *He always wears a long coat.*
Adverbs	Modify verbs, adjectives, and other adverbs	• Often come after verbs • Often end with *-ly*	*The woman types quickly.*
Prepositions	Show the time, space, or logic relationship between things	• Can be part of the subject or object clause	*The computer on the table does not function.*

QUICK TIP

Remember that you will always be given the singular form of a noun and the base form of a verb. Thus, you will have to choose the correct form in order to fit the situation shown in the photo.

TASK Write the part of speech for each of the words in the pairs.

1. umbrella/hold _____ / _____

2. helmet/on _____ / _____

3. hair/scissors _____ / _____

4. take/camera _____ / _____

5. refrigerator/empty _____ / _____

» **TIP 2 Identify the connection between the words provided and the photo.** When you first see the photograph, scan it quickly for its connection to the pair of words provided. For example, if one of the words is a verb, look for this action in the photo. By doing this, you will understand the relationship between the words in the pair. For example, you will know if a word is an adjective describing a noun or a verb showing what is happening.

TASK 1 Look at the photo. Then read the word pairs. Write what the subject, verb, and object for each pair might be. There may be more than one possible answer.

Word Pairs	Possible Subjects	Possible Verbs	Possible Objects
1. woman/suit			
2. whiteboard/behind			
3. hold/documents			

TASK 2 Complete each sentence using the correct form of the word in parentheses.

1. The server _____ (set) the plate on the table.

2. The _____ (chair) are stacked on top of each other.

3. He _____ (look) at the menu.

TIP 3 Look for function words. If the word pair includes a function word, be sure to consider the possible role of the function word in the sentence first. Look at this photo and explanation.

barefoot/although

Explanation: First, consider the function word *although*. It is a subordinating conjunction used to express contrast. Next, scan the photo for the other word in the pair (*barefoot*), and use it to make a sentence: *This person is barefoot.* Finally, complete the sentence using the function word, making sure that you express the meaning of the function word: *This person is **barefoot** **although** there is snow on the ground.* The words can be used in any order, so you can also write: ***Although** there is snow on the ground, this person is **barefoot.*** Notice the comma when the clause is used first.

TASK Look at the photo in TIP 2 TASK 1 on page 102. Then read the word pairs. Look back at the chart of function word types on page 100. Decide the meaning of each function word below and write a possible first and second clause. There may be more than one possible answer.

Word Pairs	Function Word Meaning	Possible First Clause	Possible Second Clause
pen/and			
whereas/stand			
point/as			

Two-Clause Responses

» **TIP Look for conjunctions.** Word pairs that include conjunctions (typically Questions 4 and 5) will often require you to write one sentence with two clauses. A clause is a group of words that includes a subject and a verb. An **independent clause** can stand on its own as a complete sentence, while a **dependent clause** is not a complete sentence and must be combined with another sentence. Look at these examples; pay special attention to the negative verbs.

Independent clauses: *They are waiting, but they are not talking.*
Dependent clause: *They are not talking while they are waiting.*

In some cases, both words in the word pair can go in the same clause or in separate clauses. Look at these examples.

read/while

***While** the woman **reads** the newspaper, she drinks her coffee.*
***While** the woman drinks her coffee, she **reads** the newspaper.*

TASK Choose the correct conjunction to complete each sentence.

1. You will miss your flight (unless / if) you hurry.

2. (Because / Even though) it was dark, we turned on the lights.

3. He only has a light jacket, (but / so) he must be cold.

4. The woman is driving, (nor / yet) she is talking on her cell phone.

Relevancy

» **TIP Be sure your response is relevant to the photo.** In addition to your use of correct grammar, raters will be grading you based on whether your sentence accurately describes the photo. Be sure to only mention objects that are obvious from the photo. Also, don't guess about how people in the photo feel or what they think.

TASK Look at the photo and word pair. Then answer the questions.

cart/aisle

1. Which sentence best describes the photo?

    a. The woman is pushing the cart through the aisle.

    b. The woman thinks the aisle is too narrow for the cart to fit.

2. Why was the incorrect answer in number 1 NOT a good response?

    a. The sentence mentions the woman's thoughts.

    b. The sentence mentions an object that isn't in the photo.

PROGRESSIVE PRACTICE: Get Ready

A Look at the photos and word pairs. Next, circle the correct part of speech for each word given. Then circle the most appropriate subject, object, and verb to fit the photo.

Photo 1

Word Pair: flower/table

Word 1:	noun	verb	preposition
Word 2:	noun	verb	preposition

Subj. / Obj.:	flower	flowers	table	tables
Verb:	is	are		

Photo 2

Word Pair: man/kick

Word 1:	noun	verb	preposition
Word 2:	noun	verb	preposition

Subj. / Obj.:	man	men	ball	balls
Verb:	kick	is kicking		

Photo 3

Word Pair: woman/by

Word 1:	noun	verb	preposition	
Word 2:	noun	verb	preposition	

Subj. / Obj.:	woman	women	door	doors
Verb:	stand	is standing		

B Look at the photos and word pairs in Part A. Read the possible responses. Check (✓) the best response for each photo. For each incorrect response, write the letter of the reason it is wrong. Use the reasons in the box.

a. grammar error	**b.** forgotten key word	**c.** not relevant to photo

1. ___Are flowers on the table.   ___The flowers are on the table.
2. ___The man is in the stadium.   ___The man is kicking the ball.
3. ___The woman is standing by the door.   ___There is a woman by her house.

C Write your own sentences for the photos in Part A. Use the word pairs given.

1. vase/on

_____

2. play/stadium

_____

3. carry/tray

_____

D Now, evaluate your responses in Part C using the checklist below. How well did your responses meet the scoring criteria? Check (✓) *Yes* or *No*. Keep practicing until all of your answers are *Yes*.

Response Checklist: Questions 1–5	Yes	No
1. My response has a subject and a verb.	☐	☐
2. I used correct verb forms.	☐	☐
3. I used correct noun forms (singular / plural).	☐	☐
4. I used both key words.	☐	☐
5. My response is relevant to the photo.	☐	☐

PROGRESSIVE PRACTICE: Get Set

A Look at each photo and word pair. Then complete the information. Write the correct part of speech for each word in the word pair. Then choose a possible subject and verb.

Photo 1

Word Pair: box/very

Part of Speech: Word 1 _____ Word 2 _____
Subject: _____
Verb: _____

Photo 2

Word Pair: sit/on

Part of Speech: Word 1 _____ Word 2 _____
Subject: _____
Verb: _____

Photo 3

Word Pair: even though/rain

Part of Speech: Word 1 _____ Word 2 _____

Clause 1 Subject: _____

Clause 1 Verb: _____

Clause 2 Subject: _____

Clause 2 Verb: _____

B Write a response for each photo by answering the questions with complete sentences. Don't forget to use both key words in your response.

1. Is the box very heavy or very light? _____

2. Where is the man sitting? _____

3. What is the woman doing even though it is raining? _____

C Now create your own responses for the photos using these new word pairs.

1. carry/back _____

2. sit/while _____

3. woman/cold _____

D Now, evaluate your responses using the checklist below. How well did your responses meet the scoring criteria? Check (✓) *Yes* or *No*. Keep practicing until all of your answers are *Yes*.

Response Checklist: Questions 1–5		
	Yes	**No**
1. My response has a subject and a verb.	☐	☐
2. I used correct verb forms.	☐	☐
3. I used correct noun forms (singular / plural).	☐	☐
4. I used both key words.	☐	☐
5. My response is relevant to the photo.	☐	☐

PROGRESSIVE PRACTICE: Go for the TOEIC® Test

Writing Test

HELP ?   BACK ←   NEXT →

Questions 1–5: Write a sentence based on a picture

Directions: You will write <u>one</u> sentence about a photo. You will be given <u>two</u> words or phrases. You must use them in your sentence. You can change the word forms, and you can use the words in a different order. Your sentences will be scored on

- appropriate use of grammar.
- relevance of the sentence to the photo.

Give yourself eight minutes to complete this part of the test.

1.

wind/hard

2.

hang/in

3.

woman/eat

_____

_____

4.

if/fit

_____

_____

5.

while/phone

_____

_____

Time Used: _____ minutes

To read sample responses, see page **159.**

TOEIC® Test Writing Questions 6–7

For Writing Questions 6 and 7, you will read an e-mail and respond to it. You will be given specific tasks for each response. You may be asked to provide information, ask questions, make a request or suggestion, or explain a problem. You will have ten minutes to read each e-mail and write your response to it. You will be scored on your ability to write grammatically correct sentences that are varied, use appropriate vocabulary, and organize your ideas.

The e-mails may deal with topics such as:

» *Office issues*

» *Job ads and applications*

» *Ads for products and services*

» *Orders and shipments*

» *Schedules*

» *Appointments*

QUICK GUIDE: Respond to a Written Request

Definition	Questions 6 and 7 test your ability to respond to written requests using a variety of well-organized sentences and appropriate grammar and vocabulary.
Targeted Skills	In order to correctly respond to Questions 6 and 7, you should be able to: • organize your ideas in writing. • use appropriate connecting words. • write a variety of sentence types. • write grammatically correct sentences. • use appropriate vocabulary. • respond to the given tasks.
Question Types	You will be given specific tasks to address in each response. The tasks will be relevant to the e-mail and may be worded such as the following. • Ask THREE questions. • Make TWO requests for information. • Make ONE suggestion. • Give TWO pieces of information. • Explain ONE problem.
A Good Response	A good response addresses all the tasks, has a variety of sentences, has logically organized ideas, and contains few or no grammar or vocabulary errors.
Things to Remember	1. Begin your e-mail with an appropriate introduction. 2. Keep your audience in mind. You may be responding to an e-mail from a boss, a job hunter, a repairperson, or someone else. Use language appropriate for the audience. 3. Be sure to address all the tasks in your response.

WALK THROUGH: Respond to a Written Request

A What You'll See

For Writing Questions 6 and 7, you will see and hear the directions, and then you will see an e-mail and a response area on the screen. Read the directions and the sample e-mail. Think about how you could address the three tasks that follow the e-mail.

Writing Test    HELP BACK NEXT

Questions 6–7: Respond to a written request

Directions: In this part of the test, you will write a response to an e-mail.

Your response will be scored on

- the quality and variety of your sentences.
- vocabulary.
- organization.

You will have 10 minutes to read and answer the e-mail.

Directions: Read the e-mail.

From: update@dailyjobseeker.com
To: Anna Billings
Subject: Daily Jobseeker update
Sent: March 14, 20—

Dear Daily Jobseeker subscriber,

Here is the most recent job opening:
Marleyhome Inc. is looking for an experienced accountant to fill a vacancy in its Accounting Department. The company needs someone with an accounting degree and at least three years of experience. Contact Ralph Kramer, r_kramer@marleyhome.com.

Directions: Respond to the e-mail as if you are interested in applying for the position. Make ONE statement about your professional background and TWO requests for information about the job.

(*write your response here*)

QUICK TIP

- Before you start writing,
- think about how you
- will address the tasks.
- Then organize your
- response around them.

Glossary:

⊜ POWERED BY COBUILD

recent: happening only a short while ago

experienced: knowing a lot or being very skillful at a job or activity

vacancy: a job or position that has not been filled

B What You'll Do

For Writing Questions 6 and 7, you will write a response to the e-mail. You must include information as directed. Now, write a response to the e-mail in Part A in less than 10 minutes. Then read the sample response that follows. Notice how it is organized and how it addresses the tasks. Compare your response to the sample.

SAMPLE RESPONSE ▶ Dear Mr. Kramer:

I understand that you want to hire someone to work in your Accounting Department. I have worked as an accountant at the Hiram Company for five years. Could you please send me a job application? Also, I would like to know when the job will begin. Thank you very much for your help.

Sincerely,
Mary Clark

GET IT RIGHT: Tips and Tasks for Answering Correctly

UNDERSTANDING THE E-MAILS AND THE QUESTIONS

» **TIP 1 Quickly identify the subject of the e-mail.** For Questions 6 and 7, you will read e-mails about a variety of business-related subjects. You should practice quickly identifying what the subject of an e-mail is.

For e-mails, always look first at the **header**. This information at the top of the e-mail tells you important information. A header includes these things:

- The **sender**, the sender's e-mail address, and often the sender's title or company
- The **recipient** (who the e-mail is sent to)
- The **date**
- The **subject** of the e-mail

In many cases, the subject line in the header will tell you much of what you need to know. For Questions 6 and 7, specific requests may also be in the directions (see the next section for more information on directions). In other cases, you will have to look in the body of the message. Always search in this order: (1) subject line, (2) directions, (3) body of the message.

TASK Look at the headers in the sample e-mails and underline the information in each that answers the questions below. Then use the underlined information to answer the question that follows each e-mail.

- Who wrote the e-mail?
- What is the writer's position?
- Who is the recipient of the e-mail?
- What is the subject of the e-mail?

Sample E-mail 1

> **From:** Elisa Hays, Front Desk Supervisor
> **To:** Front desk agents, Hotel Mediterraneo
> **Subject:** Reservation system
> **Sent:** December 1, 20—
>
> It has come to my attention that several of you have experienced problems with the reservation system recently. In order to address these problems, we need to compile a complete list of the issues that each of you have encountered. Please send me this list at your earliest convenience.
>
> Sincerely,
> Elisa Hays
> Front Desk Supervisor

1. What is the main purpose of the e-mail?

   a. To describe a problem with the current reservation system

   b. To gather information about problems with the reservation system

Sample E-mail 2

> **From:** Daniel Olivares, Olivares Shipping Inc.
> **To:** Administrative Staff
> **Subject:** Vacation
> **Sent:** February 19, 20—
>
> Sheila Weston, the head administrative coordinator, will be out of the office from March 10–15. We will need to redistribute her various tasks among the rest of the administrative staff while she's out. Also, please be advised that you must give at least two weeks' notice of any plans to take vacation.
>
> Sincerely,
> Daniel Olivares
> Owner, Olivares Shipping, Inc.

2. What is the main purpose of the e-mail?

    a. To inform employees about changes to the vacation policy

    b. To explain an employee's extended absence

Sample E-mail 3

> **From:** Walter Terborg
> **To:** Rita Chen
> **Subject:** Application for employment
> **Sent:** October 10, 20—
>
> Dear Ms. Chen:
>
> Thank you for your interest in the accountant position at Garrison and Associates. I am writing because your online application is currently incomplete. To see which materials are missing, please log in to your online account. Please feel free to contact me if you have any questions about the position or the application process.
>
> Thank you,
> Walter Terborg, Human Resources

3. What is the main purpose of the e-mail?

    a. To alert the recipient about a problem with her application

    b. To inform the recipient that the application has been received

» **TIP 2 Read the directions carefully.** The directions for Questions 6 and 7 provide you with key information about what to include in your response. The directions are typically worded as follows.

> **Directions:** Respond to the e-mail <u>as if you are a front desk employee for the Hotel Mediterraneo</u>. In your e-mail, <u>give ONE date you are available to meet with the client</u> and <u>TWO suggestions for travel</u>.

Notice that the directions provide important information about:

- the <u>role</u> you should play in your response.

- <u>three</u> specific tasks that you must address in your response. Note that the number of tasks to be included in your response is in capital letters.

The tasks described in the directions vary and may involve:

- requests for more information.
- specific actions.
- discussion of a problem.
- a description of something.
- instructions.
- an opinion.

TASK The following directions are based on the e-mails in the TIP 1 TASK on pages 113–114. Read the directions and underline the information that helps you understand the required tasks. Then place a check mark (✓) next to information that you would include in your response based on the directions.

1. **Directions:** Respond to the e-mail as if you are a front desk agent at Hotel Mediterraneo. In your e-mail, describe THREE problems with the reservation system.

☐ Information about reservations was lost. ☐ A new reservation could not be booked.

☐ A guest's room was not cleaned. ☐ A guest wanted a discount on the room.

☐ The system shut down suddenly. ☐ The front desk supervisor was not available.

2. **Directions:** Respond to the e-mail as if you are on the administrative staff at Olivares Shipping Inc. In your e-mail, give TWO administrative tasks that you can perform while Ms. Weston is gone and ONE range of dates during which you plan to be on vacation.

☐ Tuesday from 1 p.m. to 3 p.m. ☐ File any incoming documents

☐ Submit a vacation request form ☐ April 3 to April 7

☐ Collect time sheets from employees ☐ Confirm Ms. Weston's flight

3. **Directions:** Respond to the e-mail as if you are Rita Chen. In your e-mail, describe TWO application materials you submitted and ask ONE question about the position.

☐ A list of references ☐ How much does the position pay?

☐ An updated résumé ☐ Where is the office located?

☐ A letter from Mr. Garrison ☐ How many employees work at the office?

QUICK TIP

Remember, you will lose points if you don't address all the tasks in the prompt! You must also be careful to play the role that is assigned.

STRUCTURING YOUR RESPONSE

» **TIP 1 Learn the basic template for a successful response.** Though the responses for Questions 6 and 7 may vary according to the specific e-mail and directions, a good response will usually include these parts.

Greeting
– Greet the person the e-mail is directed to.

Opening Statement
– First sentence of your response.
– Explain the purpose of your e-mail.
– Introduce yourself if necessary.

Supporting Information 1
– Address the first task as specified by the directions.

Supporting Information 2
– Address the second task as specified by the directions.

Supporting Information 3
– Address the third task as specified by the directions.

Concluding Statement and Request for Action
– Conclude the e-mail.
– Explain any further action that may be needed.

Closing
– Sign the e-mail as the role indicates.

QUICK TIP

Typically, a complete response is no more than <u>five</u> sentences long.

TASK Match the sample responses (A–C) to the correct sample e-mails (1–3) from pages 113–114. Note the structure of the responses and how each sentence fits the template in TIP 1 on page 115.

A. Response A is for sample e-mail _____.

[greeting]
Dear Mr. Olivares,

[opening statement] I just wanted to quickly respond to the e-mail you sent on February 19 regarding Ms. Weston's absence. **[supporting information 1 and 2]** While Ms. Weston is out, I can collect the employee timesheets and file incoming documents. Please let me know if there is any other way I can help.

[supporting information 3] I also want to let you know that I plan to be on vacation from April 3 to April 7. **[concluding statement]** Please tell me if you need more information about my vacation plans.

[closing]
Sincerely,
Eric Redding, Administrative Assistant

B. Response B is for sample e-mail _____.

[greeting]
Dear Mr. Terborg:

[opening statement] Thank you for the update on the status of my application. **[supporting information 1 and 2]** Since receiving your e-mail on October 10, I have sent the missing materials by mail to your office. These materials include a list of references as well as an updated résumé.

[supporting information 3] If it is not a problem, I wanted to ask how much the accountant position pays. **[request for action]** Thank you again for your previous e-mail, and please let me know about the salary when you can.

[closing]
Best,
Rita Chen

C. Response C is for sample e-mail _____.

[greeting]
Hello Ms. Hays,

[opening statement] I am writing in response to your e-mail dated December 1 regarding problems with the reservation system. **[supporting information 1]** One problem that I had was that the system lost reservation information. **[supporting information 2]** A second problem was that the system shut down suddenly while I was using it. **[supporting information 3]** Finally, the system did not allow me to make a new reservation. **[concluding statement]** Please let me know if you require any further information.

[closing]
Sincerely,
Jaime Sanchez, Front Desk Agent

» **TIP 2 Learn common language used to respond.** You should familiarize yourself with the language that is typically used in responses for Questions 6 and 7. Remember that you will want to use more or less formal language, depending to whom the response is addressed. Generally, if your response is addressed to someone with a higher position (such as a manager or an owner), you should use more formal language. In contrast, if your response is addressed to a co-worker or peer, you should use less formal language. This chart shows some examples of common language for responses.

Common Language	More Formal	Less Formal
Greetings	• *Dear Mr. Park / Ms. Garcia / Mrs. Smith / Dr. Swanson [Family name]:* • *Hello Mr. King / Ms. Brown,* If you do not know the name of the recipient, you can use: • *Dear Sir or Madam:* • *To whom it may concern:* Notice that formal greetings often have a colon.	• *Hi [First name],* Notice that informal greetings have a comma.
Introductions	• *I am writing in response to . . .* • *It seems that . . .* • *My name is X, and I am interested in . . .* • *I am writing because (of) . . .* Notice that the most formal writing does not include contractions except on negatives.	• *I just wanted to respond to your e-mail about . . .* • *I thought I would write to let you know (that) . . .* • *I'm writing because (of) . . .* Notice that informal writing includes contractions.
Polite Requests	• *I would appreciate it if you could . . .* • *If you don't mind, could you . . . ?* • *Would it be possible for you to . . . ?* • *If it isn't too much trouble, would you . . . ?*	• *Could you please . . . ?* • *I'd like it if you would . . .* • *Please [do something].* • *It would be terrific if you could . . .* • *Would you mind . . . ?*
Giving Information	• *I would like to let you know that . . .* • *One important thing about X is . . .* • *Please be advised that . . .* • *One thing to remember . . .*	• *I'd like to . . .* • *Just wanted you to know that . . .* • *I just want to let you know about . . .* • *Don't forget that . . .*
Mentioning Problems	• *One problem that I have encountered is . . .* • *Unfortunately, I have had an issue with . . .*	• *The problem is . . .* • *The issue here is . . .* • *I've had lots of problems with . . .*
Providing Explanations	• *The main reason for this is . . .* • *Due to X . . .* • *Because of this, . . .* • *The reason (why) X is . . .*	• *That's because . . .* • *The reason is . . .* • *Because I'm . . .* • *I'm writing because . . .*

(continued)

Common Language	More Formal	Less Formal *(continued)*
Providing Instructions or Suggestions	• *I believe we should . . .* • *It may be wise to . . .* • *It would be a good idea to . . .* • *I suggest that . . .*	• *I think we should . . .* • *How about . . . ?* • *Why don't you . . . ?* • *Let's . . .*
Giving Opinions	• *I maintain that . . .* • *From my point of view, . . .* • *It is my belief that . . .* • *I hold the opinion that . . .*	• *I think (that) . . .* • *I'm assuming (that) . . .* • *I feel (that) . . .* • *Personally, I feel (that) . . .*
Concluding Statements	• *Thank you very much for your prompt attention to this matter.* • *Please let me know if you have any questions or need any further information.* • *Thank you.*	• *I'm looking forward to hearing from you.* • *Let me know if you need anything else.* • *Thanks!*
Closings	• *Sincerely,* • *Yours truly,* Some business e-mails have only a full name or a name and title.	• *Talk to you soon!* • *See you soon.* • *Nice hearing from you.* Informal e-mails often close with only a first name.

TASK Read the language commonly used in responses. Circle the expression that is not the same as the other two and note why it is different.

1. Dear Sir or Madam: To whom it may concern: Dear Lisa,

_____

2. I'm writing because . . .   Talk to you soon!   My name is . . .

_____

3. I feel that . . .   Why don't you . . . ?   I suggest that . . .

_____

4. Would it be possible for you . . . ?   I'd like to . . .   Don't forget that . . .

_____

5. Thanks.   Thank you.   Sincerely,

_____

PROGRESSIVE PRACTICE: Get Ready

A Read each e-mail and the directions. Then answer the questions.

Question 6

From:	Steven Appleby
To:	Martha Simon
Subject:	Small Business Magazine
Sent:	June 11, 20—

Dear Ms. Simon:

I work for *Small Business Magazine.* I am writing an article about small-business owners in your city, and I would like to interview you for the article. Would you be available to meet with me sometime next week?

Thank you.
Steven Appleby

Directions: Respond to the e-mail as if you are Martha Simon. Say ONE time you are available and ask TWO questions.

1. What is this e-mail about?

  a. A request for an interview

  b. Information about a new magazine

  c. A subscription order

2. What pieces of information must you include in your response? How many must you include? Circle the correct tasks and the number you need for each.

  a. Question(s)   1 2 3

  b. Request(s)   1 2 3

  c. Time(s) available   1 2 3

  d. Piece(s) of information 1 2 3

  e. Order(s)   1 2 3

Question 7

From:	Samantha Hawkins
To:	Hampton Human Resources
Subject:	Positions at Hampton
Sent:	August 10, 20—

Dear Sir or Madam:

I am interested in applying for a position at Hampton Inc. I recently graduated from the university and am interested in any openings you may have in your Marketing Department. If you have any positions open, please let me know what they are and how I can apply.

Thank you.
Samantha Hawkins

Directions: Respond to the e-mail as if you are a human resources officer at Hampton, Inc. In your e-mail, ask ONE question and give TWO pieces of information.

1. What is this e-mail about?

   a. An advertisement for a job

   b. An application for a job

   c. A request for information about jobs

2. What pieces of information must you include in your response? How many must you include? Circle the correct tasks and the number you need for each.

   a. Question(s)   1 2 3

   b. Request(s)   1 2 3

   c. Time(s) available   1 2 3

   d. Piece(s) of information   1 2 3

   e. Order(s)   1 2 3

B Now, read the sample responses to the e-mails in Part A. Note which response is for the Question 6 e-mail and which response is for the Question 7 e-mail. Write the number of the question. Then write the correct numbers to label the parts of the response. Use the answer choices in the box.

---

1. Closing

2. Supporting information 2

3. Supporting information 1

4. Opening statement

5. Concluding statement

6. Greeting

QUICK TIP

You do <u>not</u> need to include a header in your e-mail response. You can begin with the greeting.

Response to Question ____

___ Dear Ms. Hawkins:

___ Thank you for your e-mail inquiring about positions at Hampton, Inc. ___ I understand that you are interested in working in our Marketing Department. We currently have an open position for a Market Researcher. We plan to review applications next week. ___ Do you have any experience in that area? ___ Let me know if you are interested in this position.

___ Sincerely,
Michael White
Hampton Human Resources

Response to Question ____

___ Dear Mr. Appleby,

___ I will be very happy to let you interview me for your article. ___ I will be free next Tuesday afternoon at 2:00. I hope that is a good time for you. ___ I have a couple of questions. How long do you think the interview will last? Also, could you tell me exactly what the subject of your article is? ___ I'm looking forward to meeting you.

Martha Simon

C Write your own responses to the e-mails in Part A by completing the templates.

Question 6

Dear _____,

I received your _____ about _____. I will be available _____. I would like to ask you some things. First, _____ _____. Also, _____ _____. I look forward to seeing you next _____.

Sincerely,

_____

Question 7

Dear _____,

Thank you for _____. You asked about _____.

We have _____ in our Marketing Department. It requires _____. How much _____? I look forward to hearing from you.

Sincerely,

_____

D Now, evaluate your responses in Part C using the checklist below. How well did your responses meet the scoring criteria? Check (✓) *Yes* or *No*. Keep practicing until all of your answers are *Yes*.

Response Checklist: Questions 6–7	Yes	No
1. I included a greeting.	☐	☐
2. I began with an opening statement and ended with a concluding statement.	☐	☐
3. I addressed all tasks given in the directions.	☐	☐
4. I used a variety of sentence types and vocabulary.	☐	☐
5. I used correct grammar and spelling.	☐	☐

PROGRESSIVE PRACTICE: Get Set

A Read each e-mail and the directions. Then answer the questions.

Question 6

From:	Mark Hayes
To:	Easton Office Supply Company
Subject:	Order
Sent:	November 30, 20—

I put in a large order for office supplies from your company several weeks ago. I received the order yesterday; however, it was not complete. It did not contain the two boxes of manila envelopes that I ordered. Can you please resolve this problem for me?

Thank you.
Mark Hayes

Directions: Respond to the e-mail as if you are an employee of the Easton Office Supply Company. In your e-mail, explain TWO problems and make ONE request.

1. What is this e-mail about?

_____

2. What tasks and how many of each are you asked to address in your response?

_____

Question 7

From:	Mary Wilson
To:	All staff
Subject:	Tokyo visit
Sent:	April 15, 20—

Greetings to all,

As you know, next week we will receive guests from our Tokyo office. I need some ideas for interesting activities and places of interest they should visit. Also, I would like to know if any of you are available to take our visitors out for a meal or to visit some special place.

Thanks for your help.
Mary Wilson

Directions: Respond to the e-mail as if you are a staff member. In your e-mail, make TWO suggestions and offer to help with ONE task.

1. What is this e-mail about?

_____

2. What tasks and how many of each are you asked to address in your response?

_____

B Write numbers 1–7 to put the responses in the correct order. Then write the number of the question in Part A to which each response belongs.

Response to Question _____

___ Second, the person who packed your order forgot to include a note of explanation about the envelopes.

___ Dear Mr. Hayes:

___ Let me explain what happened.

___ First, we are currently out of envelopes but will get more at the end of the month.

___ I apologize again and will complete your order as soon as possible.

___ I have received your message about the problem with your order.

___ Please let me know if you will still want the envelopes then.

Response to Question _____

___ First, I think the guests should visit the art museum.

___ I have a couple of suggestions for you.

___ Second, I think they would also enjoy a walk in the City Gardens.

___ I read your e-mail about the guests from the Tokyo office.

___ Hi Mary,

___ Let me know if I can help in any other way.

___ Also, I would be happy to invite them to my house for dinner on Wednesday.

C Write your own responses to the e-mails in Part A by completing the templates.

Question 6

> [Greeting] _____
>
> [Opening statement] _____
>
> _____
>
> [Supporting information 1] _____
>
> _____
>
> [Supporting information 2] _____
>
> _____
>
> [Supporting information 3] _____
>
> _____
>
> [Concluding information] _____
>
> _____
>
> [Closing] _____

QUICK TIP

Remember to check your response for spelling and grammar. When you check your response, make sure that your sentences are well constructed and that you have used a variety of vocabulary words.

Question 7

[Greeting] _____

[Opening statement] _____

_____

[Supporting information 1] _____

_____

[Supporting information 2] _____

_____

[Supporting information 3] _____

_____

[Concluding statement] _____

_____

[Closing] _____

D Now evaluate your responses in Part C using the checklist below. How well did your responses meet the scoring criteria? Check (✓) *Yes* or *No*. Keep practicing until all of your answers are *Yes*.

Response Checklist: Questions 6–7	Yes	No
1. I included a greeting.	☐	☐
2. I began with an opening statement and ended with a concluding statement.	☐	☐
3. I addressed all tasks given in the directions.	☐	☐
4. I used supporting statements.	☐	☐
5. I used a variety of sentence types and vocabulary.	☐	☐

PROGRESSIVE PRACTICE: Go for the TOEIC® Test

Writing Test   HELP ?   BACK ◄   NEXT ►

Questions 6–7: Respond to a written request

Directions: In this part of the test, you will write a response to an e-mail.

Your response will be scored on

- the quality and variety of your sentences.
- vocabulary.
- organization.

Give yourself 10 minutes to read and answer each e-mail.

Question 6

Writing Test   HELP ?   BACK ◄   NEXT ►

Question 6 of 8

From: Samuel George
To: Janet Jones
Subject: Changing banks
Sent: February 23, 20—

Dear Ms. Jones,

We understand that you have moved your accounts to another bank. We are very sorry to lose your business. To help us provide better service in the future, would you mind telling us why you made the decision to change banks? Thank you very much.

Sincerely,
Samuel George
National City Bank Customer Service

Directions: Respond to the e-mail as if you are Janet Jones. In your e-mail, explain ONE problem and make TWO suggestions.

_____
_____
_____
_____
_____
_____
_____

TIME USED: _____ MINUTES.

TO READ SAMPLE RESPONSES, SEE PAGE 160.

Question 7

From:	John Jenkins
To:	Shirley Park
Subject:	Budget report
Sent:	February 23, 20—

Shirley,

I am working on the annual budget report as you requested. You asked me to have it finished by next Friday; however, it's taking longer than I thought. Could I have one more week to complete the report? That way I would have time to do a thorough job.

Thank you.
John

Directions: Respond to the e-mail as if you are Shirley Park. In your e-mail, ask ONE question and give TWO pieces of information.

_____

_____

_____

_____

_____

_____

_____

_____

_____

_____

TIME USED: _____ MINUTES.

TO READ SAMPLE RESPONSES, SEE PAGE 160.

TOEIC® Test Writing Question 8

For Question 8 in the Writing Test, you will be asked to write an essay in which you explain your opinion about an issue. You will have to state your opinion and then support it with specific reasons and examples. You will have 30 minutes to plan and write your essay. Your essay should be about 300 words long. You will be scored on your ability to organize and support your ideas and to use appropriate grammar and vocabulary.

You may be asked to express your opinion on such topics as:

» *Work issues*

» *Travel and transportation choices*

» *Friendships and family*

» *Shopping practices*

» *Leisure time activities*

QUICK GUIDE: Write an Opinion Essay

Definition	Question 8 tests your ability to develop an opinion essay with a clear thesis statement and supporting ideas.
Targeted Skills	In order to correctly respond to Question 8, you should be able to: • express your opinion in a thesis statement. • develop paragraphs that support your thesis statement. • connect your ideas with transition words. • write grammatically correct sentences. • use appropriate and varied vocabulary.
Question Types	In Question 8, you will be asked to write an essay in which you do one of the following: • Express a general opinion • Agree or disagree with a statement • Discuss the advantages and disadvantages of a situation • Explain your preference for something • Explain the importance of something
A Good Response	A good response has a clear thesis statement, two or three supporting ideas that are developed in separate paragraphs, and a strong conclusion. Grammar and vocabulary errors are minimal and don't interfere with understanding the ideas.
Things to Remember	1. First, write a thesis statement that clearly and simply states the opinion that your essay will support. 2. Think of two or three ideas to support your opinion. Use these ideas to develop your essay, writing one paragraph about each idea. 3. Restate your opinion in the conclusion.

WALK THROUGH: Write an Opinion Essay

A What You'll See

For Question 8, you will see and hear the directions, and then you will see an opinion question. The question will remain on the screen while you write. Read the question below. Think about how you could state your opinion about this issue.

Writing Test   HELP ?   BACK ●   NEXT ●

Question 8: Write an opinion essay

Directions: You will write an essay that responds to an opinion question. You will need to state your opinion, explain it, and support it. Your essay should have at least 300 words.

Your response will be scored on

- how well your opinion is supported by reasons and examples.
- the quality of the grammar used.
- the variety and accuracy of vocabulary.
- the organization.

You must plan, write, and revise your essay in 30 minutes.

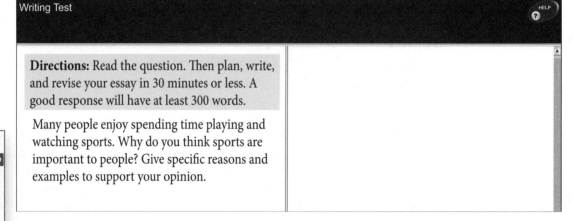

Writing Test   HELP ?

Directions: Read the question. Then plan, write, and revise your essay in 30 minutes or less. A good response will have at least 300 words.

Many people enjoy spending time playing and watching sports. Why do you think sports are important to people? Give specific reasons and examples to support your opinion.

Glossary:

⊑ POWERED BY COBUILD

spending time: using your time or effort to do something

specific: a particular fixed area, problem or subject

B What You'll Do

For Question 8, you will write a complete essay. Now, try to write an essay about the question in Part A in 30 minutes or less. Then read the sample response. Note how the paragraphs that follow the introduction develop the supporting ideas and give a conclusion.

SAMPLE RESPONSE ▶

    Sports are popular all around the world. People enjoy sports because sports bring several advantages to people's lives. Sports encourage people to get exercise, they provide opportunities for interacting with others, and they give a sense of belonging to a group.

    An interest in sports encourages people to get exercise. People who play sports get a lot of exercise. People who are serious about their sport spend a lot of effort getting in good physical shape so that they can play their sport well. Other people play sports just for fun, but they still get good exercise when they play. Of course, some people just watch sports on

TV, and that isn't very good exercise. But sometimes fans become motivated to imitate their favorite athletes, and they try playing the sport themselves.

An interest in sports provides opportunities for interacting with others. When you play on a team, you have to work with your teammates to play the game as well as you can. Or you may just interact with a single opponent when you play a sport such as tennis. Even if you just watch sports, you have opportunities to interact with other fans of your favorite teams.

An interest in sports gives a sense of belonging to a group. If you play on a team, then the team is your group. You are also part of the larger group of people who enjoy playing that sport. If you enjoy watching sports, you can feel that you are part of the group of fans who support your teams. You can also feel pride in being a resident of the city that your favorite team represents.

Sports bring a lot of positive things to people's lives. Sports encourage people to exercise, to spend time with others, and to belong to groups. These are the reasons why sports are important to people everywhere.

GET IT RIGHT: Tips and Tasks for Answering Correctly

UNDERSTANDING THE TOPIC AND THE QUESTION

» **TIP 1 Familiarize yourself with the types of questions you may see.** For Question 8, you may encounter a number of different questions or prompts. By familiarizing yourself with the different types of prompts you may see, you will understand what type of information to include in your response and how to create a complete and successful response. This chart gives an explanation of the most common types of prompts and examples of each.

Prompt Types	Descriptions	Example Prompts
Advantage / Disadvantage	Asks you to choose the advantages or disadvantages of a topic and to support that position	*What are the advantages or disadvantages of living near work? Give reasons or examples to support your opinion.*
Preference	Presents you with a number of options and asks you to choose which of those options you prefer	*Some people prefer to work for a large company, while others prefer to work in a small office. Which size company do you prefer to work in? Use specific examples to support your choice.*
General Opinion	Asks for your opinion on a topic	*At some jobs, employees are allowed to listen to music while they work. What is your opinion of this? Give reasons or examples to support your opinion.*
Agree / Disagree	Asks if you agree or disagree with a statement or idea	*Do you agree or disagree with the following statement: Learning an additional language is a good way to improve one's job prospects in any field. Use specific reasons and examples to support your answer.*
Importance	Asks you to explain why something is important to some people	*References from previous employers are important for some employers when making hiring decisions. Why do you think that references are important to employers? Use specific reasons and examples to explain your answer.*

QUICK TIP

Remember that the prompt will remain on the screen while you are writing, so you will be able to refer to it while you write.

TASK Read the example prompts above and underline key words and information that help you recognize the prompt type.

» **TIP 2 Read the question carefully.** Once you understand the type of question you have been given, read the question carefully and decide what information you must include in your response. This chart gives you tips for quickly finding important information in the prompts.

Prompt Types	What to Look For
Advantage / Disadvantage	Be careful. Does the prompt ask you to discuss <u>both</u> the advantages and disadvantages of a topic, only the advantages, or only the disadvantages?
Preference	Read the options carefully. Make sure you understand what options you are supposed to choose among. For example, are you choosing the <u>best</u> option, the <u>most useful</u>, or something else?
Opinion, Agree / Disagree, and Importance	Carefully read the given statement or opinion and the context given to be sure you understand how they relate to each other.

TASK Read the sample prompts from the chart in TIP 1 on page 129. Choose the answers that best describe the information you need to give for each prompt.

1. What are the advantages or disadvantages of living near work? Give reasons or examples to support your opinion.
   a. The advantages and disadvantages of owning a home
   b. The pros or cons of living near one's place of employment

2. Some people prefer to work for a large company, while others prefer to work in a small office. Which size company do you prefer to work in? Use specific examples to support your choice.
   a. My opinion on work environments
   b. My work environment preference

3. At some jobs, employees are allowed to listen to music while they work. What is your opinion of this? Give reasons or examples to support your opinion.
   a. My music preferences
   b. My thoughts on a specific company policy

4. Do you agree or disagree with the following statement: Learning an additional language is a good way to improve one's job prospects in any field. Use specific reasons and examples to support your answer.
   a. My beliefs about learning new languages
   b. My position on corporate language requirements

5. References from previous employers are important for some employers when making hiring decisions. Why do you think that references are important to employers? Use specific reasons and examples to explain your answer.
   a. My explanation of why something is important to some people
   b. My opinion of how managers make hiring decisions

STRUCTURING YOUR RESPONSE

» **TIP 1 First, brainstorm ideas for your essay.** When you brainstorm, you think about a lot of possible ideas in a short time. Before you start typing your response, you should take 2–3 minutes to brainstorm. Think about the following questions.

- **What is my position?** The prompt for Question 8 will always require you to take a position about the topic. For example, you might have to choose whether you agree or disagree with a given statement, but you may not have strong feelings about the prompt. In such cases, take a minute to write down all the points you can think of that you may be able to use either for or against the prompt. Based on the number of

QUICK TIP

Don't spend a lot of time trying to figure out what your opinion on the question is. If you don't have strong feelings about it, just make up an opinion and write about that. The scorers grade on how well the essay is written, <u>not</u> on what the opinion is.

130

points you come up with for each viewpoint, you can then choose the position that will be easiest for you to support.

- **What is my thesis?** The thesis is the main idea that you will support throughout your essay. Your thesis should express your position on the topic in one sentence. By starting with a strong thesis statement, you will be able to easily organize the rest of your essay. One strategy for creating a strong thesis statement is to <u>restate the information from the prompt</u>. The relevant information from the prompt may be in question form, so you will have to change it to a statement. When you restate the prompt, you should add your opinion about the topic.

- **What do I want to say?** Return to the list of points you made when you were trying to decide on your position. Choose the three strongest points and quickly write down some details or examples that you can use to support those points.

TASK Match the prompts (1–5) from the TIP 2 TASK on page 130 to the correct restatements (a–e). Notice how each of the restatements is changed from the original question to create a strong thesis statement.

____ **a.** Personally, I prefer to work in a small office rather than at a large company for several reasons.

____ **b.** It is my belief that learning an additional language is a great way to improve one's chances of getting a job.

____ **c.** There are several advantages of living near the office.

____ **d.** My opinion is that it is a bad idea for employers to allow workers to listen to music at the office.

____ **e.** I think that references from previous employers are important to some bosses for a number of reasons.

» **TIP 2 Second, create a basic outline of what you want to write.** An outline is the first step in developing your ideas and organizing your essay. This chart is a guide for creating your outline.

Parts of the Essay	What to Include
Thesis Statement	Use the one-sentence thesis that you wrote while you were brainstorming. Remember, this sentence should state your position on the given topic.
Main Point 1	Write what the main point of each paragraph in the body will be. You should also write down any examples and details you might use to support the main points of the body paragraphs.
Main Point 2	
Main Point 3	
Concluding Statement	Restate your position on the given topic.

After you have written a basic outline, check the organization of your response. Make sure that the response is logical and that the ideas flow naturally from one paragraph to the next. Also, make sure that your outline contains all of the information you want to include in your essay.

TASK Match these model outlines (A–E) to the writing prompts (1–5) from the TIP 2 TASK on page 130.

Sample Outline A ____

[Thesis statement] It is my belief that learning an additional language is a great way to improve one's chances of getting a job.

[Main point 1] Access to more jobs

   [Examples / Details] many jobs require more than one language

[Main point 2] Create new opportunities

   [Examples / Details] friend who speaks German was able to bring in new contracts with German companies

[Main point 3] Become indispensable to your employer

   [Examples / Details]

   –friend is the only one who speaks German in his office

   –he's a necessary part of communicating with important clients

Sample Outline B _____

[Thesis statement] I think that references from previous employers are important to some bosses for a number of reasons.

[Main point 1] Helps employers understand the applicant's personality

[Examples / Details] I'm very helpful and friendly, but there's no place on an application for that.

[Main point 2] Tests honesty

[Examples / Details] When my boss was hiring a new employee, she called the references for one application. Boss found out that the applicant had lied on the application.

[Main point 3] Explains why person left former job

[Examples / Details] Someone might not want to hire someone who was fired from the last job, but someone who was laid off might work out well.

Sample Outline C _____

[Thesis statement] Personally, I prefer to work in a small office rather than at a large company for several reasons.

[Main point 1] More interaction with managers

[Examples / Details] better training

[Main point 2] Better relationships with co-workers

[Examples / Details] friend worked for big company, never had any friends there because their offices were so far away

[Main point 3] Faster promotions

[Examples / Details] not as much competition

Sample Outline D _____

[Thesis statement] There are several advantages of living near the office.

[Main point 1] Less time commuting

[examples/details] I spend over an hour driving to and from work every day. Cutting down on that would mean less stress and more time for family.

[Main point 2] Cheaper

[examples/details] An apartment near my office might be a little more expensive, but I'd save on transportation costs.

[Main point 3] Convenient

[examples/details] would be nice to go home for lunch and get back to the office quickly

Sample Outline E _____

[Thesis statement] My opinion is that it is a bad idea for employers to allow workers to listen to music at the office.

[Main point 1] Too distracting

[Examples / Details]

–clerks at store listening to music, not paying attention to customers

–will not return to that store now

[Main point 2] Hurts teamwork

[Examples / Details] everyone is listening to music, not helping each other

[Main point 3] Not everyone has the same musical taste

[Examples / Details]

–what some people like, others may find annoying

–my friend has to listen to country music at work, it makes her unproductive

QUICK TIP

Take no more than three minutes to create your outline. To make sure you don't spend too much time on any part of the writing process, check the on-screen clock from time to time.

» **TIP 3 Third, write a rough draft of your essay.** When you write your rough draft, you expand on the ideas that you wrote in your outline. Don't worry if your writing isn't perfect in the rough draft. You should just focus on writing your ideas down and thinking of ways to strongly support your thesis. Remember that you will be writing on computer, and you will be able to move and change what you write easily. The information below shows how to structure each part of your response.

Introduction

Your first paragraph should introduce the main topic and clearly state your position. In general, it will follow the structure shown below.

[Topic Sentence]	Introduce the main topic of the essay.
[Thesis Statement]	Restate the prompt using your opinion. You may also briefly mention the three main points you will use to support your thesis.

Body Paragraphs

Paragraphs 2, 3, and 4 will be the body of your essay. In the body, you will present three main points to support your thesis. See below for the typical structure of each of the body paragraphs.

[Topic Sentence]	Express the major point that supports the main thesis.
[Details / Examples]	Mention the details / examples that you will use to support your opinion.
[Transition Statement]	Signal to the reader that you have finished talking about the point and will move on to the next point.

Conclusion

Paragraph 5 will conclude your essay. The conclusion is usually structured as shown below.

[Restate Thesis]	Express the main supporting detail that supports the main thesis.
[Review of Major Points]	Briefly mention the three major points used to support the thesis, and be sure to mention how these points support your opinion.
[Concluding Sentence]	Wrap up the content of the paragraph.

TASK Put the paragraphs in this sample essay in the correct order (1–5). Make sure to notice the structure of each of the paragraphs.

Sample Draft Essay

___ To start with, I think that listening to music at work is distracting for employees. This is bad because distracted employees can lead to bad customer service. Many times I've gone to a store, and the clerks are too busy listening to music on personal music players to even help me. Experiences like this have made me stop shopping at certain stores. So I think that if companies want to avoid losing customers, they should not allow behaviors like listening to music that lead to bad customer service.

___ Some offices allow employees to listen to music, while others do not. In my opinion, I think that employers should not allow workers to listen to music at the office because it is distracting, it hurts teamwork, and it can lead to disagreements.

___ Second of all, listening to music hurts teamwork. I've worked at places where employees are allowed to listen to music while they work. People listened to music all day long and never even spoke to each other. We never worked together or tried to solve problems together, which, again, could hurt the quality of the work.

___ To summarize, I think that it is a bad idea to allow employees to listen to music at work. I think this because allowing music in the workplace distracts employees, hurts teamwork, and leads to disagreements. In the end, it is important to remember that work is for work, and people should listen to music at home.

___ Finally, I think listening to music at work can lead to disagreements. The fact is, not everybody has the same musical taste. In cases where music is played over a loudspeaker, this could lead to arguments. That is what happened to my friend. At her job, they play country music over the loudspeaker all day. My friend hates country music, and she is really annoyed about having to listen to it all day. It makes her less productive and, thus, her work suffers.

» **TIP 4 Learn useful language to use in writing your essay.** For several parts of the essay, you will find that you will be able to use similar language. This chart presents useful language to include in different parts of your essay. (See also Speaking Question 11 for more language for giving opinions.)

Useful Language for Question 8 Essays	
Functions	**Examples of Language to Use**
Stating an opinion	• *In my opinion . . .* • *I feel that . . .* • *Personally, I feel / believe / prefer . . .* • *It is my opinion that . . .*
Showing sequence	• *First, / First of all, . . . ; Second, . . . ; Third, . . .* • *Next, . . .* • *Then, . . .* • *After that, . . .* • *Finally, . . .* • *To summarize, . . .* • *In conclusion, . . .*
Transitioning into a new paragraph	• *In general, . . .* • *Generally, . . .* • *Overall, . . .*
Introducing an example	• *For example, . . .* • *For instance, . . .* • *In my experience, . . .* • *. . . such as*

Useful Language for Question 8 Essays *(continued)*	
Functions	**Examples of Language to Use**
Contrasting	• *On the other hand, . . .* • *In contrast, . . .* • *On the contrary, . . .*
Adding information	• *Furthermore, . . .* • *Additionally, . . .* • *Also, . . .*

TASK Choose the correct word or phrase from the box to complete the sample essay. In some cases, more than one answer is possible.

Conversely	Personally	Next	Generally
To summarize	Lastly	For example	First of all

Sample Draft Essay

   Today, people have many choices about where they work. People can work for large companies with equally large offices or at smaller offices. **(1)** _____, I prefer to work in a small office rather than at a large company because working in a small office means more interaction with managers, better relationships with co-workers, and faster promotions.

   (2) _____, I think that by working in a small office, I can spend more time with managers. This is a good thing because managers have a lot to teach, and interacting with them often means that I can get better training and improve my skills. **(3)** _____, I don't think that people at bigger companies have that kind of opportunity.

   (4) _____, working at a small office usually leads to strong, close relationships with co-workers. I had a friend who worked for a company with over 100 employees. She told me that she never had any friends there because there were simply too many people. **(5)** _____, she said that they were really far away from each other because the building was so big. I like having friends where I work, so this would be a bad thing for me. Clearly, working at a small office is much better.

   (6) _____, I've found that it's possible to earn promotions faster at smaller companies than at huge companies. The reason for this is that there isn't as much competition. I had worked at my job at a small office for only six months before I got my first promotion. **(7)** _____, I know people who have worked at big companies for more than three years and have never gotten a promotion.

   (8) _____, my preference is to work in a small office rather than at a big one. By working at a small office, I think employees have more time with managers, have better relationships with their co-workers, and get promoted faster. For me, these three things are really important, and that's why I'll always choose a small office over a big one.

QUICK TIP

Stay focused! It can be easy to get away from the main purpose of the task or focus of the question. Be sure not to move away from your opinion or include information that is not relevant to the question. This can use up time and also lower your score. Refer to your question and thesis statement again and again if you need to.

» **TIP 5 Revise your essay.** When you complete your first draft, take about five minutes to carefully read and revise your essay. The purpose of revising is to perfect your essay by:

• rearranging words, sentences, or sections to improve organization and make the essay clear and easy to follow.

• taking out or adding parts to make your meaning clearer.

• replacing words or expressions that are overused or don't make sense.

• adding words or expressions that you are comfortable using to add variety.

TASK Read the sample essay. Then choose the best way to improve the underlined parts of the essay. You may notice some other errors that you will fix later in the TIP 6 TASK.

Sample Draft Essay

One thing that many people don't consider when they're choosing where to live is distance from the office. There are several advantages to living near the office, including saving time and money, and it is very convenient?

To start with, living near the Office can help save time because employees spend less time driving back and forth from work every day. For example, I spend more than an hour **1.** <u>driving to and from work every day</u>. All of that time in traffic can be really stressful. Cutting down on that travel time by moving closer to work would **2.** <u>not only mean less stress and more time with my family.</u>

Second, I think that living near the office can be cheaper in some ways. **3.** <u>My office is located downtown, the apartments there are a little more expensive than the ones farther away.</u> However, I have to spend just as much money on gas so that I can drive to work downtown. In fact, it would be cheaper for me to live close to my office and just walk to work. That way, I could save the money I am now paying for gas and car maintenance.

Third, live near work is more convenient than living far away. This is because if you live close by, you can always run home and back to work in a short time. Nice to go home for lunch. It is also much less expensive eating at home than eating out for lunch every day.

In conclusion, I know that there are probably some disadvantages to living close to work, but the way I see it, there are far more advntges. Not only does it save time and money, but it is also very convenient.

---

1. a. no change needed
   b. *driving to work all the time*
   c. *not traveling to and from work*

2. a. delete underlined part
   b. *not only mean less stress, but also more time with my family.*
   c. *only mean less time with my family and more stress.*

3. a. *Because my office is located downtown, the apartments there are a little more expensive than the ones that are farther away.*
   b. *My office is located downtown. On the other hand, the apartments there are a little more expensive than the ones farther away.*
   c. *Unlike the apartments located far away, the apartments near the office are located downtown.*

» **TIP 6 Finally, correct your essay.** The final step before you submit your essay is making final corrections. This involves reading and paying special attention to the format, style, and correctness of your essay. Allow at least five minutes for this important last step.

- Check that all sentences are complete and make sense.

- Check that all sentences are grammatically correct (e.g., check subject-verb agreement, pronoun use, etc.).

- Check for correct spelling, capitalization, and punctuation.

TASK Read the sample essay from the TIP 5 TASK again. Not including the underlined portions from the previous task, find and underline these things. Make a check mark [✓] when you have found the item.

☐ 1 incomplete sentence   ☐ 1 capitalization error
☐ 1 grammar error   ☐ 1 punctuation error
☐ 1 spelling error

PROGRESSIVE PRACTICE: Get Ready

A Read the sample question. Then answer the questions that follow.

> **Sample Question 8**
>
> Do you agree or disagree with the following statement? A small town is a better place than a big city to raise children. Support your answer with specific reasons and examples.

1. This question asks about

   a. preference.

   b. advantages and disadvantages.

   c. agreement.

   d. importance.

2. The topic is about

   a. the best place to live.

   b. the best place to work.

   c. the best place to take a vacation.

B Complete the brainstorming notes for the question in Part A by answering the questions. Use the sentences given to respond.

> **Brainstorming Notes**
>
> 1. What is the question asking for? _____
>
> _____
>
> 2. What is my viewpoint? _____
>
> _____
>
> 3. What is my thesis? _____
>
> _____
>
> 4. Why do I feel this way? _____
>
> _____

> **Sentences for Notes**
>
> *I agree with the statement.*
>
> *Small towns are safer, people in small towns are nicer, and life in small towns is less expensive.*
>
> *I agree that a small town is a better place to raise children.*
>
> *Do I agree or disagree that a small town is better than a city for raising children?*

C Read the sample response to the question in Part A. Then choose the correct number from the box to label each part of the response.

> 1. Body paragraph
>
> 2. Concluding paragraph
>
> 3. Introductory paragraph
>
> 4. First supporting idea
>
> 5. Second supporting idea
>
> 6. Third supporting idea
>
> 7. Thesis statement

Sample Response

___ While many families live in cities, many other people believe that a small town is better for children. ___ I agree that a small town is a better place to raise a family than a big city. I think that small towns are safer than cities, the people there are nicer, and life is less expensive.

___ Everybody knows that small towns are safer than cities. There is a lot less crime, so parents know that their children aren't in danger. ___ In addition, people in small towns are usually nicer than people in big cities. It is much better for children to grow up in the friendly atmosphere of a small town. ___ Finally, life in a small town is much less expensive than life in a big city. It is easier for parents to provide their children with everything they need.

___ Life in a small town is better than life in a big city in several ways. A small town is a safer, nicer, and cheaper place to raise children. When I have children, I will certainly move to a small town.

D Write your own response to the question in Part A by completing the template.

> While many families live in cities, many other people believe that a small town is better for children. I agree / disagree that a small town is a better place to raise a family than a big city. I think this because _____,
> _____, and
> _____.
>
> In the first place, I think _____
> because _____. I also think
> _____ because
> _____.
>
> Finally, _____ because
> _____.
>
> Life in a _____ is better than life in a
> _____ in several ways. A _____ is
> _____ , _____,
> and _____. Therefore,
> _____.

E Now, evaluate your response in Part D using the checklist below. How well did your response meet the scoring criteria? Check (✓) *Yes* or *No*. Keep practicing until all of your answers are *Yes*.

Response Checklist: Question 8	Yes	No
1. I wrote a thesis statement that stated my opinion clearly.	☐	☐
2. I gave reasons for my opinion.	☐	☐
3. I supported my reasons with details.	☐	☐
4. I included a conclusion.	☐	☐
5. I used correct grammar and vocabulary.	☐	☐
6. My essay was well organized and flowed easily from each paragraph to the next.	☐	☐

PROGRESSIVE PRACTICE: Get Set

A Read the sample question. Then complete the brainstorming notes in your own words.

Sample Question 8

Some people use public transportation (buses and subways) to get around a city. Others use private cars. Which do you prefer? Support your answer with specific reasons and examples.

Brainstorming Notes

1. What is the question asking for? _____

_____

2. What is my viewpoint? _____

_____

3. What is my thesis? _____

_____

4. Why do I feel this way? _____

_____

B Number the sentences in each paragraph to put them in the correct order to create a response to the question in Part A.

Introduction (number 1–3)

_____ My preference is definitely for public transportation.

_____ I believe that it is cheaper, more convenient, and better for the environment than private cars are.

_____ In order to get around a city, you can use public transportation or private cars.

Body Paragraph 1 (number 1–4)

_____ On the other hand, you also have to pay money to buy a car, to maintain it, and to park it.

_____ It is much cheaper to use public transportation than it is to drive a private car.

_____ I believe that the costs of driving a car add up to a lot more than the costs of paying bus and subway fares.

_____ Of course, you have to pay a fare every time you ride a bus or subway.

Body Paragraph 2 (number 1–4)

_____ In addition to being cheaper, public transportation is also more convenient than private cars.

_____ To use a car, however, you have to pay attention while you drive it, and you have to worry about finding a parking place at your destination.

_____ In addition, you have to spend time and money keeping your car maintained.

_____ To use public transportation, you just get on, pay your fare, and ride to your destination.

Body Paragraph 3 (number 1–4)

_____ Buses may cause air pollution, but they also carry a lot of passengers.

_____ Overall, public transportation is cleaner than private cars.

_____ If you look at the amount of pollution per passenger, I am sure that cars dirty the air more than buses do.

_____ Finally, public transportation is better for the environment than private cars are.

Conclusion (number 1–3)

_____ It is cheap, convenient, and clean.

_____ I think public transportation is the best way to get around a city.

_____ I take buses and subways whenever I can.

C Use the template to write your own response to the question in Part A.

Draft Essay Template

Introduction Paragraph

[Introductory sentence] _____

[Thesis statement] _____

[Supporting ideas that will be in essay] _____

_____

Body Paragraph 1

[Topic sentence] _____

[Supporting sentence 1] _____

[Details and examples 1] _____

_____

[Supporting sentence 2] _____

[Details and examples 2] _____

_____

[Supporting sentence 3] _____

[Details and examples 3] _____

_____

[Concluding/transition sentence] _____

Body Paragraph 2

[Topic sentence] _____

[Supporting sentence 1] _____

[Details and examples 1] _____

_____

[Supporting sentence 2] _____

[Details and examples 2] _____

_____

[Supporting sentence 3] _____

[Details and examples 3] _____

_____

[Concluding/transition sentence] _____

Body Paragraph 3

[Topic sentence] _____

[Supporting sentence 1] _____

[Details and examples 1] _____

_____

[Supporting sentence 2] _____

[Details and examples 2] _____

_____

[Supporting sentence 3] _____

[Details and examples 3] _____

_____

[Concluding/transition sentence] _____

Conclusion

[Topic sentence] _____

[Restate thesis] _____

[Restate supporting ideas] _____

[Concluding sentence] _____

D Now, evaluate your response in Part C using the checklist below. How well did your response meet the scoring criteria? Check (✓) *Yes* or *No*. Keep practicing until all of your answers are *Yes*.

Response Checklist: Question 8	Yes	No
1. I wrote a thesis statement that stated my opinion clearly.	☐	☐
2. I gave reasons for my opinion.	☐	☐
3. I supported my reasons with details.	☐	☐
4. I included a conclusion.	☐	☐
5. I used correct grammar and vocabulary.	☐	☐
6. My essay was well organized and flowed easily from each paragraph to the next.	☐	☐

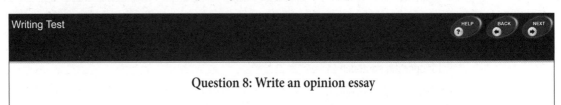

PROGRESSIVE PRACTICE: Go for the TOEIC® Test

Read the question and write an essay in response. If possible, write on a computer. Give yourself no more than 30 minutes to complete your essay.

Writing Test

Question 8: Write an opinion essay

Directions: You will write an essay that responds to an opinion question. You will need to state your opinion, explain it, and support it. Your essay should have at least 300 words.

Your response will be scored on

- how well your opinion is supported by reasons and examples.
- the quality of the grammar used.
- the variety and accuracy of vocabulary.
- the organization.

You must plan, write, and revise your essay in 30 minutes.

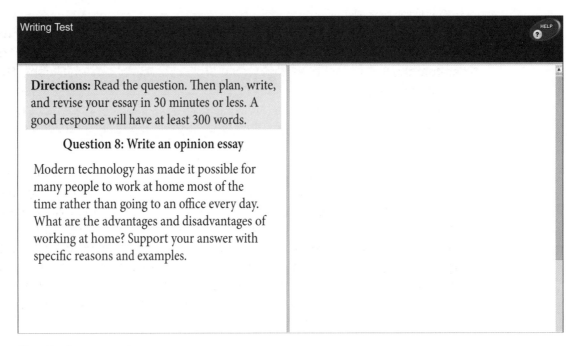

Writing Test

Directions: Read the question. Then plan, write, and revise your essay in 30 minutes or less. A good response will have at least 300 words.

Question 8: Write an opinion essay

Modern technology has made it possible for many people to work at home most of the time rather than going to an office every day. What are the advantages and disadvantages of working at home? Support your answer with specific reasons and examples.

Time Used: _____ minutes

TO READ SAMPLE RESPONSES, SEE PAGE 161.

Practice TOEIC® Test: Writing

TAKING THE PRACTICE TEST

The following Writing Practice Test will help you evaluate the TOEIC test-taking skills that you have learned for the Writing Section. The Writing Practice Test is divided into three parts, just as on the actual test. The level of difficulty of the material is like that of the TOEIC test. Your timing should be set like the actual test as well, so plan to complete the Writing Practice Test questions in the time limits given.

We advise you to simulate the actual test when you take the Writing Practice Test. Take the test in a quiet setting. Be sure to follow the directions exactly as instructed and write your responses on a computer if possible.

SCORING THE TEST

For the actual test, your responses will be sent to graders who will assign a score for each question. Questions 1–5 are scored on a scale of 0–3. Questions 6 and 7 are scored on a scale of 0–4, and Question 8 is scored on a scale of 0–5. Therefore the last three questions carry more weight in your overall score. The specific requirements for these scoring scales are available from any testing center. These scores are then translated into Writing Proficiency Levels that give a detailed description of writing ability. These Proficiency Level indicators are meant to assign a general writing level to each test taker.

For this Writing Practice Test, you or a qualified evaluator may want to check your responses against the checklists given for each question in the *Progressive Practice* sections of the book when you are finished. This will help you assess if you are meeting the main scoring criteria used to measure TOEIC test performance. If you answer *No* to any areas, you may want to practice more on those points by reviewing and taking the test again. In addition, a model response for each question has been provided in the answer key at the back of this book. Reviewing these model responses will give you a better idea of what you will need to be successful on the test.

WRITING PRACTICE TEST

Questions 1–5: Write a sentence based on a picture

Directions: You will write <u>one</u> sentence about a photo. You will be given <u>two</u> words or phrases. You must use them in your sentence. You can change the word forms, and you can use the words in a different order.

Your sentence will be scored on

- appropriate use of grammar.
- relevance of the sentence to the photo.

During the actual test, you will be able to move to the next question by clicking on "Next." You will be able to return to a previous question by clicking on "Back." You will have eight minutes to complete this part of the test.

woman/pay

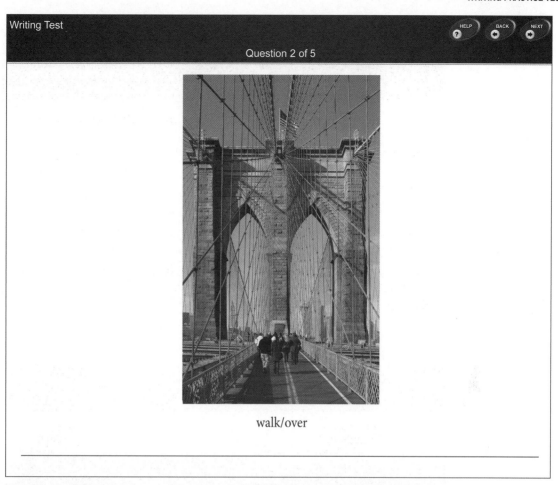

walk/over

passenger/board

outside/although

_____

as soon as/serve

_____

Questions 6–7: Respond to a written request

Directions: In this part of the test, you will write a response to an e-mail. Your response will be scored on

- the quality and variety of your sentences.
- vocabulary.
- organization.

In the actual test, you will have 10 minutes to read and answer the e-mail.

Directions: Read the e-mail.

From: George Pinkney
To: Social Committee members
Subject: Meeting
Sent: April12, 20—

It is time for a meeting of the Social Committee. We need to start planning the annual year-end party. I would like all members of the committee to meet next Friday morning from 9 to 11 in Conference Room A. Please let me know as soon as possible if you are available to attend this meeting.

Thank you.
George Pinkney
Social Committee Chair

Directions: Respond to the e-mail as if you are a member of the Social Committee. In your e-mail, explain ONE problem and make TWO suggestions.

(Write your response here or on a computer.)

_____

_____

_____

_____

_____

_____

_____

_____

_____

_____

_____

Directions: Read the e-mail.

From:	Journal of Business News
To:	Business professionals
Subject:	Subscribe
Sent:	December 2, 20—

Dear Business Professional,

The *Journal Of Business News* brings you all the latest news about important developments in the international business world. It is read by thousands of businesspeople just like you in over 40 countries around the world. Subscribe today and receive a 30% discount off the regular price.

Directions: Respond to the e-mail as if you are a businessperson interested in subscribing to the *Journal of Business News*. In your e-mail, ask THREE questions.

(Write your response here or on a computer.)

_____

_____

_____

_____

_____

_____

_____

_____

_____

_____

_____

_____

_____

_____

_____

_____

_____

_____

_____

_____

Question 8: Write an opinion essay

Directions: You will write an essay that responds to an opinion question. You will need to state your opinion, explain it, and support it. Your essay should have at least 300 words.

Your response will be scored on

- how well your opinion is supported by reasons and examples.
- the quality of the grammar used.
- the variety and accuracy of vocabulary.
- the organization.

You must plan, write, and revise your essay in 30 minutes.

Cut | Paste | Undo | Redo

Directions: Read the question. Then plan, write, and revise your essay in 30 minutes or less. A good response will hove at least 300 words.

Do you agree or disagree with the following statement? It is more important to work at a job you enjoy than to make a lot of money. Support your answer with specific reasons and examples.

(Write your response here or on a computer.)

_____

_____

_____

_____

_____

_____

_____

_____

_____

_____

_____

Answer Key and Audio Scripts

ANSWER KEY

Speaking Questions 1–2

GET IT RIGHT: Pronunciation

TIP 1 TASK 1 pg 5

1. thin	6. lunch	11. fans
2. laughed	7. bright	12. veer
3. sip	8. stare	13. zinc
4. clothes	9. she'll	14. than
5. junk	10. watch	

TIP 1 TASK 2 pg 6

1. den	5. right	9. wind
2. though	6. tow	10. clean
3. think	7. then	11. cream
4. sink	8. light	12. vend

TIP 2 TASK 1 pg 6

1. corporate: 2 syllables	6. frequently: 3 syllables
2. invaluable: 4 syllables	7. cooperation: 5 syllables
3. February: 4 syllables	8. athletics: 3 syllables
4. automatically: 5 syllables	9. librarian: 4 syllables
5. candidate: 3 syllables	10. unfortunately: 5 syllables

TIP 2 TASK 2 pg 6

1. car/eer	7. asked
2. carr/i/er	8. in/tell/i/gent
3. ad/ver/tise/ment	9. de/pen/da/bil/i/ty
4. im/pro/ba/ble	10. a/cqui/si/tion
5. cor/por/a/tion	11. re/gion/al
6. clothes	12. li/a/bil/i/ty

GET IT RIGHT: Stress

TIP 1 TASK 1 pg 7

1. verb	5. noun
2. noun	6. noun
3. verb	7. verb
4. verb	8. verb

TIP 1 TASK 2 pg 7

1. authorize*	4. validate	7. geographic
2. interruption	5. version	8. appreciate
3. recreation	6. geography	9. accommodations

10. estimate	14. location	18. recognize
11. interpretation	15. cooperate	19. suspension
12. notarize	16. direction	20. charity
13. policy	17. evaluate	21. democracy

*pronunciation stress is marked—stress and syllable breaks on some words may vary

TIP 1 TASK 3 pg 8

1. descendent*	7. dislocate	13. redundant
2. underestimate	8. extract	14. inspect
3. overuse	9. outstanding	15. unusable
4. belated	10. completely	16. contented
5. renew	11. unable	17. reduction
6. extensive	12. respectable	18. complaint

*pronunciation stress is marked—stress and syllable breaks on some words may vary

TIP 1 TASK 4 pg 8

1. Please use this software to **record** the day's sales. (verb)
2. All employees are expected to follow the company code of **conduct.** (noun)
3. Let's not **overestimate** the amount of work we can do. (verb)
4. Before we create our business plan for the month, let's **coordinate** our schedules. (verb)
5. **Prosperity** is the goal of all nations. (noun)
6. After you receive your pass code, you will have **authorization.** (noun)
7. This year, we decided to **recognize** our supervisor for his 10 years of service. (verb)
8. We **project** that our product sales will **increase** over the next two years. (verb / verb)
9. It was a great **comfort** to **receive** your letter. (noun / verb)
10. She studied **biology** at the **university**. (noun / noun)
11. As we **progress** with this **project**, we will give everyone a monthly **report**. (verb / noun / noun)
12. The marketing team really **outdid** themselves with this **detailed explanation**. (verb / noun)

TIP 2 TASK 1 pg 9

1. The correct numbers are 13 and 17, not 30 and 70.
2. We strongly suggest that you back up your computer files at the end of the day.
3. Our genealogists will conduct a very thorough search of your family tree.

4. On the <u>new</u> schedule, you will see that the bus departs on <u>Tuesday</u> at 1 p.m.

5. Your estimated wait time to speak to a representative is <u>ten</u> minutes.

6. The parking spaces are clearly marked <u>"visitor."</u>

TIP 2 TASK 2 pg 9

1. The real estate office is located in the <u>green</u> house on the left.

2. You will receive a credit card within <u>ten days</u> after receipt of your application.

3. The message said to phone their office between <u>9 and 5</u>, Monday to Friday.

4. We are currently reviewing your request and will respond <u>within 30</u> days.

5. Please turn <u>down</u> the volume on the TV, not up.

GET IT RIGHT: Intonation and Pausing

TIP 1 TASK pg 10

1. We will need ushers↗, ticket takers↗, and box office staff↘ at the theater this weekend.↘

2. At this time, there is no one available to take your call.↗ Please leave a message after the beep.↘

3. Our number is 202-555-4567. Please call if you have any problems.↘

4. Because the application forms were late↗, we'll need to adjust the start date.↘

5. Please turn off all cell phones and pagers before the movie begins.↘

6. In conclusion↗, we'd like to thank all of our guests for their participation.↘

TIP 2 TASK pg 11

1. What do you think? ↘

2. If Friday is not a good day, can we meet on Saturday? ↗

3. I'm sorry, could you repeat that, please? ↗

4. We didn't hear that. What did he say? ↘

5. What did John bring to the party? ↘

6. How can I help you today? ↘

7. Is this your first day here? ↗

8. Have you sent the latest market reports? ↗

TIP 3 TASK pg 11

1. They have not yet determined what the problem was. ↘

2. Would you like the three-month or the six-month plan? ↘

3. Do you know what time it is? ↗

4. You wouldn't have an extra pencil, would you? ↗

5. Would you mind closing the window? ↗

6. When you need a reliable copy service, Tip Top Copy Shop has everything you need. ↘

Speaking Question 3

WALK THROUGH: Describe a Picture

A What You'll See and Hear pg 17

(Answers will vary.) **Important Details:** a woman and a man in a bakery; the woman works there

GET IT RIGHT: Tips and Tasks for Answering Correctly pg 18

Nouns: people, picture, bakery, man, right, back, camera, shirt, customer, counter, something, woman, center, picture, camera, jacket, uniform, cap, hair, tray, rolls, baker, tray, bread, oven, oven, bread, customer, rolls, something, bakery *(pronouns not included)*

Verbs: see, think, must be, 's, 's wearing, must be, seems to be, waiting, to buy, 's, 's facing, 's wearing, to cover, 's . . . carrying, think, must be, looks, took, is, smells, was waiting to buy, 's going to buy

GET IT RIGHT: Grammar and Vocabulary

TIP 1 TASK pg 19

1. woman; She

2. bread; It

3. customer / man; He

4. It

5. baker / woman; She

6. man / customer; He

7. man / customer; he

8. She

TIP 2 TASK pg 20

1. is standing

2. walks

3. is waiting

4. There are

5. is wearing

6. There is

TIP 3 TASK pg 20

1. behind

2. in front of

3. on

4. in

5. at the back of

TIP 4 TASK pg 21

1. three big black cars

2. a tall dark-haired customer

3. some fresh French bread

4. nice blue cotton shirt

TIP 5 TASK pg 21

1. quietly

2. probably

3. patiently

4. quickly

5. probably

GET IT RIGHT: Cohesion and Structuring a Response

TIP 1 TASK pg 22

6, 3, 2, 5, 4, 1

TIP 2 TASK pg 22

1. There are two people, a man and a woman, in this photo.

2. The people are in an office.

3. They are talking and looking at a document while standing next to a copy machine.

4. Other details: *(Answers will vary.)* The man is wearing a white shirt and gray slacks.; The man is holding a pair of glasses.; The woman is wearing a blouse and black slacks.; The woman is holding a document.; Both people are about 30 years old.; Inside the room, there are office machines and four rows of boxes filled with paper and envelopes.; The document has a lot of pages.; The document may be a report or a manual for an office machine.

TIP 3 TASK pg 22

(Answers will vary.)

1. I think that the woman **might be** the man's boss.

2. I'm **not sure if** the man is waiting for a document.

3. The woman **could be** the children's mother.

4. It's possible that the man is there to repair the computer.

5. The man and woman **may be** running in a race.

6. Possibly, the man is a new employee at the company.

Progressive Practice: Get Ready pg 23

Part A

shirt [7]	computer [4]	younger man [1]
desk [6]	cables [5]	
glasses [3]	older man [2]	

Part B pg 23

2, 5, 1, 6, 3, 4

Part C pg 23

Sample Response: *(Answers will vary.)* There are two men at a desk. The younger man has brown hair and a white shirt. He is hooking up wires on the back of a computer. The older man is wearing glasses, and he is watching the younger man work on the computer. The younger man is probably from technology support. He is most likely fixing the older man's computer.

Progressive Practice: Get Set

Part B pg 24

5, 1, 3, 6, 2, 7, 8, 4

Part C pg 24

Sample Response: *(Answers will vary.)* Well, in this picture, there are four people. It's a really nice, sunny day. They're sitting next to a lake, probably in a park. They're probably a family—a mother and father and their two young sons. They're having a picnic lunch. They have cups, a basket, some fruit, sandwiches, and other things, and these things are on a blanket on the ground. The father and son in the center are eating their watermelon. The mother is sitting on the right, and it looks like she just cut a piece of watermelon for herself. They're probably having a good time.

Progressive Practice: Go for the TOEIC Test pg 25

Sample Response: *(Answers will vary.)* In this picture, there's a young woman in an orange car. I think maybe she is lost because she has stopped her car and rolled down her window so that she can ask for directions. There's also an older woman with short hair in the picture. She's wearing a white jacket, and she has a map in her hands. She's standing next to the car door and pointing to the map. She looks like she's talking to the younger woman and is probably explaining where the younger woman needs to go. The older woman looks very sure of herself and more confident, while the younger woman looks like she's confused.

Speaking Questions 4–6

GET IT RIGHT: Understanding the Questions

TIP 1 TASK pg 29

1. sports: gardening

2. movies: photography

3. emergency services: limousine

4. public parks: school playground

5. materials to read for enjoyment: employee handbooks

TIP 2 TASK pg 30

1. Where do you	**4.** Why do you
2. What is	**5.** What kind of
3. What do you	

TIP 3 TASK pg 30

1. How often	**4.** When
2. How much	**5.** How long
3. How many	

TIP 4 TASK pg 30

1. What kind of; a type	**4.** How do you think; an opinion
2. How important is it; an opinion	**5.** What do you think; an opinion
3. Describe; a description	**6.** Do you believe it; an opinion

GET IT RIGHT: Structuring Your Response

TIP 1 TASK pg 32

(Answers will vary.)

1. My preferred method of transportation is . . .

2. I usually do my food shopping at . . .

3. The kind of music I usually listen to is . . .

4. I have lived at my current residence for . . .

TIP 2 TASK 1 pg 33

Question 4: 4, 1, 3, 2; **Question 5:** 3, 1, 4, 2; **Question 6:** 5, 2, 3, 1, 4

TIP 2 TASK 2 pg 33

(Answers will vary.)

1. I really like rock music, especially if the song has great lyrics. One of my favorite things to do is sing along.

2. The beach is one of my favorite places to go on vacation. I really like to take vacations in Australia because the beaches are so beautiful and I enjoy swimming.

3. A popular place to meet friends in my neighborhood is at my neighborhood café. It has a great atmosphere and good food, so people really like to go there.

TIP 3 TASK 1 pg 34

1. d (Sports statistics are not considered literature.)

2. c (Potato chips are a snack food, not a dessert.)

3. a (A birthday is a type of day; no season is mentioned.)

TIP 3 TASK 2 pg 34

Question 4: Response A is correct. Response B is not complete because it does not give an explanation. Response C is off topic, as it does not restate the prompt or address the importance of the park.

Question 5: Response A is correct. Response B is not complete because it is not a personal response to the question. Response C is off topic because it does not mention the park.

Question 6: Response B is correct. Response A is off topic and doesn't discuss how a park could be improved. Response C is incomplete because it does not directly answer the question.

Progressive Practice: Get Ready pg 35
Part A
Question 4
Restatement: I usually take the subway.
Supporting: The subway is very inexpensive.
Supporting: And it is not far from my house, which makes it very convenient.

Question 5
Restatement: My commute to work is really long.
Supporting: It usually takes me 45 minutes to get to work every day.
Supporting: It takes a long time for me to get to work because I live outside of the city.

Question 6
Restatement: The subway is the quickest way to get around, especially when there is a lot of traffic.
Supporting: The subway is the fastest and easiest method of travel.
Supporting: I think this because there are many lines, and every stop is close to major city areas.

Part B pgs 35–36

Question 4: 1, 2, 3, 4, 5
Question 5: 1, 2, 3, 4, 5
Question 6: 1, 2, 3, 4, 5, 6, 6

Progressive Practice: Get Set pg 38
Part A
Response A: Question 6
Response B: Question 4
Response C: Question 5

Speaking Questions 7–9

WALK THROUGH: Respond to Questions Using Information Provided pg 42
A What You'll See
(Answers will vary.) **Purpose**: a city tour; **Activities**: bus tour of downtown, history museum tour, lunch, walking tour of gardens, bus tour of waterfront, optional dinner

GET IT RIGHT: Understanding the Information Texts and Questions
TIP 1 TASK 1 pg 45

a. Text 3
b. Text 2
c. Text 1

TIP 1 TASK 2 pg 45
Text 1: a tour of a work site
Text 2: a gathering of professional writers
Text 3: a meeting at Government Center

TIP 2 TASK pg 45
Text 1: 1. You can take the tour Monday through Friday at 11:00 a.m. **2.** The tour lasts about four hours, from 10:45 a.m. until 3:00 p.m. You will see the finished part of the tunnel and the drill area.
Text 2: 1. The main speakers at the conference are Jenny Hill, Marlon Thomson, and Angela Moeller. **2.** In the afternoon, you can see Marlon Thomson or Angela Moeller speak. You can also visit the publisher exhibits or go to the open forum with the guest speakers.
Text 3: 1. The delegation arrives at 7:00 in the morning, and Secretary Sullivan is picking them up. **2.** The delegation has about one hour and forty-five minutes for lunch. The time might be shortened if the presentation before lunch runs over.

TIP 3 TASK pg 46
Part 1: *(Answers will vary.)* **1.** When, flight, arrive; **2.** Who's, picking up; **3.** Where, lunch; **4.** earlier, train; **5.** fees, involved; **6.** have to stay, hotel; **7.** break, coffee; **8.** what time, starts; **9.** what, to do, evenings; **10.** seats, left; **11.** speakers, all day; **12.** problem, coming early
Part 2: *(Answers will vary.)* **1.** tickets, cost; **2.** speaking, first, morning session; **3.** stay, all day; **4.** Mr. Lee, free, afternoon; **5.** Professor Hunt, speak, days and times; **6.** can't meet, Ms. Johnson, Thursday; **7.** time, answering e-mails; **8.** registration, costs; **9.** meet, 1:00; **10.** pay, fees, first day, exhibition

GET IT RIGHT: Structuring Your Responses
TIP 1 TASK pg 48
a: 8 **b:** 9 **c:** 6 **d:** 7 **e:** 4 **f:** 3 **g:** 2 **h:** 1 **i:** 5 **j:** 10

TIP 2 TASK pg 50
Text 1: 1. You need to meet for the tour at ten forty-five. **2.** There's a walking tour of the finished part of the tunnel. Then you'll have lunch in the underground break room. After that, there's a talk about drill site safety. Finally, they're offering open viewing of the drill area, with a guide available.
Text 2: 1. Angela Moeller is the CEO of the Editorial Advisory Group. She will be speaking in Room 12 of Carver Hall in Thorpe Center on West University Campus. **2.** At the exhibits, you can browse through the booths. They offer valuable information on how to get published, what's new in the field, and where to send your work.
Text 3: 1. Secretary Sullivan will be taking the Southeast delegation to the airport. Their flight leaves at seven o'clock in the evening. **2.** After the first presentation, the delegation is taking a taxi to a restaurant. Then they're having lunch with the CEO of HCG Incorporated. They'll be going back to Government Center at about a quarter to two.

Progressive Practice: Get Ready pg 51

Part A

(B) A special dinner

Part B pg 51

Question 7: Appetizers will be served in the Green Room.

Question 8: No. There will be an awards ceremony first.

Question 9: Yes. Both the membership secretary and the president will speak.

Part C pg 52

Question 7:

> The main meal? Just let me check that for you. OK. The main meal will be served in the East Dining Room at 8 o'clock.

Question 8:

> No, I don't think so, but let's see here. There will be music and dancing, but the music will be played by the Moonlight Swing Band.

Question 9:

> So you'd like to know what will happen during the ceremony? OK. Well, let me take a look. There are several parts to the ceremony. First, there will be a welcome speech by Peter Harris. Then Rose Smith will receive an award. Finally, everyone will enjoy a slide show. I hope that answers your question.

Progressive Practice: Get Set pg 53

Part A

The information is an itinerary for Mr. Green's visit to the New York headquarters.

Part C pgs 53–54

Sample Responses

Question 7: Good question. Let me just check the itinerary. OK, it says that Mr. Green will arrive at the airport at 5 p.m. on April 15.

Question 8: At 12:15? Well, according to the itinerary, it looks like the lunch begins at twelve, so I think you will have to pick him up earlier than that.

Question 9: So you need his schedule for later in the day? Let me take a look. Well, I'm looking at the itinerary, and it shows several activities after lunch. First, you'll need to take Mr. Green to the Hotel Dominion for a reception at four o'clock. Then he has a private tour at the City Museum of Art at seven. He's scheduled to return to the hotel at nine.

Progressive Practice: Go for the TOEIC Test pg 55

Sample Responses

Question 7: OK, it looks like *Romeo and Juliet* will be performed on July 10, and—let me check—there's another performance on July 31, and that's all. So two performances.

Question 8: Yes, it's true that the plays will be performed at the outdoor theater, but if the weather is bad, the performances will be moved to City Auditorium, so no performances will be canceled.

Question 9: Let me just check the schedule. It looks like there will be three different plays performed in August. First we have *The Tempest,* with performances on August 7 and 8. Then *Comedy of*

Errors will be performed on August 14 and 15, and finally, there will be one last performance of *King Lear* on August 21.

Answer Analysis: All of these answers are long enough to demonstrate fluency. They make use of words and expressions like *Let me check, In fact, It looks like,* and so on to give the speaker time to think while formulating an answer. The grammar and vocabulary are appropriate, and the information is correct.

Speaking Question 10

WALK THROUGH: Propose a Solution pg 57

A What You'll See

Message Topic: a problem with the elevator; **Role:** building manager

B What You'll Hear

Problem: The caller is complaining about a broken elevator.

Sentence: I'm calling about the elevator, which doesn't seem to be working again.

GET IT RIGHT: Understanding the Voicemail Messages

TIP 1 TASK pg 59

1. request   **2.** complaint   **3.** both

TIP 2 TASK pg 60

Message 1: John Green, Swift Plumbing; needs pipe ASAP; main line broke on job site; customer will get angry; needs by this afternoon

Message 2: Charlotte Strand, Room 128; disappointed with room; reserved deluxe double and got small room with one bed, no TV, problem with heating; not acceptable because paid for bigger and better room

Message 3: Peter Arnold; problem with credit card while on vacation in Europe; tried in three stores and bank card not accepted; planned to use card for most of his shopping; needs fixed ASAP

GET IT RIGHT: Structuring Your Response

TIP 1 TASK 1 pg 62

1. **Expressions to greet and introduce:** Hi, Mr. Green. This is Janet Day, and I'm returning your call from earlier today. **Expressions to apologize or acknowledge requests:** I understand that you're interested in having some pipes delivered.

2. **Expressions to greet and introduce:** Hello. I'm calling for Ms. Strand. My name's Percy Rogers with Smith Hotels, and we just got your message. **Expressions to apologize or acknowledge requests:** We'd like to apologize for the problem with your room. **Expressions to show understanding:** We understand that you're upset that you didn't get the room you wanted.

3. **Expressions to greet and introduce:** Good morning, Mr. Arnold. This is Karen Stall with First Bank. I just wanted to get back to you about your message. **Expressions to apologize or acknowledge requests:** We're sorry to hear that your card isn't working. **Expressions to show understanding:** I know this is especially frustrating because you're traveling, so we want to help you as soon as possible.

TIP 1 TASK 2 pg 62

(Answers will vary.)

1. Hi. I'm calling for Susan Jones. This is Emi Sugiyama with Hayashi Hotels.

2. Please accept our apologies for the missing computer part.

3. Thank you very much for asking about our driving course.

TIP 2 TASK 1 pg 63

1. a   **2.** b   **3.** b

TIP 2 TASK 2 pgs 63–64

(Answers will vary.)

1. It seems that the repairmen didn't clean up. / There must have been a problem with the door.

2. As you know, we don't usually take emergency appointments. / I'm afraid there's a problem with that because we are full today.

3. I checked, and it seems that the driver can't find the address. / There could be heavy traffic.

TIP 3 TASK 1 pg 65

1. b, c   **2.** a, b   **3.** a, c

TIP 3 TASK 2 pg 65

(Answers will vary.)

1. I'd like to suggest that we resend the DVD express delivery. For the inconvenience, we'd like to offer free shipping.

2. If you can meet at 10:00 instead, we can change the meeting. Another option would be to schedule the meeting for the day after tomorrow.

3. We just need to stop by, and then we can repair the lock. I can arrange for someone to come this afternoon.

4. I've checked, and it seems the bill is wrong. In order to fix that quickly, let's get the date of your repair and your personal information. Then I'll adjust the bill and resend it. For your inconvenience, we'd like to offer you a reduced rate on your next repair.

5. Normally we don't send repair crews out this late, but I'll see what I can do. Or if you prefer, we can send someone early tomorrow. For your inconvenience, we'd like to offer a 10 percent discount on your next bill.

Progressive Practice: Get Ready pg 66
Part A

1. a   **2.** c   **3.** b

Part B pg 66

2, 3, 6, 1, 5, 4

Progressive Practice: Get Ready

Part C pg 67

(Answers will vary.)

Thank you for calling, Mr. Jones. Your message said that you can't take the Saturday morning Spanish class because of your new job. I'm sorry to hear about this difficulty with your schedule, but I think this problem is easy to solve. You said that you're available on Monday and Tuesday afternoons. We have an advanced Spanish

class you can attend on either of those days. Please choose which day you want and let me know. I hope this will work well for you.

Progressive Practice: Get Set pg 68
Part A

1. George Smith

2. Complaint and request

3. His new coffeemaker doesn't work.

4. He followed the instructions for using the coffeemaker, but it doesn't work.

5. He needs a coffeemaker that works because he is expecting guests.

6. He wants to know if there is an easy way to fix it or what he can do.

Part B pg 68

(Answers will vary.)

1. I understand that you haven't been able to get your new coffeemaker to work. I realize how frustrating this must be.

2. There could be an issue with the coffeemaker or a problem with the programming.

3. a. Look in the manual for instructions about fixing the coffeemaker.

   b. Return the coffeemaker to us, and we will send you a new one.

4. Thanks so much for calling, and please accept our apologies for the inconvenience.

Part C pg 69

(Answers will vary.)

Hi, there. I'm calling for Mr. Smith. This is Amy Martin from Winston Appliance. I received the message that your new coffeemaker is not working. I know this must be frustrating for you, especially with guests coming to stay with you soon, and we apologize that this has caused you frustration. It's possible that the coffeemaker you received is defective. It may have been damaged in shipping. I'd like to suggest that you send the coffeemaker back to us, and we will send you a replacement model right away. For your inconvenience, we'd like to offer you free express shipping so that your new coffeemaker will arrive by next week. Thank you for contacting us, and I hope this solves your problem.

Progressive Practice: Go for the TOEIC Test pg 70

Sample Response: Hello, Ms. Clark. This is John Peters. I got your message about rescheduling our appointment for our meeting. I understand how busy you are at this time of the year. I appreciate that you're still willing to meet with me. If we can get together early next week, that will be fine. Can we meet on Monday? Anytime Monday morning or afternoon works for me. If you don't have time to meet on Monday, then perhaps we could talk for a short while on the phone. It would take less time than an actual meeting. Please let me know which solution works best for you. Thank you.

Sample Response Analysis: This response addresses the caller by name, restates the problem, apologizes, and expresses sympathy for the caller's situation. The two solutions that are offered are relevant to the information provided in the message. The language is fluent, and it uses appropriate vocabulary and correct grammar.

Speaking Question 11

WALK THROUGH: Express an Opinion pg 72
A What You'll See and Hear
Main Questions: Would you rather live in a big city or a small town? Why?

GET IT RIGHT: Understanding the Topic and Question
TIP 1 TASK pg 74

1. f	**3.** d	**5.** e
2. a	**4.** b	**6.** c

TIP 2 TASK pg 74

1. b	**3.** a	**5.** c
2. c	**4.** c	**6.** a

GET IT RIGHT: Structuring Your Response
TIP 1 TASK pg 76

1. d	**3.** b	**5.** a
2. c	**4.** f	**6.** e

TIP 2 TASK pg 76
(*Answers will vary.*)

1. In my opinion, attending a yearly three-day company trip is a lot to ask. There are a number of reasons I feel this way.
2. If I were planning a vacation, I would prefer to go to the beach. I prefer the beach for a few different reasons.
3. I would rather keep vacation days than get a raise. While some people may think that getting a raise is better, I don't feel that way.
4. I believe that young people should be able to drive before they're 21. I have this opinion for the following reasons.

TIP 3 TASK pg 77

1. **Key Point 1:** relaxing is important for feeling good
   Key Point 2: relaxing can help you sleep better
   Key Point 3: being busy all the time makes you tired / cuts focus
2. **Key Point 1:** hate crowds
   Key Point 2: can compare prices more easily
   Key Point 3: like getting delivery
3. **Key Point 1:** not fair
   Key Point 2: don't like people getting rewards for doing a bad job
   Key Point 3: should actually reduce pay for doing a bad job
4. **Key Point 1:** more convenient / don't need to drive to work
   Key Point 2: can do other things while you work
   Key Point 3: can get more done
5. **Key Point 1:** all young people should have a chance to study / helps them get jobs

Key Point 2: use taxes for education instead of other things
Key Point 3: cost is not that high
6. **Key Point 1:** Why pay for other people's Internet? / big cost to some people
   Key Point 2: city should pay for it
   Key Point 3: free wireless not a big advantage anymore

TIP 4 TASK 1 pg 78
(*Answers will vary.*)

1. <u>So basically,</u> I think that electric cars will not solve the world's pollution problems.
2. <u>In general,</u> I agree that if you work hard, you will be successful.
3. <u>All in all, I'd have to say</u> I would rather work for a small company.

TIP 4 TASK 2 pg 78
Answers will vary.

Progressive Practice: Get Ready pg 79
Part A
b. preferences about something

Part B pg 79
3, 8, 1, 6, 5, 2, 7, 4

Part C pg 80
Sample Response: I think I would prefer to <u>eat most of my meals at home.</u> I have several reasons for this. First, I think the food tastes better at <u>home.</u> This is because <u>I am a good cook, and I have a lot of delicious recipes.</u> In addition to that, I think it is more enjoyable to eat at <u>home</u> because <u>it's more relaxing to eat in your own house than at a noisy restaurant.</u> Finally, I think <u>you can save a lot of money by eating at home.</u> The reason I feel this way is <u>because it's usually cheaper to buy groceries than to buy food at a restaurant.</u>

Progressive Practice: Get Set pg 81
Part A

1. support or opposition
2. (*Answers will vary.*) I disagree with the statement. I believe that young people should be able to drive cars when they turn sixteen.
3. (*Answers will vary.*) The main reasons, details, and examples to support my opinion are:
   a. Young people are mature enough to drive when they turn sixteen (not all teenagers are irresponsible).
   b. Letting young people drive encourages them to be independent (they can get jobs).
   c. Parents will have more free time (they won't have to drive their children to school, sports practice, etc.).

Part B pg 81
3, 6, 1, 5, 7, 8, 4, 2, 9

Part C pg 82
Sample Response:

[State opinion] I disagree with the statement that young people should not be allowed to drive cars until they are twenty-one years old.

[Introduce supporting information] I feel this way for several reasons.

[Key point 1] First, I think that young people are mature enough to drive when they turn sixteen years old.

[Supporting details 1] Most people think people who are sixteen are immature, but this is not true—there are a lot of teenagers who are responsible at this age.

[Key point 2] Second, letting young people drive encourages them to be independent at an early age.

[Supporting details 2] When young people start to drive, they can easily find jobs and start to make their own money.

[Key point 3] Finally, letting young people drive when they're sixteen means their parents will have more free time.

[Supporting details 3] Parents won't have to drive their children to school and to sports practice, because the teenagers can drive themselves to those things.

[Restate opinion] So overall, I'd have to say I think young people should be able to drive long before they are twenty-one years old.

Progressive Practice: Go for the TOEIC Test pg 83

Sample Response: I support the plan to build a large shopping mall in my neighborhood because it would benefit the neighborhood in several ways. First of all, it would make shopping a lot more convenient for local residents. Currently, we have only a few small stores in the area, and they mostly sell groceries and a few other things. If we want to buy clothes or things for the house or books or just about anything, we have to travel several miles to get to the nearest shopping mall. The other important reason why I support this plan is because it would bring more jobs to our neighborhood. There are a lot of opportunities for employment at a shopping mall. There are jobs in stores and restaurants, management jobs, and maintenance jobs, for example. I think a new shopping mall would definitely be a good thing.

Sample Response Analysis: This response clearly states the speaker's opinion and supports the opinion with two main supporting ideas and many details. It uses appropriate vocabulary and correct structures. The ideas are well organized, and the connections are smooth.

Speaking Practice Test pgs 86–89

Question 3 Sample Response: Two people are walking down a sidewalk—a man and a woman. I think they are businesspeople because they are dressed in business suits. The man is carrying a briefcase, and the woman is also carrying something in her hand. They are looking at each other as they walk, so maybe they are having a conversation about something. It looks like they are walking in a park. There are trees behind them, and there's also grass on the ground. Behind them are some tall buildings, so they are in a city.

Question 4 Sample Response: The sport that I enjoy the most is bicycle riding. I really love getting on my bike and riding all through the park near my house. That's really the only sport I practice.

Question 5 Sample Response: I ride my bike at least once a week, on Saturday mornings. Sometimes I also take a ride during the week if I have time.

Question 6 Sample Response: Yes, I think it is important for children to practice sports. First, children need to get a lot of exercise, so if they have sports that they enjoy, then it is easy for them to get the exercise they need. Also, learning to play on a team is important for children. It helps them learn how to work together with other children, and it helps them learn about competition.

Question 7 Sample Response: Certainly. Let me check. It looks like the tour begins at the front entrance to the gardens, located at number 301 South Main Street.

Question 8 Sample Response: Yes, of course. Tickets are 25 dollars each, but there's a special discount. If you buy your ticket before May 15, it will cost only 20 dollars.

Question 9 Sample Response: Yes, there will be two meals, so you don't need to worry about getting hungry. First, there will be lunch served in the Garden Café at 12 o'clock. Then, at the end of the tour, tea and pastries will be served in the outdoor garden.

Question 10 Sample Response: Hello, Mr. Webster. Thank you for your call about the books you ordered. I'm sorry you've been waiting so long to receive them. I know how important those books are to you. It seems that there was a delay in sending your package, so unfortunately it might be another week before it arrives. However, I am going to send you a new package with the same books. I am going to send it by express mail this afternoon. That way it should arrive at your house in two days, so you will still have some time to start reading the books before your class begins. Of course there will be no extra charge for this. Thank you very much for your patience. Please let me know if you have more questions.

Question 11 Sample Response: My preference is definitely for public transportation. There are several reasons for this. The first one is convenience. In the city where I live, I can take a bus or subway to almost any place I want to go. When I get to my destination, I don't have to worry about finding a parking space. It's so easy. Public transportation is also cheaper. It's true that I have to pay the fare every time I ride the bus or subway, but I think the costs of owning a car are greater. You have to buy the car, pay for gasoline, pay for repairs, and maybe even pay for a place to keep it. I think that costs more than bus and subway fare. Finally, there are a lot of traffic problems in my city, but when I am riding the bus or subway, I don't have to worry about traffic. I can just relax and enjoy the ride. I think public transportation is a much better way to get around than a private car is.

Writing Questions 1–5

GET IT RIGHT: Grammar and Vocabulary
TIP 1 TASK pg 97

1. She rides a bike.
2. Sally looks at the screen.
3. The map is folded.
4. The book is on the table.
5. The refrigerator is empty.

TIP 2 TASK pg 98

1. I need to order some pens.

2. We went to New York in June.

3. Did Mr. Smith call you?

4. The Spanish book is on the desk.

5. Has the flight from Paris, France arrived?

TIP 3 TASK pg 98

1. are

2. are making

3. is

4. is writing

5. is

GET IT RIGHT: Prepositions and Modifiers

TIP 1 TASK pg 99 *(Answers will vary.)*

1. There is a clock hanging in between two photo frames.

2. There is a laptop on top of the table.

3. There are two bottles and a glass next to the phone.

TIP 2 TASK pg 100

1. The ☐ cookies ☐ were ☑.

2. The ☑ film ☐ starts ☐ at ☐ 8:00.

3. The ☑ man ☐ looks ☐ at ☐ his ☐ watch ☐.

TIP 3 TASK pg 100

1. yet

2. Whereas

3. either; or

4. about

GET IT RIGHT: Writing Your Response

TIP 1 TASK pg 101

1. noun / verb

2. noun / preposition

3. noun / noun

4. verb / noun

5. noun / adjective

TIP 2 TASK 1 pg 102

(Answers will vary.)

1. The woman / is wearing / a suit.

2. The whiteboard / is / behind the woman.

3. The woman / is holding / the documents.

TIP 2 TASK 2 pg 102

1. is setting

2. chairs

3. is looking

TIP 3 TASK pg 103

(Answers will vary.)

connecting: The woman is holding a pen / and some papers.

contrast: Whereas the woman is standing, / her colleagues are sitting.

stating a condition: As the woman points to the whiteboard, / she faces the audience.

GET IT RIGHT: Two-Clause Responses

TIP TASK pg 103

1. unless

2. Because

3. so

4. yet

GET IT RIGHT: Relevancy

TIP TASK pg 104

1. a

2. a

Progressive Practice: Get Ready pg 105

Part A

Photo 1 – Word 1: noun; Word 2: noun; Subj. / Obj: flowers, table; Verb: are

Photo 2 – Word 1: noun; Word 2: verb; Subj. / Obj: man, ball; Verb: is kicking

Photo 3 – Word 1: noun; Word 2: preposition; Subj. / Obj: woman, door; Verb: is standing

Part B pg 106

1. a, [✓]

2. b, [✓]

3. [✓], c

Part C pg 106

1. The vase is on the table.

2. The man is playing soccer in the stadium.

3. The woman is carrying a tray.

Progressive Practice: Get Set pg 107

Part A

Photo 1 – Word 1: noun; Word 2: adverb; Subject: box; Verb: is

Photo 2 – Word 1: verb; Word 2: preposition; Subject: man; Verb: is sitting

Photo 3 – Word 1: subordinating conjunction; Word 2: verb; Clause 1 Subject: it; Clause 1 Verb: is raining; Clause 2 Subject: women; Clause 2 Verb: is standing

(Clauses 1 and 2 could be reversed; the order doesn't matter.)

Part B pg 108

1. The box is very heavy.

2. The man is sitting on a bench.

3. Even though it is raining, the woman is standing outside.

(or The woman is standing outside even though it is raining.)

Part C pg 108 *(Answers will vary.)*

1. The man is carrying the box on his back.

2. The man is sitting on the bench while he is reading.

3. The woman is very cold.

Progressive Practice: Go for the TOEIC Test pg 109

Sample Responses

Photo 1: The wind is blowing hard.

Photo 2: The clothes are hanging in the closet.

Photo 3: The woman is eating spaghetti for lunch.

Photo 4: She will buy the shoes if they fit well.

Photo 5: He is writing while he talks on the phone.

Analysis: These responses contain no grammatical errors. In addition, they use both key words appropriately and are relevant to the photo.

Writing Questions 6–7

GET IT RIGHT: Understanding the E-mails and the Questions
TIP 1 TASK pg 113

Sample E-mail 1: Elisa Hays; Front Desk Supervisor; Front desk agents, Hotel Mediterraneo; Reservation system; **Correct Answer:** b

Sample E-mail 2: Daniel Olivares; Owner, Olivares Shipping Inc.; Administrative Staff; Vacation; **Correct Answer:** b

Sample E-mail 3: Walter Terborg; Human Resources; Rita Chen; Application for employment; **Correct Answer:** a

TIP 2 TASK pg 115

1. describe THREE problems with the reservation system; ☑ Information about reservations was lost.; ☑ The system shut down suddenly.; ☑ A new reservation could not be booked.

2. give TWO administrative tasks that you can perform while Ms. Weston is gone and ONE range of dates during which you plan to be on vacation; ☑ Collect time sheets from employees; ☑ File any incoming documents; ☑ April 3 to April 7

3. describe TWO application materials you submitted and ask ONE question about the position; ☑ A list of references; ☑ An updated résumé; ☑ How much does the position pay?

GET IT RIGHT: Structuring Your Response
TIP 1 TASK pg 116

Response A: 2   Response B: 3   Response C: 1

TIP 2 TASK pg 118

1. Dear Lisa,; informal greeting

2. Talk to you soon!; closing

3. I feel that . . .; opinion

4. Would it be possible for you . . . ?; polite request

5. Thanks.; informal concluding statement *or* Sincerely,; closing

Progressive Practice: Get Ready pg 119
Part A
Question 6
1. a   **2.** a – 2, c – 1
Question 7
1. c   **2.** a – 1, d – 2

Part B pg 120
Question 7 ; 6, 4, 3, 2, 5, 1
Question 6 ; 6, 4, 3, 2, 5

Progressive Practice: Get Set pg 122
Part A
Question 6
1. A problem with an order
2. Explain a problem – 2; Make a request – 1
Question 7
1. Entertaining guests
2. Make a suggestion – 2; Help with a task – 1

Part B pg 123
Question 6
6, 1, 3, 4, 7, 2, 5

Question 7
4, 3, 5, 2, 1, 7, 6

Progressive Practice: Go for the TOEIC Test pg 125

Sample Responses
Question 6 E-mail
Dear Mr. George,

I have received your e-mail about my decision to change banks. I would be happy to explain this decision to you. I decided to use another bank because your bank doesn't have any branches close to my job. You might be able to get more customers if you opened more branches in different neighborhoods. I also suggest that you place cash machines in more locations around the city. If you make going to your bank more convenient, I think your customers will be happier.

Sincerely,
Janet Jones

Sample Answer Analysis: This e-mail addresses all three tasks. It explains one problem (no branches close to the writer's job) and makes two suggestions (open more branches and have more cash machines). It is well organized with opening and concluding statements and has good transitions between ideas. It is also free of grammar and vocabulary errors.

Question 7 E-mail
Hi John,

I got your message about the budget report. I'm sorry, but I really need to have that report finished by next Friday. If I asked two other people to help you, would you be able to finish it by then? I need the report because we are going to discuss the budget at a meeting on Friday. We will have more money for our department next year, so it is important to know how we spent our money this year. Let me know if you want more help.

Thanks.
Shirley

Sample Answer Analysis: This e-mail addresses all three tasks. It asks one question ("If I asked two other people to help you, would you be able to finish it by then?") and gives two pieces of information ("we are going to discuss the budget at a meeting on Friday" and "we will have more money for our department next year"). It is well organized with opening and concluding statements and has good transitions between ideas. It is also free of grammar and vocabulary errors.

Writing Question 8

GET IT RIGHT: Understanding the Topic and the Question
TIP 1 TASK pg 129

(1) advantages or disadvantages

(2) do you prefer

(3) your opinion of this

(4) agree or disagree

(5) Why do you think that references are important to employers?

TIP 2 TASK pg 130

1. b **3.** b **5.** a
2. b **4.** a

GET IT RIGHT: Structuring Your Response
TIP 1 TASK pg 131

a. 2 **d.** 3
b. 4 **e.** 5
c. 1

TIP 2 TASK pg 131–132

A. 4 **D.** 1
B. 5 **E.** 3
C. 2

TIP 3 TASK pg 132–133

2, 1, 3, 5, 4

TIP 4 TASK pg 135

1. Personally **5.** Lastly
2. First of all **6.** Conversely
3. Generally **7.** On the other hand
4. Next **8.** To summarize

TIP 5 TASK pg 136

1. a **2.** b **3.** a

TIP 6 TASK pg 136

Incomplete sentence: Nice to go home for lunch.; **Grammar error:** Third, live near work is more convenient . . .; **Spelling error:** advntges; **Capitalization error:** the Office; **Punctuation error:** There are several advantages to living near the office, including saving time and money, and it is very convenient?

Progressive Practice: Get Ready pg 137
Part A

1. c **2.** a

Part B pg 137 *(Answers will vary.)*

1. agree or disagree that a small town is better than a city for raising children.
2. I agree with the statement.
3. I agree that a small town is a better place to raise children.
4. small towns are safer; people in small towns are nicer; life in small towns is less expensive

Part C pgs 137–138

3, 7, 1, 4, 5, 6, 2

Progressive Practice: Get Set pg 139
Part B page 139

Introduction: 3, 2, 1
Body Paragraph 1: 3, 1, 4, 2
Body Paragraph 2: 1, 2, 4, 3
Body Paragraph 3: 2, 3, 4, 1
Conclusion: 2, 1, 3

Progressive Practice: Go for the TOEIC Test pg 142
Sample Response

Because of modern technology, many people do most of their work at home instead of at an office. There are both advantages and disadvantages to this situation. Working at home is very convenient for the employee. However, it makes supervision of work and collaborating with co-workers more difficult.

The main advantage of working at home is convenience for the employee. A person who works at home does not have to get up early to get dressed and ready for work. The person doesn't have to spend time traveling between home and the office. This means the employee has more time to pay attention to home and family as well as having more energy to devote to work.

On the other hand, there are several disadvantages for the employer. An important one is supervision. It is much more difficult for a supervisor to manage the work of several employees if each one is working in a different place. It is hard for the supervisor to provide support and to make sure that each employee is actually working during work hours.

It is also difficult for co-workers to collaborate on projects if each one is working at home. When co-workers are working in different places, then formal meetings are difficult to schedule and informal meetings become impossible. This can have a major effect on the quality of the work. It also makes it difficult for the employer to form work teams and organize projects.

There is a current trend toward working at home. These days, more and more people are doing it. There are certainly advantages to following this trend, but there are also disadvantages. Each employer has to take several things into consideration before deciding if allowing employees to work at home is the best plan for the company.

Sample Response Analysis: This essay clearly addresses the topic. It has a clear thesis with supporting ideas that are developed in the body of the essay with examples and details. It has an introduction and a conclusion. There are smooth transitions between ideas. It uses a variety of sentence types, is free of grammar and vocabulary errors, and is the proper length.

Writing Practice Test

Question 1 Sample Response pg 144 The woman is paying for her groceries.

Question 2 Sample Response pg 145 They're walking over the bridge.

Question 3 Sample Response pg 145 The passenger is boarding the bus.

Question 4 Sample Response pg 146 They are taking a walk outside although it is cold.

Question 5 Sample Response pg 146 As soon as the food is ready, she will serve it.

Analysis: These responses contain no grammatical errors. In addition, they use both key words appropriately and are relevant to the picture.

Question 6 Sample Response pg 147

Hi George,

I got your message about the Social Committee meeting next Friday. I am sorry but I will be unable to attend because I have a dentist appointment at that time. I would like to suggest that you ask all the committee members when they are free for a meeting and then choose a new meeting time based on that information. Also, I think that Conference Room B is a better place for a meeting because it is a larger and more comfortable room. I am looking forward to working on the plans for the year-end party.

Samantha

Analysis: This e-mail addresses all three tasks. It explains one problem (she can't attend the meeting because of a dentist appointment) and makes two suggestions (ask committee members when they are free and have the meeting in Conference Room B). In addition, it is well organized with opening and concluding statements and has good transitions between ideas. It is also free of grammar and vocabulary errors.

Question 7 Sample Response pg 148

Dear *Journal of Business News*,

I have received the information about subscribing to your journal. I have a few questions about your journal. First, you offer a 30% discount off the regular price. What is the regular price? Also, I would like to know how frequently your journal is published. Finally, would you be able to send me a sample issue before I pay for a subscription? Thank you for your help.

Thanks,
David Jones

Analysis: This e-mail addresses all three tasks. It asks three questions (what is the regular price, how frequently is the journal published, and can you send a sample issue). In addition, it is well organized with opening and concluding statements and has good transitions between ideas. It is also free of grammar and vocabulary errors.

Question 8 Sample Response pg 149

Some people think that it is more important to work at a job you enjoy than to make a lot of money. I have to say that I agree with this statement. If you work at a job you enjoy, you will probably do your job better than if you work at a job only to earn money. You will also feel happier. Money has its uses, but everyone knows that it doesn't buy happiness.

Most people do their work better when they have a job they enjoy. If they are interested in their work, they are willing to put more effort into it. They will take the time to learn more about their profession and improve their skills. They don't mind spending extra time on the job when that is required. Overall, they have a good attitude toward their job, and that can improve the way they do it.

When people enjoy their jobs, they feel happier. They are happy to go to work. They are also happy outside of work hours because they don't feel the stresses of an unpleasant job. Since most people spend a large percentage of their lives at their jobs, it is important to have a job that brings happiness.

Earning a lot of money is a goal for many people, but money does not lead to a happy life. If you focus on making money, you may miss the opportunity to bring other things into your life, such as self-fulfillment, love and friendships, and just relaxing and enjoying yourself. If, on the other hand, you focus your work on doing something you enjoy, you will be happy whether or not you also earn a lot of money.

The best way to have a good life is to do work that you enjoy. That may or may not be work that earns you a lot of money. It will, however, be something that makes your life better.

Analysis: This essay clearly addresses the topic. It has a clear thesis with supporting ideas that are developed in the body of the essay with examples and details. It has an introduction and a conclusion. There are smooth transitions between ideas. It uses a variety of sentence types, is free of grammar and vocabulary errors, and is the proper length. This essay is 324 words long.

Audio Scripts for Speaking

Questions 1–2

Track 01-02.01 pg 3
Narrator: Speaking Questions 1 and 2
WALK THROUGH: Read a Text Aloud
What You'll See and Hear
Directions: In this part, you will read a text aloud. You will have 45 seconds to prepare and 45 seconds to read the text aloud.

Track 01-02.02 pg 3
Narrator: Speaking Questions 1 and 2
WALK THROUGH: What You'll Do
Sample Response
Man: The city's annual summer festival will take place next Saturday and Sunday. There will be activities that are fun for the whole family. You can try a variety of food, hear different kinds of music, and enjoy games for all ages. Tickets cost fifteen dollars at the gate. However, if you buy your ticket in advance, you will get a ten percent discount. Tickets are available at many local stores, as well as at City Hall. Don't miss this fun event!

Track 01-02.03 pg 3
Narrator: Speaking Questions 1 and 2
GET IT RIGHT: Pronunciation
Woman: pronunciation or pronunciation [prə-ˌnən-sē-ˈā-shən or prə-ˌnənt-sē-ˈā-shən]

Track 01-02.04 pg 4
Narrator: Speaking Questions 1 and 2
GET IT RIGHT: Stress
Man: The meeting will be in the conference room.

Track 01-02.05 pg 4

Narrator: Speaking Questions 1 and 2

GET IT RIGHT: Intonation

Man: We have a meeting on Tuesday.

Man: We'll be talking about sales, earnings, and future plans.

Man: What time is the meeting?

Man: Is the meeting at 2:00?

Track 01-02.06 pg 4

Narrator: Speaking Questions 1 and 2

GET IT RIGHT: Sample Response

Man: Could we have your attention, please? We'd like to take this time to thank you for attending this athletic banquet. This has been a fantastic year for our team and our athletes. We now hold a new record for most wins in our state's division. Your support has allowed us to purchase new uniforms and a new scoreboard for our field. To show our appreciation for the coaches, the staff, and our fans, we'd like to invite you to view the new scoreboard, enjoy some refreshments, and meet the team. Let's give a round of applause for the three candidates for player of the year.

Track 01-02.07 pgs 4–5

Narrator: Speaking Questions 1 and 2

GET IT RIGHT: Pronunciation
TIP 1

Woman: /th/, /thl/, /thr/, /ths/   thing, athlete, throw, months

Woman: /ð/   then, clothes

Woman: /kl/, /kr/   clear, create

Woman: /l/   like, whole, shelf, flake, place, blend

Woman: /r/   repair, server, trip, prescribe, clerk, course

Woman: /s/   silence, ceremony, study, streets, script

Woman: /z/   zero, wisdom, wins

Woman: /w/   window, wagon

Woman: /sh/   shield, motion, wish

Woman: /ch/   child, lunch, watch

Woman: /j/   jump, dodge, lounge

Woman: /v/   volume, curve, shelves

Track 01-02.08 pg 5

Narrator: Speaking Questions 1 and 2

GET IT RIGHT: Pronunciation
TIP 1 TASK 1
Number 1.

Man: /th/   thin

Narrator: Number 2.

Man: /l/   laughed

Narrator: Number 3.

Man: /s/   sip

Narrator: Number 4.

Man: /ðz/   clothes

Narrator: Number 5.

Man: /j/   junk

Narrator: Number 6.

Man: /nch/   lunch

Narrator: Number 7.

Man: /br/   bright

Narrator: Number 8.

Man: /st/   stare

Narrator: Number 9.

Man: /sh/   she'll

Narrator: Number 10.

Man: /ch/   watch

Narrator: Number 11.

Man: /f/   fans

Narrator: Number 12.

Man: /v/   veer

Narrator: Number 13.

Man: /z/   zinc

Narrator: Number 14.

Man: /ð/   than

Track 01-02.09 pg 6

Narrator: Speaking Questions 1 and 2

GET IT RIGHT: Pronunciation
TIP 1 TASK 2
Number 1.

Woman: den

Narrator: Number 2.

Man: though

Narrator: Number 3.

Woman: think

Narrator: Number 4.

Man: sink

Narrator: Number 5.

Woman: right

Narrator: Number 6.

Man: tow

Narrator: Number 7.

Woman: then

Narrator: Number 8.

Man: light

Narrator: Number 9.

Woman: wind

Narrator: Number 10.

Man: clean

Narrator: Number 11.

Woman: cream

Narrator: Number 12.

Man: vend

Track 01-02.10 pg 6

Narrator: Speaking Questions 1 and 2

GET IT RIGHT: Pronunciation
TIP 2 TASK 1
Number 1.

Woman: corporate

Narrator: Number 2.

Man: invaluable

Narrator: Number 3.

Woman: February

Narrator: Number 4.

Man: automatically

Narrator: Number 5.

Woman: candidate

Narrator: Number 6.

Man: frequently

Narrator: Number 7.

Woman: cooperation

Narrator: Number 8.

Man: athletics

Narrator: Number 9.

Woman: librarian

Narrator: Number 10.

Man: unfortunately

Track 01-02.11 pg 6

Narrator: Speaking Questions 1 and 2

GET IT RIGHT: Pronunciation
TIP 2 TASK 2
Number 1.

Woman: career

Narrator: Number 2.

Man: carrier

Narrator: Number 3.

Woman: advertisement

Narrator: Number 4.

Man: improbable

Narrator: Number 5.

Woman: corporation

Narrator: Number 6.

Man: clothes

Narrator: Number 7.

Woman: asked

Narrator: Number 8.

Man: intelligent

Narrator: Number 9.

Woman: dependability

Narrator: Number 10.

Man: acquisition

Narrator: Number 11.

Woman: regional

Track 01-02.12 pg 7

Narrator: Speaking Questions 1 and 2

GET IT RIGHT: Stress

TIP 1

Woman: CON-duct / con-DUCT

Man: CON-test / con-TEST

Woman: EX-port / ex-PORT

Man: IM-port / im-PORT

Woman: IN-crease / in-CREASE

Man: PRO-ject / pro-JECT

Woman: PER-mit / per-MIT

Man: PRO-duce / pro-DUCE

Woman: OB-ject / ob-JECT

Man: SUB-ject / sub-JECT

Woman: SUR-vey / sur-VEY

Man: RE-fund / re-FUND

Track 01-02.13 pg 7

Narrator: Speaking Questions 1 and 2

GET IT RIGHT: Stress

TIP 1 TASK 1

Number 1.

Woman: You really need to learn how to <u>conduct</u> yourself in a meeting.

Narrator: Number 2.

Man: There are several important <u>projects</u> coming up.

Narrator: Number 3.

Woman: We have to <u>address</u> the problems to avoid issues later.

Narrator: Number 4.

Man: They <u>import</u> most of their auto parts.

Narrator: Number 5.

Woman: He set a new sales <u>record</u> last month.

Narrator: Number 6.

Man: We've made most of our money in <u>produce</u>.

Narrator: Number 7.

Woman: Business is set to <u>increase</u> next year.

Narrator: Number 8.

Man: She decided to <u>contest</u> the decision to fire the people.

Track 01-02.14 pg 7

Narrator: Speaking Questions 1 and 2

GET IT RIGHT: Stress

TIP 1 TASK 2

Number 1.

Woman: authorize

Narrator: Number 2.

Man: interruption

Narrator: Number 3.

Woman: recreation

Narrator: Number 4.

Man: validate

Narrator: Number 5.

Narrator: Number 12.

Man: liability

Woman: version

Narrator: Number 6.

Man: geography

Narrator: Number 7.

Woman: geographic

Narrator: Number 8.

Man: appreciate

Narrator: Number 9.

Woman: accommodations

Narrator: Number 10.

Man: estimate

Narrator: Number 11.

Woman: interpretation

Narrator: Number 12.

Man: notarize

Narrator: Number 13.

Woman: policy

Narrator: Number 14.

Man: location

Narrator: Number 15.

Woman: cooperate

Narrator: Number 16.

Man: direction

Narrator: Number 17.

Woman: evaluate

Narrator: Number 18.

Man: recognize

Narrator: Number 19.

Woman: suspension

Narrator: Number 20.

Man: charity

Narrator: Number 21.

Woman: democracy

Track 01-02.15 pg 8

Narrator: Speaking Questions 1 and 2

GET IT RIGHT: Stress

TIP 1 TASK 3

Number 1.

Man: descendent

Narrator: Number 2.

Woman: underestimate

Narrator: Number 3.

Man: overuse

Narrator: Number 4.

Woman: belated

Narrator: Number 5.

Man: renew

Narrator: Number 6.

Woman: extensive

Narrator: Number 7.

Man: dislocate

Narrator: Number 8.

Woman: extract

Narrator: Number 9.

Man: outstanding

Narrator: Number 10.

Woman: completely

Narrator: Number 11.

Man: unable

Narrator: Number 12.

Woman: respectable

Narrator: Number 13.

Man: redundant

Narrator: Number 14.

Woman: inspect

Narrator: Number 15.

Man: unusable

Narrator: Number 16.

Woman: contented

Narrator: Number 17.

Man: reduction

Narrator: Number 18.

Woman: complaint

Track 01-02.16 pg 8

Narrator: Speaking Questions 1 and 2

GET IT RIGHT: Stress

TIP 1 TASK 4

Number 1.

Man: Please use this software to <u>record</u> the day's sales.

Narrator: Number 2.

Woman: All employees are expected to follow the company code of <u>conduct</u>.

Narrator: Number 3.

Man: Let's not <u>overestimate</u> the amount of work we can do.

Narrator: Number 4.

Woman: Before we create our business plan for the month, let's <u>coordinate</u> our schedules.

Narrator: Number 5.

Man: <u>Prosperity</u> is the goal of all <u>nations</u>.

Narrator: Number 6.

Woman: After you receive your pass code, you will have <u>authorization</u>.

Narrator: Number 7.

Man: This year, we decided to <u>recognize</u> our supervisor for his 10 years of service.

Narrator: Number 8.

Woman: We <u>project</u> that our product sales will <u>increase</u> over the next two years.

Narrator: Number 9.

Man: It was a great <u>comfort</u> to <u>receive</u> your letter.

Narrator: Number 10.

Woman: She studied <u>biology</u> at the <u>university</u>.

Narrator: Number 11.

Man: As we <u>progress</u> with this <u>project</u>, we will give everyone a monthly <u>report</u>.

Narrator: Number 12.

Woman: The marketing team really <u>outdid</u> themselves with this <u>detailed</u> <u>explanation</u>.

Track 01-02.17 pg 9

Narrator: Speaking Questions 1 and 2

GET IT RIGHT: Stress

TIP 2, Example 1

Woman: Would you like some tea?

Man: I'd like some <u>black</u> tea.

Woman: Sure, here you are.

Man: Sorry, but this is <u>green</u> tea. I asked for <u>black</u> tea.

Track 01-02.18 pg 9

Narrator: Speaking Questions 1 and 2

GET IT RIGHT: Stress

TIP 2, Example 2

Man: The <u>employees</u> are the ones to <u>thank</u>.

Woman: There's really not a lot to <u>say</u> about that.

Track 01-02.19 pg 9

Narrator: Speaking Questions 1 and 2

GET IT RIGHT: Stress

TIP 2, Example 3

Man: We <u>really</u> don't have much time.

Woman: I <u>completely</u> forgot the conference.

Track 01-02.20 pg 9

Narrator: Speaking Questions 1 and 2

GET IT RIGHT: Stress

TIP 2 TASK 1

Number 1.

Man: The correct numbers are <u>13</u> and <u>17</u>, not 30 and 70.

Narrator: Number 2.

Woman: We <u>strongly</u> suggest that you back up your computer files at the end of the day.

Narrator: Number 3.

Man: Our genealogists will conduct a very <u>thorough</u> search of your family tree.

Narrator: Number 4.

Woman: On the <u>new</u> schedule, you will see that the bus departs on <u>Tuesday</u> at 1 p.m.

Narrator: Number 5.

Man: Your estimated wait time to speak to a representative is <u>ten</u> minutes.

Narrator: Number 6.

Woman: The parking spaces are clearly marked "<u>visitor.</u>"

Track 01-02.21 pg 9

Narrator: Speaking Questions 1 and 2

GET IT RIGHT: Stress

TIP 2 TASK 2

Number 1.

Man: The real estate office is located in the <u>green</u> house on the left.

Narrator: Number 2.

Woman: You will receive a credit card within <u>ten days</u> after receipt of your application.

Narrator: Number 3.

Man: The message said to phone their office between <u>9 and 5</u>, Monday to Friday.

Narrator: Number 4.

Woman: We are currently reviewing your request and will respond <u>within 30</u> days.

Narrator: Number 5.

Man: Please turn <u>down</u> the volume on the TV, not up.

Track 01-02.22 pg 10

Narrator: Speaking Questions 1 and 2

GET IT RIGHT: Intonation and Pausing

TIP 1, Example 1

Woman: We've had a lot of success with the new plan.

Man: There are a multitude of reasons for the problem.

Woman: She really hasn't done much in her new position.

Track 01-02.23 pg 10

Narrator: Speaking Questions 1 and 2

GET IT RIGHT: Intonation and Pausing

TIP 1, Example 2

Man: The key points here are time, expense, and quality.

Woman: Hotel management, health care, accounting, and education are all good career options.

Man: Our new number is 218-555-3675.

Track 01-02.24 pg 10

Narrator: Speaking Questions 1 and 2

GET IT RIGHT: Intonation and Pausing

TIP 1, Example 3

Woman: Because we don't have the reports yet, we can't have the meeting.

Man: We really wanted to leave at 5:00; however, the plane was delayed.

Woman: I really wanted to go to the conference until I saw the huge entry fees.

Man: Although I usually enjoy my job, this past month has been tough.

Track 01-02.25 pg 10

Narrator: Speaking Questions 1 and 2

GET IT RIGHT: Intonation and Pausing

TIP 1 TASK

Number 1.

Woman: We will need ushers, ticket takers, and box office staff at the theater this weekend.

Narrator: Number 2.

Man: At this time, there is no one available to take your call. Please leave a message after the beep.

Narrator: Number 3.

Woman: Our number is 202-555-4567. Please call if you have any problems.

Narrator: Number 4.

Man: Because the application forms were late, we'll need to adjust the start date.

Narrator: Number 5.

Woman: Please turn off all cell phones and pagers before the movie begins.

Narrator: Number 6.

Man: In conclusion, we'd like to thank all of our guests for their participation.

Track 01-02.26 pg 11

Narrator: Speaking Questions 1 and 2

GET IT RIGHT: Intonation and Pausing

TIP 2, Example 1

Woman: What did you do last weekend?

Man: Where is the meeting?

Woman: Why didn't he call?

Man: When do we need to be there?

Woman: How many people are coming?

Man: How much does it cost?

Track 01-02.27 pg 11

Narrator: Speaking Questions 1 and 2

GET IT RIGHT: Intonation and Pausing

TIP 2, Example 2

Woman: Do you want to join the call?

Man: Have you seen the report?

Woman: Those are my files, aren't they?

Man: Could you open that file?

Track 01-02.28 pg 11

Narrator: Speaking Questions 1 and 2

GET IT RIGHT: Intonation and Pausing

TIP 2 TASK

Number 1.

Woman: What do you think?

Narrator: Number 2.

Man: If Friday is not a good day, can we meet on Saturday?

Narrator: Number 3.

Woman: I'm sorry, could you repeat that, please?

Narrator: Number 4.

Man: We didn't hear that. What did he say?

Narrator: Number 5.

Woman: What did John bring to the party?

Narrator: Number 6.

Man: How can I help you today?

Narrator: Number 7.

Woman: Is this your first day here?

Narrator: Number 8.

Man: Have you sent the latest market reports?

Track 01-02.29 pg 11

Narrator: Speaking Questions 1 and 2

GET IT RIGHT: Intonation and Pausing

TIP 3, Example 1

Woman: According to the monthly report, our production has increased 300% over the past five years. There's only one group to thank for this: you. Our support staff and team members have done so much to help over the past year; we couldn't have done it without you. Our thanks go out to everyone. We really appreciate it.

Track 01-02.30 pg 11

Narrator: Speaking Questions 1 and 2

GET IT RIGHT: Intonation and Pausing

TIP 3, Example 2

Man: Nonetheless, he got the promotion.

Woman: Unfortunately, there's nothing more we can do.

Man: By the time we got to the airport, the plane had gone.

Woman: As a result of the sale, we all got raises.

Track 01-02.31 pg 11

Narrator: Speaking Questions 1 and 2

GET IT RIGHT: Intonation and Pausing,

TIP 3 TASK

Number 1.

Man: They have not yet determined what the problem was.

Narrator: Number 2.

Woman: Would you like the three-month or the six-month plan?

Narrator: Number 3.

Man: Do you know what time it is?

Narrator: Number 4.

Woman: You wouldn't have an extra pencil, would you?

Narrator: Number 5.

Man: Would you mind closing the window?

Narrator: Number 6.

Woman: When you need a reliable copy service, Tip Top Copy Shop has everything you need.

Track 01-02.32 pg 12

Narrator: Speaking Questions 1 and 2

Progressive Practice: Get Ready
Part A Text 1

Woman: Welcome to sunny Yorktown and thank you for joining us today at our first national New Marketers training conference. Please make sure to check in at the booth so that we can record your attendance. The trainers will be on hand to conduct tours of the facilities. You will be given a training handbook and a new employee packet. At the end of today's training session, we'll be handing out surveys. Does anyone have any questions?

Track 01-02.33 pg 12

Narrator: Speaking Questions 1 and 2

Progressive Practice: Get Ready
Part A Text 2

Man: Have you ever been late for work or an appointment because you couldn't find a parking space? If you said yes, then Stop and Park is the answer to all your parking problems. Just call us or go online and tell us your car size and model, give us the address of your destination, and your estimated time of arrival. We'll find a parking space for your car within walking distance and hold it for you until you arrive. For your parking needs, Stop and Park is your best bet!

Track 01-02.34 pg 13

Narrator: Speaking Questions 1 and 2

Progressive Practice: Get Ready
Part B Text 1

1. thank you	9. conduct
2. national	10. facilities
3. marketers	11. handbook
4. conference	12. employee packet
5. sure	13. training session
6. both	14. surveys
7. record	15. anyone
8. attendance	16. questions

Track 01-02.35 pg 13

Narrator: Speaking Questions 1 and 2

Progressive Practice: Get Ready
Part B Text 2

1. late	6. problems
2. appointment	7. model
3. parking	8. address
4. park	9. destination
5. answer	10. estimated

11. arrival	14. for you
12. within	15. arrive
13. distance	

Track 01-02.36 pg 14

Narrator: Speaking Questions 1 and 2

Progressive Practice: Get Set
Part B Text 1: Sample Response

Man: Good afternoon, everyone, and welcome to the county fair! It's wonderful to have you here today as we celebrate the 120th anniversary of our city. We commemorate this day with great pride. Please make sure you visit the exhibits and game booths. Later today there will be competitive events, such as our famous pie-baking contest. I strongly suggest that you get over to the pie table early, or there might not be anything left. It's also my pleasure to introduce you to our mayor, Mr. James Moon. Mr. Moon will lead us in singing our national anthem. Then we'll begin the festivities.

Track 01-02.37 pg 14

Narrator: Speaking Questions 1 and 2

Progressive Practice: Get Set
Part B Text 2: Sample Response

Woman: Are you ready for an adventure? Extreme Sports Center offers the latest in adventurous outdoor sports—skydiving, hang gliding, scuba diving, or rock climbing. We can expedite the process of getting you a scuba diving permit and train you to dive in just a few intensive sessions. Our specialized training sessions with expert instructors will give you all the basics. We also organize packages for extreme-sport vacations. So wherever you want to go, we'll take you there! Go Extreme!

Track 01-02.38 pg 15

Narrator: Speaking Questions 1 and 2

Progressive Practice: Go for the TOEIC Test
Question 1: In this part, you will read a text aloud. You will have 45 seconds to prepare and 45 seconds to read the text aloud.

Track 01-02.39 pg 15

Narrator: Speaking Questions 1 and 2

Progressive Practice: Go for the TOEIC Test
Question 2: In this part, you will read a text aloud. You will have 45 seconds to prepare and 45 seconds to read the text aloud.

Track 01-02.40 pg 15

Narrator: Speaking Questions 1 and 2

Progressive Practice: Go for the TOEIC Test
Question 1 Sample Response

Woman: Good day, everyone, and welcome to the Faraway Spa and Resort. We'd like to call your attention to a few important items. Make sure you register at the front desk and pick up your room keys and introductory packets. Next, you will receive a complimentary certificate for dinner at our gourmet restaurant. Dinner will be served at 6 p.m. and 8 p.m. In your room, you will find a robe, towels, and a gift basket of products, such as bath soaps and lotions. Please feel free to contact us if you have forgotten to bring any personal items with you. We hope you find your stay at Faraway Spa and Resort relaxing and enjoyable.

Track 01-02.41 pg 15

Narrator: Speaking Questions 1 and 2

Progressive Practice: Go for the TOEIC Test

Question 2 Sample Response

Man: Could I have everyone's attention, please? Due to mechanical problems, this bus will now be taken out of service. We apologize for any inconvenience this might cause you. Please exit the bus safely by using the front or back doors and stepping away from the side of the road. We have contacted the main bus depot, and a shuttle bus is presently en route to our location. The shuttle's approximate arrival time is fifteen minutes. Again, we apologize for the delay and appreciate your patience. All connecting buses will be held at the station until our bus arrives. Are there any questions?

Question 3

Track 3-01 pg 17

Narrator: Speaking Question 3

WALK THROUGH: Describe a Picture

What You'll See and Hear

Directions: In this part, you will describe the photo on the screen with as much detail as possible. You will have 30 seconds to prepare. You will have 45 seconds to describe the photo.

Track 3-02 pg 17

Narrator: Speaking Question 3

WALK THROUGH: What You'll Do

Sample Response

Man: Well, there are two people inside a bakery in this photo. The woman who is facing us is probably a baker because she's wearing a white uniform and a black hat to cover her hair. And she's coming out of the kitchen carrying bread. It looks like she has just taken the hot bread out of the oven, and she's carrying the tray to the counter. We can see the oven behind her. The bakery looks very modern. I'd guess that the baker is going to put the bread on some kind of bread rack or a shelf to cool so that people can buy it. She's smiling at the customer. Um, next, she's probably going to help the man in the blue shirt, who's waiting in front of the counter. His back is to us. He's probably hoping to buy some of that delicious fresh bread.

Track 3.03 pg 18

Narrator: Speaking Question 3

GET IT RIGHT: Sample Response 2

Woman: I see two people in this picture. I think this must be a bakery. There's a man on the right with his back to the camera. He's wearing a blue shirt. He must be a customer because he seems to be at the counter waiting to buy something. There's also a woman in the center of the picture. She's facing the camera. She's wearing a white jacket or uniform and a black cap to cover her hair. She's also carrying a large tray of rolls, so I think she must be a baker. It looks like she just took the tray of bread out of the oven. The oven is behind her. The bread probably smells delicious. Maybe the customer was waiting to buy some of the delicious, fresh rolls, or maybe he's going to buy something else at the bakery.

Track 3.04 pg 22

Narrator: Speaking question 3

GET IT RIGHT: Cohesion and Structuring a Response

TIP 2 TASK Sample Response

Man: There are two people in this photo. The man, who is on the right, is wearing a white shirt and gray slacks. He's holding a pair of glasses. The woman, who is on the left, is wearing an orange short-sleeved blouse and black slacks. She is holding a document of some kind in her hand. Both seem to be about 30 years old. It looks like they're in an office because there are office machines and four rows of boxes with slots that are filled with different types of paper and envelopes. The two people are standing next to a copy machine, looking at a document, and talking about something. The document has a lot of pages, so maybe it's a report. Or perhaps it's a manual for some type of office machine.

Track 3.05 pg 23

Narrator: Speaking Question 3

Progressive Practice: Get Ready

Part B Sample Response

Man: There is a computer unit on the right side of the table. On the left, there is a young man with a white shirt leaning over a desk. He's probably a technology expert. The computer cables are at the back of the computer unit, where the young man is working. The younger man is connecting the computer cables. An older man is sitting behind the desk. He's wearing glasses. The older man is watching the younger man fix his computer.

Track 3.06 pg 24

Narrator: Speaking Question 3

Progressive Practice: Get Set

Part A Sample Response

Woman: Well, in this picture, there are four people. It's a really nice, sunny day. They're sitting next to a lake, probably in a park. They're probably a family—a mother and father and their two young sons. They're having a picnic lunch. They have cups, a basket, some fruit, sandwiches, and other things, and these things are on a blanket on the ground. The father and son in the center are eating their watermelon. The mother is sitting on the right, and it looks like she just cut a piece of watermelon for herself. They're probably having a good time.

Track 3.07 pg 25

Narrator: Speaking Question 3

Progressive Practice: Go for the TOEIC Test

In this part, you will describe the photo on the screen with as much detail as possible. You will have 30 seconds to prepare. You will have 45 seconds to describe the photo.

Track 3.08 pg 25

Narrator: Speaking Question 3

Progressive Practice: Go for the TOEIC Test

Sample Response

Man: In this picture, there's a young woman in an orange car. I think maybe she is lost because she has stopped her car and rolled down her window so that she can ask for directions. There's also an older woman with short hair in the picture. She's wearing a white jacket, and she has a map in her hands. She's standing next to the car door and pointing to the map. She looks like she's talking to the younger woman and is probably explaining where the younger woman needs to go. The older woman looks very sure of herself and more confident, while the younger woman looks like she's confused.

Questions 4–6

Track 04-06.01 pg 27

Narrator: Speaking Questions 4 to 6
WALK THROUGH: Respond to Questions
What You'll See and Hear
Directions: In this part, you will answer three questions. Begin responding as soon as you hear the beep for each question. You will have 15 seconds for Questions 4 and 5 and 30 seconds for Question 6. There is no preparation time.

Imagine that an American marketing firm is doing research in your country. You have agreed to participate in a telephone survey about food shopping.

Question 4: What types of food stores are there in your neighborhood?

Question 5: How often do you go food shopping and when do you usually go?

Question 6: Describe what you buy and why you make those purchases.

Track 04-06.02 pg 27

Narrator: Speaking Questions 4 to 6
WALK THROUGH: What You'll Do
Question 4 Sample Response
Man: Well, there are a lot of small general stores and some specialty meat shops in my neighborhood, but I usually like to go to a big supermarket that's not far from where I live.

Narrator: Question 5 Sample Response

Man: I usually go food shopping once or twice a week, and most of the time, I go on Thursday evening. I try to get there between 8 and 9 p.m., when it's not so busy.

Narrator: Question 6 Sample Response

Man: Well, there are so many things—mostly, I like to buy fresh fruit and vegetables and organic foods. I like to eat healthy food, so I think it's really important to shop for natural products. That's what I usually buy. I also like to purchase things on sale, so sometimes I stock up on canned goods and frozen foods.

Track 04-06.03 pg 28

Narrator: Speaking Questions 4 to 6
GET IT RIGHT: Sample Response
Woman: My favorite kind of museum to visit is a natural history museum. I really enjoy seeing exhibits related to Earth, dinosaurs, different animals, and things like geology. For me, those are the most interesting exhibits. I usually spend hours looking around in that kind of museum.

Track 04-06.04 pg 31

Narrator: Speaking Questions 4 to 6
GET IT RIGHT: Structuring Your Response
Question and Sample Response for Speaking Question 4 or 5
Question: What's your favorite place to buy clothing?

Man: My favorite place to buy clothing is Del's Department Store. I like it because the prices are good and the selection is nice. Last year, I got a new winter coat for only $30. I also like it because the clerks there are very friendly. They always say hello and are really helpful.

Track 04-06.05 pg 31

Narrator: Speaking Questions 4 to 6
GET IT RIGHT: Structuring Your Response
Question and Sample Response for Speaking Question 6
Question 6: Describe your favorite restaurant.

Woman: My favorite restaurant is really cozy and nice. It's in an old building, so the atmosphere is really "old-style." The walls are made of brick, and the restaurant is lit with candles. The restaurant serves excellent Italian food. The lasagna is my favorite.

Track 04-06.06 pg 35

Narrator: Speaking Questions 4 to 6
Progressive Practice: Get Ready
Part A
Imagine that a Canadian market research company is conducting a survey about preferred methods of public transportation.
Question 4: What kind of transportation do you take most often? Why?

Question 5: How long is your commute to work every day?
Question 6: Describe one method of public transportation in your city and why it is the best way to travel.

Track 04-06.07 pgs 35–36

Narrator: Speaking Questions 4 to 6
Progressive Practice: Get Ready
Part B Questions and Sample Responses
Question 4: What kind of transportation do you take most often? Why?

Woman: The kind of transportation I take most often is the subway. For me, the subway is a convenient and inexpensive way to travel. I saved a lot of money last year when I stopped driving to work. I also like the subway because I can read while I travel. Reading helps me relax on the way to work.

Narrator: Question 5: How long is your commute to work every day?

Woman: My commute to work takes me only 30 minutes in total every day. It's a short walk from my house to the subway stop. So I think it's very convenient and the best way for me to travel. In addition, the subway stop where I get off is close to my job. I'd have to walk farther to my office if I drove because the nearest parking lot is several blocks away.

Narrator: Question 6: Describe one method of public transportation in your city and why it is the best way to travel.

Woman: I think the best method of public transportation in my city is the subway. The subway is much faster than driving.

Because of the heavy traffic downtown, it can take twice as long to get anywhere with a car or in a taxi or bus. Also, the subway operates 24 hours a day, seven days a week, so that makes it really convenient. The buses stop running at midnight most nights, so you would have to pay for a taxi instead. Plus, the subway stops are close to all the major places in the city. If you look at a map, you don't have to walk more than a few blocks to catch the subway in most areas.

Track 04-06.08 pg 38

Narrator: Speaking Questions 4 to 6

Progressive Practice: Get Set

Part A

Imagine that a European marketing firm is doing research in your country. You have agreed to participate in a phone survey about how people spend their free time.

Question 4: What is your favorite thing to do when you have free time?

Question 5: How much free time do you have during the week, and where do you spend your free time?

Question 6: How do you think the quality of your activities during your free time could be improved?

Track 04-06.09 pg 38

Narrator: Speaking Questions 4 to 6

Progressive Practice: Get Set

Part A Sample Responses

Sample Response A

Woman: I would have to say that the quality of my activities could be greatly improved in two ways. First, the space in which I usually exercise is not as quiet as it could be. I think that the space for exercise should be very quiet and clean. The second thing is that it is not really well organized. There need to be better spaces for storing the yoga mats. Those two things would really make an improvement in the overall quality of the class.

Narrator: Sample Response B

Woman: When I have free time, my favorite thing to do is to attend yoga or another kind of exercise class. The reason I say this is because I spend a lot of time working and studying, so I really need to do something that helps me relax alone. I usually go to about three classes a week.

Narrator: Sample Response C

Woman: I usually have between six and ten hours of free time per week. So that's about one and a half hours per day, which is enough time to do a 45-minute yoga class at least three times per week. I use the rest of my free time to go shopping, do laundry, or meet friends.

Track 04-06.10 pg 38

Narrator: Speaking Questions 4 to 6

Progressive Practice: Get Set

Part B Questions and Sample Responses

Question 4: What is your favorite thing to do when you have free time?

Woman: When I have free time, my favorite thing to do is to attend yoga or another kind of exercise class. The reason I say this is because I spend a lot of time working and studying, so I

really need to do something that helps me relax alone. I usually go to about three classes a week.

Narrator: Question 5: How much free time do you have during the week, and where do you spend your free time?

Woman: I usually have between six and ten hours of free time per week. So that's about one and a half hours per day, which is enough time to do a 45-minute yoga class at least three times per week. I use the rest of my free time to go shopping, do laundry, or meet friends.

Narrator: Question 6: How do you think the quality of your activities during your free time could be improved?

Woman: I would have to say that the quality of my activities could be greatly improved in two ways. First, the space in which I usually exercise is not as quiet as it could be. I think that the space for exercise should be very quiet and clean. The second thing is that it is not really well organized. There need to be better spaces for storing the yoga mats. Those two things would really make an improvement in the overall quality of the class.

Track 04-06.11 pg 40

Narrator: Speaking Questions 4 to 6

Progressive Practice: Go for the TOEIC Test

Imagine that a marketing firm is doing research in your country. You have agreed to participate in a survey about live music and concerts.

Question 4: What kinds of concerts or live music performances do you attend?

Question 5: How often do you listen to live music?

Question 6: Describe where you go to listen to live music and why you like it there.

Track 04-06.12 pg 40

Narrator: Speaking Questions 4 to 6

Progressive Practice: Go for the TOEIC Test

Questions and Sample Responses

Question 4: What kinds of concerts or live music performances do you attend?

Woman: I attend a lot of different concerts and live performances because I like a lot of different kinds of music. I really love loud rock concerts in big stadiums and concert halls. But I also like listening to singers and musicians in small theaters and clubs.

Narrator: Question 5: How often do you listen to live music?

Woman: I try to listen to live music as often as I can, but it depends on the price of tickets. If I can afford it, I'll go to a concert at least once a month. Sometimes my friends and I go for the weekend. There are some free concerts in the park, so I usually go to those two or three times per month.

Narrator: Question 6: Describe where you go to listen to live music and why you like it there.

Woman: One of my favorite places to go to listen to live music is a small club near the university. I like it because on Friday and Saturday nights anyone can perform there. Musicians and singers from the area get to perform onstage for a half hour each. All they have to do is sign up when they arrive at the club. Some solo performers just play musical instruments. Last week, for example, there was a terrific saxophone player.

The ones who play guitar and sing are my favorites. Some bands play there, too. It's great listening to new performers, and you get to hear all types of music.

Questions 7–9

Track 07-09.01 pg 42

Narrator: Speaking Questions 7 to 9

WALK THROUGH: Respond to Questions Using Information Provided

What You'll Hear

Man: Hello. I'm interested in taking a tour of Danville, but I'm afraid it might be a bit too expensive.

Narrator: Question 7.

Man: Can you tell me how much it costs to take the tour?

Narrator: Question 8.

Man: I heard that the tour includes dinner as well as lunch. Is that correct?

Narrator: Question 9.

Man: Does the tour take place mostly in the morning, or will we also visit some places after lunch?

Track 07-09.02 pg 43

Narrator: Speaking Questions 7 to 9

WALK THROUGH: What You'll Do

Question 7 Sample Response

Woman: Sure. Let me check the information on the schedule. The tour costs 75 dollars for adults, and for children under 12, the cost is 50 dollars.

Narrator: Question 8 Sample Response

Woman: Let's see. According to the schedule, there's an optional dinner at the end of the tour. This costs an extra 25 dollars over and above the cost of your tour ticket.

Narrator: Question 9 Sample Response

Woman: Yes, the tour includes visits to several places after lunch. First, there's a walking tour of Danville City Park and Gardens, which begins at two o'clock. Then after that, at three thirty, the tour goes by bus to the Danville waterfront. Then you'll get back to the hotel by five fifteen.

Track 07-09.03 pg 43

Narrator: Speaking Questions 7 to 9

GET IT RIGHT: Sample Response

Speaker: Just a moment, sir. Let me check that for you. I'm really sorry, but the 3:00 presentation has been canceled. There's a similar presentation at 2:00. It covers increasing sales, motivating employees, and improving your work environment. I can give you more information on that, if you'd like.

Track 07-09.04 pg 46

Narrator: Speaking Questions 7 to 9

GET IT RIGHT: Understanding the Information Texts and Questions

TIP 3 TASK

Number 1.

Man: Could you let me know how much the tickets cost?

Narrator: Number 2.

Woman: Who's speaking first in the morning session?

Narrator: Number 3.

Man: We don't have to stay all day long, do we?

Narrator: Number 4.

Woman: What time is Mr. Lee free in the afternoon?

Narrator: Number 5.

Man: I'd like to see Professor Hunter speak. What days and times will he be there?

Narrator: Number 6.

Woman: Why can't I meet with Ms. Johnson on Thursday?

Narrator: Number 7.

Man: I need to keep up with my regular work. Will we have time for answering e-mails?

Narrator: Number 8.

Woman: Do you have any idea how much the registration costs?

Narrator: Number 9.

Man: Does anyone have time to meet at 1:00 instead of 3:00?

Narrator: Number 10.

Woman: May I pay the fees on the first day of the exhibition?

Track 07-09.05 pg 47

Narrator: Speaking Questions 7 to 9

GET IT RIGHT: Structuring Your Responses

Question and Sample Response for Speaking Question 7 or 8

Man: Can you tell me how much it costs to attend the conference?

Woman: Certainly, sir. Let me check for more information on that. Let's see, it looks like one-day registration will cost $235.

Track 07-09.06 pg 47

Narrator: Speaking Questions 7 to 9

GET IT RIGHT: Structuring Your Responses

Question and Sample Response for Speaking Question 9

Woman: What other events are happening in the evening, after the conference?

Man: Hmm . . . that's a good question. Let me see here. I've got a schedule in front of me. It looks like there's a reception for the attendees on Tuesday. That starts at 5:00 and goes until 7:00. It's in the lobby. Then on Wednesday evening there's a dinner in the main dining room. That starts at 7:30. I hope that answers your question.

Track 07-09.07 pg 51

Narrator: Speaking Questions 7 to 9

Progressive Practice: Get Ready

Part B

Question 7.

Man: Where will appetizers be served?

Woman: Appetizers will be served in the Green Room.

Narrator: Question 8.

Man: Will there be dancing immediately following dinner?

Woman: No. There will be an awards ceremony first.

Narrator: Question 9.

Man: Will there be any speakers during the banquet?

Woman: Yes. Both the membership secretary and the president will speak.

Track 07-09.08 pg 53

Narrator: Speaking Questions 7 to 9

Progressive Practice: Get Set

Part B

Question 7.

Woman: Hi. This is Martha in the Public Relations Office. I'm supposed to pick up Mr. Green when he arrives. Can you tell me the exact date and time of his arrival?

Narrator: Question 8.

Woman: I'm also supposed to transport him to his lunch with the Board of Directors. If I pick him up at the office at 12:15, would that be early enough?

Narrator: Question 9.

Woman: What about after lunch? Will he be needing transportation to any other place that afternoon or evening?

Track 07-09.09 pg 53

Narrator: Speaking Questions 7 to 9

Progressive Practice: Get Set

Part B Questions and Sample Responses

Question 7.

Woman: Hi. This is Martha in the Public Relations Office. I'm supposed to pick up Mr. Green when he arrives. Can you tell me the exact date and time of his arrival?

Man: Good question. Let me just check the itinerary. OK, it says that Mr. Green will arrive at the airport at 5 p.m. on April 15.

Narrator: Question 8.

Woman: I'm also supposed to transport him to his lunch with the Board of Directors. If I pick him up at the office at 12:15 would that be early enough?

Man: At 12:15? Well, according to the itinerary, it looks like the lunch begins at twelve, so I think you will have to pick him up earlier than that.

Narrator: Question 9.

Woman: What about after lunch? Will he be needing transportation to any other place that afternoon or evening?

Man: So you need his schedule for later in the day? Let me take a look. Well, I'm looking at the itinerary, and it shows several activities after lunch. First, you'll need to take Mr. Green to the Hotel Dominion for a reception at four o'clock. Then he has a private tour at the City Museum of Art at seven. He's scheduled to return to the hotel at nine.

Track 07-09.10 pg 55

Narrator: Speaking Questions 7 to 9

Progressive Practice: Go for the TOEIC Test

You will answer three questions based on information on the screen. You will have 30 seconds to read the information. You will have 15 seconds to respond to Questions 7 and 8, and you will have 30 seconds to respond to Question 9. For each

question, begin to answer as soon as you hear the beep. No preparation time is provided.

Woman: Hello. I'm interested in seeing a few of the plays during the Outdoor Shakespeare Theater Festival this summer, but I have a few questions about the schedule.

Narrator: Question 7.

Woman: How many performances of *Romeo and Juliet* will there be throughout the summer?

Narrator: Question 8.

Woman: I understand that the plays will be performed in the outdoor theater, so that means that performances will be canceled if it rains, right?

Narrator: Question 9.

Woman: I'll be out of town for most of July, so I'm wondering whether there will be any plays performed in August.

Track 07-09.11 pg 55

Narrator: Speaking Questions 7 to 9

Progressive Practice: Go for the TOEIC Test

Question and Sample Responses

Question 7.

Woman: How many performances of *Romeo and Juliet* will there be throughout the summer?

Man: OK, it looks like *Romeo and Juliet* will be performed on July 10, and—let me see—there's another performance on July 31. So two performances.

Narrator: Question 8.

Woman: I understand that the plays will be performed in the outdoor theater, so that means that performances will be canceled if it rains, right?

Man: Yes, the plays will be performed at the outdoor theater, but if it rains, the performances will be moved to the City Auditorium, so no performances will be canceled.

Narrator: Question 9.

Woman: I'll be out of town for most of July, so I'm wondering whether there will be any plays performed in August.

Man: Let me check the schedule. There will be three different plays performed in August. First is *The Tempest*, with performances on August 7 and 8. Then *Comedy of Errors* will be performed on August 14 and 15, and finally, there will be one last performance of *King Lear* on August 21.

Question 10

Track 10.01 pg 57

Narrator: Speaking Question 10

WALK THROUGH: Propose a Solution

What You'll Hear

Directions: In Question 10, you will hear a problem and you will propose a solution. You will have 30 seconds to prepare your response. You will have 60 seconds to speak.

Respond as if you are the building manager.

In your response, you should

• show that you understand the problem.

• propose a solution for the problem.

Sample Message

Man: Hi. This is Chris Robertson in Apartment 314. I'm calling about the elevator, which doesn't seem to be working again. This afternoon, when I got home, I pushed the button to call the elevator, but nothing happened. I waited and waited and pushed the button several times, but the elevator never arrived. I had a heavy bag of groceries with me, and I, you know, had to carry them all the way up the stairs to my apartment on the third floor. Can you let me know what's going to be done about this situation? Using the stairs isn't easy for me because I have a bad back—and it's especially hard when I'm carrying groceries or packages. It's really an inconvenience, and this is the third time this year that the elevator has broken down. I hope it can be repaired soon. Again, this is Chris Robertson from number 314. Thank you.

Track 10.02 pg 57

Narrator: Speaking Question 10

WALK THROUGH: What You'll Do

Sample Response

Woman: Hello, Mr. Robertson. This is Tara Conner from Rental Management. I understand you had a problem with the elevator this afternoon. I'm very sorry for the inconvenience. I know it's difficult for you because of your back. I also understand that it is frustrating because it has happened before. I think you'll be happy to know that we plan to replace the elevator. The new elevator will be installed early next week. After that, there won't be any problems with the elevator breaking down. In the meantime, I invite you to use the service elevator. It's near the entrance to the stairs. I know it's not as nice as the passenger elevator, but I think it will be easier for you than the stairs. Then next week you'll be able to use the new passenger elevator. Please let me know if you have any questions.

Track 10.03 pg 58

Narrator: Speaking Question 10

GET IT RIGHT: Sample Response

Man: Hello, Ms. Jones. This is Marco with Sunco Products returning your call. We're very sorry to hear that your package is late. We understand how frustrating that is, especially because you want it for a party this weekend. I checked into the problem. It appears that the delivery person tried to deliver the package three times. Unfortunately, there was no one at home at the time. I'd like to suggest that we set up a time this week when you know you will be home. Then we can try to deliver the package again. That way, we should be able to get your delivery to you before the weekend. Let me know if this will be OK with you or if you have any questions. And again, we're very sorry about the delay.

Track 10.04 pg 59

Narrator: Speaking Question 10

GET IT RIGHT: Understanding the Voicemail Messages

TIP 1 TASK

Number 1.

Man: Hi, there. This is John Green calling from Swift Plumbing. I'm working on a project over here in Northwood, and I've run into a problem. The main line broke going into the house I'm working on, and I have to replace about 40 feet of pipe right away. I need some two-inch plastic pipe as soon as possible. Is there any way you could send someone over to the job site with that pipe? I know you don't usually deliver, but I really need your help on this. If I don't get this fixed by this afternoon, my customer is going to be upset, and it's a pretty big job. Please give me a call as soon as you can to let me know. Again, this is John Green with Swift Plumbing, 814-555-2715.

Narrator: Number 2.

Woman: Hello. This is Charlotte Strand, and I'm a guest in Room 128. I reserved a room online last week for three nights. I just checked in, and I have to say that I'm very disappointed with it. The room is much smaller than I expected. The Web site said I'd be getting a deluxe double room with a seating area, and this room has only one bed, and there's not even a TV! There also seems to be something wrong with the heating. It must be a hundred degrees in here, and I can't get it to turn off. This is completely unacceptable. I paid for a much bigger and better room, and I'm not about to stay in something like this.

Narrator: Number 3.

Man: Uh, yeah . . . hi, there. My name's Peter Arnold, and I'm calling about a problem with my credit card. I'm on vacation in Europe, and I just tried it at three different stores and it doesn't seem to be usable. I also just tried it in a bank machine—um, ATM—and it's not working there, either. One salesclerk said that it's showing up as declined, but my bill is paid and the card is current. I'm not sure what to do, as I was planning to use the card for most of my shopping over the next few days. I'd appreciate it if you could give me a call as soon as possible. I'd like to get this taken care of today. You can reach me at 19 33 555 7256, and, again, my name's Peter Arnold.

Track 10.05 pg 61

Narrator: Speaking Question 10

GET IT RIGHT: Structuring Your Response

Sample Message

Woman: Hi, this is Sarah Brown. I'd like to make a complaint about a problem I've been having with my new stove. We just bought it two weeks ago, but the last few times I've turned it on, nothing has happened. Then, when I try again, it works. I don't know what the issue is, but I need to get it fixed right away. I have people coming over for dinner on Friday night, and it's already Tuesday. I really need someone to come out and have a look at it. I'd prefer it if someone could come today or, at the latest, tomorrow. Please call me back as soon as possible. Sarah Brown at 906-555-7272. Thank you.

Narrator: Sample Response

Man: Hello, Ms. Brown. My name is Brenden, and I'm with Miller Stoves. I'm returning your call from this morning. We're very sorry that you're having problems with your stove. I know you're worried about your dinner party, so we'll try to fix the stove right away. The problem could be that the stove was damaged in shipping, so we'll have to come and take a look at it. I need to check with our repair department first, but they might be able to come this evening. If they can't come today, we should be able to come tomorrow. I'll call back later this afternoon to check what times you are available. Thanks again for your call, and again, we're very sorry about the problem with the stove.

Track 10.06 pg 62
Narrator: Speaking Question 10
GET IT RIGHT: Structuring Your Response
TIP 1 TASK 1
Number 1.

Woman: Hi, Mr. Green. This is Janet Day, and I'm returning your call from earlier today. I understand that you're interested in having some pipes delivered.

Narrator: Number 2.

Man: Hello. I'm calling for Ms. Strand. My name's Percy Rogers with Smith Hotels, and we just got your message. We'd like to apologize for the problem with your room. We understand that you're upset that you didn't get the room you wanted.

Narrator: Number 3.

Woman: Good morning, Mr. Arnold. This is Karen Stall with First Bank. I just wanted to get back to you about your message. We're sorry to hear that your card isn't working. I know this is especially frustrating because you're traveling, so we want to help you as soon as possible.

Track 10.07 pg 63
Narrator: Speaking Question 10
GET IT RIGHT: Structuring Your Response
TIP 2 TASK 1
Number 1.

Woman: Hi, Mr. Green. This is Janet Day, and I'm returning your call from earlier today. I understand that you're interested in having some pipes delivered. As you know, we don't deliver. It's not our usual policy, and we don't have a delivery truck. However, since this is an emergency and you're such a good customer, we might be able to help. One option would be to check with East Plumbing Supply. I know they deliver. Maybe they could pick up the pipe and bring it over to you. Another option would be for us to rent a truck and bring the pipes. If we did that, then you would need to pay for the delivery and for the rental cost. Just give me a call back and let me know if one of these options will work.

Narrator: Number 2.

Man: Hello. I'm calling for Ms. Strand. My name's Percy Rogers with Smith Hotels, and we just got your message. We'd like to apologize for the problem with your room. We understand that you're upset that you didn't get the room you wanted. I've checked your reservation, and everything seems to be in order. It was probably a mistake with the computer system. It didn't record the additional request for the deluxe double room. I can arrange for another room. In order to make up for the mistake, we're going to give you the deluxe double room at the cost of a single. Someone will come to your room in the next hour or so to show you to your new room and give you your key. We're very sorry about any inconvenience.

Narrator: Number 3.

Woman: Good morning, Mr. Arnold. This is Karen Stall with First Bank. I just wanted to get back to you about your message.

We're sorry to hear that your card isn't working. I know this is especially frustrating because you're traveling, so we want to help you as soon as possible. I talked to our customer service center, and it seems that the card was stopped because there were charges in another country. This might be because of your travel. I just need to ask you a few security questions. Then we should be able to fix things or send you another card immediately. Please call me back as soon as possible. And in the future, it's usually best to let us know if you're going somewhere. That way, we can avoid stopping the card. Thank you very much for calling, and we look forward to helping you solve your problem.

Track 10.08 pg 66
Narrator: Speaking Question 10
Progressive Practice: Get Ready
Part A Sample Message
Man: Good morning. My name is Marty Jones. I signed up to take the advanced Spanish course that meets on Saturday mornings. However, I just found out that I'll be starting a new job this week, and my work schedule will include Saturday mornings. So I won't be able to take that class. Could I take it at another time? I'm free most evenings during the week and on Monday and Tuesday afternoons. If there's an advanced Spanish class that meets at one of these times, maybe I could transfer into it. Please let me know. I can be reached at 403-555-1212. Thanks.

Track 10.09 pg 66
Narrator: Speaking Question 10
Progressive Practice: Get Ready
Part B Sample Response
Woman: Hello, Mr. Jones. My name is Kim. I understand that you can't take the Saturday morning Spanish class because of your new work schedule. I'm sorry that the class schedule doesn't work for you. I know that it can be complicated to try to study and work at the same time. However, this problem is very easy to solve. We do have another advanced Spanish class. It meets on Tuesday afternoons, and there's still room for another student in it. I'll put your name on the list for that class, so all you have to do is show up next Tuesday afternoon at two o'clock. Please let me know if you have any problem with this. Otherwise, we hope to see you next Tuesday.

Track 10.10 pg 68
Narrator: Speaking Question 10
Progressive Practice: Get Set
Part A Message
Man: Hello. This is George Smith at 602-555-8943. I ordered a coffeemaker from your website. It just arrived today. When I took it out of the box, it looked fine, but I couldn't get it to work. I plugged it in and carefully followed the instructions for adding coffee and water. Then, when I pressed the power button, the little green light went on, but nothing happened. The water didn't heat up, the coffee didn't brew, and the machine didn't make any sound at all. I don't know if there is an easy way to fix this or what I should do. I really would like a coffeemaker that works, as I'm expecting guests next week. Please let me know what I can do about this. Thanks.

Track 10.11 pg 68

Narrator: Speaking Question 10

Progressive Practice: Get Set

Part B Sample Response

Woman: Thank you for calling us, Mr. Smith. My name is Carrie Jones. I understand that you haven't been able to get your new coffeemaker to work. I realize how frustrating this must be. There could be an issue with the coffeemaker or with the programming. I'd like to suggest that you look at page 10 in the instruction manual. There you will see some instructions for fixing common problems. If that doesn't solve the problem for you, you can return the coffeemaker to us. Just repack it in its box and mail it to us at the address in the manual. We will send you a new coffeemaker. We will do our best to get it to you by the beginning of next week. Thanks so much for calling, and please accept our apologies for the problem.

Track 10.12 pg 70

Narrator: Speaking Question 10

Progressive Practice: Go for the TOEIC Test

Directions: In Question 10, you will hear about a problem and you will propose a solution. You will have 30 seconds to prepare your response. You will have 60 seconds to speak.

Respond as if you are a businessperson.

In your response, you should

- show that you understand the problem.
- propose a solution for the problem.

Woman: Hello, Mr. Peters. This is Pat Clark. I'm calling about our appointment this afternoon. I had agreed to meet with you about our new construction project. Unfortunately, something has come up, and I won't be free at 2:00, so I have to cancel our appointment. I'm very sorry for this. I'm still interested in meeting with you. I'm busy most of the rest of the week—this is a really busy time of the year for us—but I will probably have some time available in my schedule next week. If there's any time next week that you're free, then I hope we can reschedule the meeting. I don't know what you wanted to discuss, so I hope next week won't be too late for you. Please call me back soon and let me know. Thank you.

Track 10.13 pg 70

Narrator: Speaking Question 10

Progressive Practice: Go for the TOEIC Test

Sample Response

Man: Hello, Ms. Clark. This is John Peters. I got your message about rescheduling our appointment for our meeting. I understand how busy you are at this time of the year. I appreciate that you're still willing to meet with me. If we can get together early next week, that will be fine. Can we meet on Monday? Anytime Monday morning or afternoon works for me. If you don't have time to meet on Monday, then perhaps we could talk for a short while on the phone. It would take less time than an actual meeting. Please let me know which solution works best for you. Thank you.

Question 11

Track 11.01 pg 72

Narrator: Speaking Question 11

WALK THROUGH: Express an Opinion

What You'll See and Hear

Directions: In Question 11, you will give your opinion about a topic. You will have 15 seconds to prepare your response. You will have 60 seconds to speak. Say as much as you can in the time you have.

Woman: Some people enjoy the excitement of city life. Other people prefer the peace and quiet of small-town living. Would you rather live in a big city or a small town? Why? Use specific examples to support your preference.

Track 11.02 pg 72

Narrator: Speaking Question 11

WALK THROUGH: Express an Opinion

What You'll Do

Part B Sample Response

Man: I would definitely prefer to live in a big city. I like the excitement of city life. There are always so many interesting activities to do, like different kinds of theater, concerts, classes you can take, and so on. You can also meet a lot of different kinds of people in your daily life—people from different places with all different kinds of interests. In addition, it's much easier to find jobs in a city than it is in a small town. That's really important. You have to work, right? So you want to live in a place where you have a chance of finding a good job. I think life in a small town is very restrictive. There aren't many options for entertainment, and you don't come across many different kinds of people. I would be really bored if I lived in a small town.

Track 11.03 pgs 72–73

Narrator: Speaking Question 11

GET IT RIGHT: Question and Sample Response

Man: Some people enjoy jobs in which they do the same work every day. Others enjoy jobs that involve changing from project to project. Which type of job would you prefer and why?

Woman: I would prefer a job that involves changing from project to project. I feel this way for a number of reasons. First of all, I don't really like doing the same thing every day. I like change and need some variety in my life. Second, I like to meet new people. Working on different projects would give me a chance to make a lot of new friends and contacts. Finally, I think doing the same thing all the time could be really boring. If I did the same thing every day, I might never learn new things. In my opinion, a job that involves changing from project to project would just be more exciting.

Track 11.04 pg 75

Narrator: Speaking Question 11

GET IT RIGHT: Structuring Your Response

Question and Sample Response

Woman: Do you agree or disagree with the following statement? "It's more important to eat a good diet than to exercise a lot." Support your choice with reasons and details.

Man: I disagree with the statement, "It's more important to eat a good diet than to exercise a lot." There are several reasons for this opinion. For one thing, exercise is a very important part of a healthy lifestyle. It's good for your heart, for your muscles, and for controlling your weight. Another reason exercise is important is that it's fun. Playing sports and moving your body can make you feel happier and feel better. Finally, eating a good diet can be healthy, but if you don't move your body, it will become weak. Good nutrition will give you energy, but you should use that energy to move! In conclusion, I have to say that exercise and diet are equally important.

Track 11.05 pg 77

Narrator: Speaking Question 11
GET IT RIGHT: Structuring Your Response
TIP 3 TASK
Number 1.

Woman: In my opinion, taking time to relax is the key to being productive. I have this opinion for the following reasons. To begin with, relaxing is very important for feeling good. If you feel good, then you'll be able to work more and enjoy life more. For another thing, relaxing can help you sleep better. If you sleep better, you can do more when you are awake. Finally, being busy all the time makes you tired, so you can't focus on your work. For example, if you have a long day at work and then come home and work some more, you might start to make mistakes. This won't help anyone. So overall, I guess I would say relaxing is an important part of everyone's day.

Track 11.06 pg 77

Narrator: Number 2.

Man: That's a good question. I guess I prefer to shop online rather than shop in the store. While some people may think that shopping in the store is better, I don't feel that way. The main reason is that I just hate crowds. Let me give you an example of what I'm talking about. I went Christmas shopping last November. There were so many people, I had to wait in line for 30 minutes to pay. I don't have time for that. Another reason I like shopping online is that you can compare prices more easily. If you find something at one price on one site, you can check to see if it's cheaper on another site. You can't do that in a store. Finally, although some people don't like the cost, I like getting delivery. That way, I don't have to carry everything up to my apartment. In general, I think that online shopping makes more sense.

Track 11.07 pg 77

Narrator: Number 3.

Woman: I strongly disagree with the statement, "People should get a pay raise every year, even if they don't perform well." I disagree for several reasons. First of all, it's just not fair. If you work hard, you should get a pay raise. If you don't, you should not. It's that simple. Why reward someone for not doing a good job? Secondly, I really don't like the stories in the news about people who get rewards when they do a bad job. For example, one company went out of business, but the president still got a one million dollar bonus—is that fair? Finally, I know it gets more expensive to live every year, but that doesn't mean people should get paid for a bad job. In fact, if someone does a bad job, the company should reduce the salary, in my opinion. The main thing for me is, it's just not fair, so people should not get a pay raise if they don't perform well.

Track 11.08 pg 77

Narrator: Number 4.

Man: Hmm . . . that's a good question. I guess I would prefer to work at home. There are advantages and disadvantages to both, but I think working at home is better because it's just more convenient. First of all, you don't need to drive to work every day. That will save you time and money for gas. In addition, you can do other things while you work, like wash clothes, cook dinner, and watch your children. Lastly, you can also usually get more done. If you work in an office, people sometimes stop by. This can disturb you and make you lose focus. As you can see, there are a lot of reasons why working at home is more convenient.

Track 11.09 pg 78

Narrator: Number 5.

Woman: In my opinion, all young people should be able to attend college for free. I have this opinion for the following reasons. My first reason is that all young people should have a chance to study. In my country, college costs are very high. Because of this, not very many people can go. This makes it harder for many poorer people to get a better job. My second reason for thinking this is that it's better to use taxes for education than some other things. Some people think that military or highway budgets are more important, but I disagree. Young people need to learn. Thirdly, the cost is not that high. If everyone pays a little more in taxes, more young people will have a chance. So basically, I would have to say that I'm in favor of having free college education for all.

Track 11.10 pg 78

Narrator: Number 6.

Man: I would not be in favor of the planned tax increase. I disagree with the idea for several reasons. To begin with, why should I pay for other people's Internet? I know this would help some businesses, but it would also be a big cost for people. Some people might not be able to afford the tax. Next, I think the city should pay for something like that itself. If they want to bring more people here with that plan, they can pay the bill. Furthermore, free wireless is not that big of an advantage anymore. Most people have mobile Internet connections. They can use their home Internet anywhere. They won't need free wireless that much. All in all, I'd have to say that it's just a bad idea.

Track 11.11 pg 78

Narrator: Speaking Question 11
GET IT RIGHT: Structuring Your Response
TIP 4 TASK 2
Number 1.

Woman: Some people like working at home better than working in an office. Which work environment do you prefer and why?

Track 11.12 pg 78

Narrator: Number 2.

Man: Do you agree or disagree with the following statement? "People should get a pay raise every year, even if they don't perform well."

Track 11.13 pg 78

Narrator: Number 3.

Woman: Would you rather shop online or go to a store? Give reasons and examples to support your shopping preference.

Track 11.14 pg 78

Narrator: Number 4.

Man: There is a plan to offer free wireless service in your city, but there will be a slight tax increase as a result. Would you be in favor of the planned tax increase? Give reasons and details to support your answer.

Track 11.15 pg 78

Narrator: Number 5.

Woman: Many people feel that taking time to relax is the key to being productive at work and at home. How do you feel about taking time to relax? Does it make people more productive? Use reasons and examples to support your opinion.

Track 11.16 pg 78

Narrator: Number 6.

Man: Some people think that all young people should be able to attend college for free. What's your opinion about free education? Support your answer with reasons and details.

Track 11.17 pg 79

Narrator: Speaking Question 11

Progressive Practice: Get Ready

Part A Sample Question

Woman: Some people enjoy cooking and eating most of their meals at home. Other people would rather eat out at a restaurant most of the time. Which do you prefer? Use specific examples to support your answer.

Track 11.18 pg 79

Narrator: Speaking Question 11

Progressive Practice: Get Ready

Part B Sample Response

Man: I prefer to eat out at restaurants most of the time. I feel this way for several reasons. The main reason for this is that I don't know how to cook very well. If I eat at a restaurant, the food always tastes better than food I cook myself. I also eat more of a variety of food at restaurants. This is because I know how to cook only a few things. Finally, there are a lot of good restaurants in the neighborhood where I live. I have lots of choices for places to eat, and the food at each one is delicious.

Track 11.19 pg 81

Narrator: Speaking Question 11

Progressive Practice: Get Set

Part A Sample Question

Man: Do you agree or disagree with the following statement? "Young people should not be allowed to drive cars until they

are twenty-one years old." Use specific reasons and examples to support your answer.

Track 11.20 pg 81

Narrator: Speaking Question 11

Progressive Practice: Get Set

Part B Sample Response

Woman: I strongly agree with the statement that people should not be allowed to drive until they are 21. I agree with this because of the following reasons. In the first place, many young people are careless, but a car can be a dangerous machine. It isn't safe to let someone have the responsibility of driving such a dangerous machine until they're mature enough to be serious and careful about it. Another reason is that most young people don't have enough money to buy and maintain a car. They should learn to use public transportation until they can afford a car of their own. Finally, many young people probably don't really need to drive a car. In my country, you can get a driver's license at age 18, but most people don't start driving regularly until they're married and have families of their own. So basically, it isn't always safe for young people to drive cars, they can't afford it, and they usually don't need to, anyway.

Track 11.21 pg 83

Narrator: Speaking Question 11

Progressive Practice: Go for the TOEIC Test

In Question 11, you will give your opinion about a topic. You will have 15 seconds to prepare your response. You will have 60 seconds to speak. Say as much as you can in the time you have.

Woman: Imagine that there is a plan to build a large shopping mall in your neighborhood. Do you support or oppose this plan? Why? Use specific reasons and examples to support your opinion.

Track 11.22 pg 83

Narrator: Speaking Question 11

Progressive Practice: Go for the TOEIC Test

Sample Response

Man: I support the plan to build a large shopping mall in my neighborhood because it would benefit the neighborhood in several ways. First of all, it would make shopping a lot more convenient for local residents. Currently, we have only a few small stores in the area, and they mostly sell groceries and a few other things. If we want to buy clothes or things for the house or books or just about anything, we have to travel several miles to get to the nearest shopping mall. The other important reason why I support this plan is because it would bring more jobs to our neighborhood. There are a lot of opportunities for employment at a shopping mall. There are jobs in stores and restaurants, management jobs, and maintenance jobs, for example. I think a new shopping mall would definitely be a good thing.

Speaking Test

Track SPT-01 pg 85

Narrator: Speaking Test Question 1: Read a text aloud

Directions: In this part, you will read a text aloud. You will have 45 seconds to prepare and 45 seconds to read the text aloud.

Track SPT-02 pg 85

Narrator: Speaking Test Question 2: Read a text aloud

Directions: In this part, you will read a text aloud. You will have 45 seconds to prepare and 45 seconds to read the text aloud.

Track SPT-03 pg 86

Narrator: Speaking Test Question 3: Describe a picture

Directions: In this part, you will describe the photo on the screen with as much detail as possible. You will have 30 seconds to prepare. You will have 45 seconds to describe the photo.

Track SPT-04 pgs 86–87

Narrator: Speaking Test Questions 4–6: Respond to questions

Directions: In this part, you will answer three questions. Begin responding as soon as you hear the beep for each question. You will have 15 seconds for Questions 4 and 5 and 30 seconds for Question 6. There is no preparation time.

Imagine that a research firm is doing a telephone survey of people in your city. You have agreed to answer some questions about sports.

Question 4: What sports do you enjoy playing?

Question 5: How often do you usually play sports?

Question 6: Do you think it is important for children to play sports? Why or why not?

Track SPT-05 pg 88

Narrator: Speaking Test Questions 7–9: Respond to questions using information provided

Directions: You will answer three questions based on information on the screen. You will have 30 seconds to read the information. You will have 15 seconds to respond to Questions 7 and 8, and you will have 30 seconds to respond to Question 9. For each question, begin to answer as soon as you hear the beep. No preparation time is provided.

Narrator: Question 7.

Man: I'm interested in taking the tour of the Botanical Gardens on June 5, but I'm not sure exactly where I should go. Can you tell me where the tour begins?

Narrator: Question 8.

Man: Can you tell me how much the tickets for the tour cost?

Narrator: Question 9.

Man: I understand that the tour lasts for several hours, and I'm afraid I might get hungry in that time. Will any meals be served during the tour?

Track SPT-06 pg 89

Narrator: Speaking Test Question 10: Propose a solution

Directions: In Question 10, you will hear about a problem and you will propose a solution. You will have 30 seconds to prepare your response. You will have 60 seconds to speak.

Man: Hello, this is Sam Webster. I'm calling about some books I ordered from your company recently. When I placed the order,

I was told that the books would arrive within five business days, but now two weeks have passed and the books still haven't arrived. I need them for a class I'm taking, which begins next Monday. I will definitely need the books by then, and I was hoping to have them before then so that I could have a chance to start reading before the class begins. Is there some way I can find out where the package with my books is and how soon it will arrive? Thank you.

Track SPT-07 pg 89

Narrator: Speaking Test Question 11: Express an opinion

Directions: In Question 11, you will give your opinion about a topic. You will have 15 seconds to prepare your response. You will have 60 seconds to speak. Say as much as you can in the time you have.

Man: Many people prefer driving their own cars, while others would rather use public transportation. Which do you prefer? Explain why.

Track SPT-08 pg 85

Narrator: Speaking Test Question 1: Read a text aloud Sample Response

Woman: Hi. This is Myra Peters calling about my appointment with Dr. Jones. I have a three o'clock appointment scheduled for this afternoon. Unfortunately, I won't be able to keep it because of an important meeting at work. So, I'll need to reschedule. I was hoping to come in sometime next week. Any time Monday, Tuesday, or Wednesday afternoon would work for me. I hope the doctor has some time available on one of those days. Please call me back and let me know. Thanks.

Track SPT-09 pg 85

Narrator: Speaking Test Question 2: Read a text aloud Sample Response

Man: Our speaker tonight is Mr. John Wilson, who has just returned from traveling in South America. Mr. Wilson spent his trip photographing scenes of small-town life across the continent. His work is well known around the world, and his photography has been featured in numerous newspapers, magazines, and books. Tonight he will share with us photographs and stories from his recent trip and will answer any questions you may have. Due to time constraints, we ask you to hold your questions until the end of the talk.

Track SPT-10 pg 86

Narrator: Speaking Test Question 3: Describe a picture Sample Response

Woman: Two people are walking down a sidewalk—a man and a woman. I think they are businesspeople because they are dressed in business suits. The man is carrying a briefcase, and the woman is also carrying something in her hand. They are looking at each other as they walk, so maybe they are having a conversation about something. It looks like they are walking in a park. There are trees behind them and there's also grass on the ground. Behind them are some tall buildings, so they are in a city.

Track SPT-11 pgs 86–87

Narrator: Speaking Test Questions 4–6: Respond to questions

Question 4 Sample Response

Man: The sport that I enjoy the most is bicycle riding. I really love getting on my bike and riding all through the park near my house. That's really the only sport I practice.

Narrator: Question 5 Sample Response

Man: I ride my bike at least once a week, on Saturday mornings. Sometimes I also take a ride during the week if I have time.

Narrator: Question 6 Sample Response

Man: Yes, I think it is important for children to practice sports. First, children need to get a lot of exercise, so if they have sports that they enjoy, then it is easy for them to get the exercise they need. Also, learning to play on a team is important for children. It helps them learn how to work together with other children, and it helps them learn about competition.

Track SPT-12 pg 88

Narrator: Speaking Test

Questions 7–9: Respond to questions using information provided

Question 7 Sample Response

Woman: Certainly. Let me check. It looks like the tour begins at the front entrance to the gardens, located at number 301 South Main Street.

Narrator: Question 8 Sample Response

Woman: Yes, of course. Tickets are 25 dollars each, but there's a special discount. If you buy your ticket before May 15, it will cost only 20 dollars.

Narrator: Question 9 Sample Response

Woman: Yes, there will be two meals, so you don't need to worry about getting hungry. First, there will be lunch served in the Garden Café at 12 o'clock. Then, at the end of the tour, tea and pastries will be served in the outdoor garden.

Track SPT-13 pg 89

Narrator: Speaking Test Question 10: Propose a solution

Question 10 Sample Response

Woman: Hello, Mr. Webster. Thank you for your call about the books you ordered. I'm sorry you've been waiting so long to receive them. I know how important those books are to you. It seems that there was a delay in sending your package, so unfortunately it might be another week before it arrives. However, I am going to send you a new package with the same books. I am going to send it by express mail this afternoon. That way it should arrive at your house in two days, so you will still have some time to start reading the books before your class begins. Of course there will be no extra charge for this. Thank you very much for your patience. Please let me know if you have more questions.

Track SPT-14 pg 89

Narrator: Speaking Test Question 11: Express an opinion

Question 11 Sample Response

Man: My preference is definitely for public transportation. There are several reasons for this. The first one is convenience. In the city where I live, I can take a bus or subway to almost any place I want to go. When I get to my destination, I don't have to worry about finding a parking space. It's so easy. Public transportation is also cheaper. It's true that I have to pay the fare every time I ride the bus or subway, but I think the costs of owning a car are greater. You have to buy the car, pay for gasoline, pay for repairs, and maybe even pay for a place to keep it. I think that costs more than bus and subway fare. Finally, there are a lot of traffic problems in my city, but when I am riding the bus or subway, I don't have to worry about traffic. I can just relax and enjoy the ride. I think public transportation is a much better way to get around than a private car is.